THE MARBLE MAN

ALSO BY THOMAS L. CONNELLY

Will Success Spoil Jeff Davis?   (1963)

Army of the Heartland:
The Army of Tennessee, 1861–1862   (1967)

Discovering the Appalachians   (1968)

Autumn of Glory:
The Army of Tennessee, 1862–1865   (1971)

The Politics of Command
(with Archer Jones, 1973)

THE MARBLE MAN

Robert E. Lee and His
Image in American Society

THOMAS L. CONNELLY

LOUISIANA STATE UNIVERSITY PRESS
Baton Rouge

LIBRARY OF CONGRESS CATALOGING IN PUBLICATION DATA

Connelly, Thomas Lawrence
The marble man, Robert E. Lee and his image in American society

Bibliography: p.
Includes index.
1. Lee, Robert Edward, 1807–1870.   I. Title.
E467.1.L4C67   1977   973.7'3'0924   [B]   76–41778
ISBN 0–394–47179–2 Cloth
ISBN 0–8071–0474–4 Paper

The paper in this book meets the guidelines for permanence and durability of the
Committee on Production Guidelines for Book Longevity of the Council
on Library Resources. ∞

Louisiana Paperback Edition, 1978
02   01   00   12

CONTENTS

	Acknowledgments	*ix*
	Preface	*xi*
PROLOGUE		3
CHAPTER I	LEE IN HIS TIME	11
CHAPTER II	THE IMAGE MOLDERS	27
CHAPTER III	THE MAKING OF A SOUTHERN IDOL	62
CHAPTER IV	BIRTH OF A NATIONAL HERO	99
CHAPTER V	LEE AND THE SOUTHERN RENAISSANCE, 1920–1940	123
CHAPTER VI	THE MIDDLE-CLASS HERO: FROM FREEMAN TO THE CENTENNIAL	141
EPILOGUE	THE MARBLE MAN: A REAPPRAISAL	163
	A Note on Sources	223
	Notes	225
	Index	245

ILLUSTRATIONS

(following page 110)

Robert E. Lee (Courtesy Washington-Custis-Lee Collection, Washington and Lee University)

Mary Custis Lee (Courtesy Washington-Custis-Lee Collection, W & L University)

Arlington in 1864 (Library of Congress)

Washington College (Courtesy Michael Miley Collection, W & L University)

Robert E. Lee (Courtesy Michael Miley Collection, W & L University)

General Custis Lee, General Robert E. Lee, and Colonel Walter Taylor (Library of Congress)

Robert E. Lee funeral cortege (Courtesy Michael Miley Collection, W & L University)

Washington College chapel (Courtesy Michael Miley Collection, W & L University)

Washington College students guarding Robert E. Lee's coffin (Courtesy Michael Miley Collection, W & L University)

Parlor and dining room of the Lee home (Courtesy Michael Miley Collection, W & L University)

General Jubal Early (Library of Congress)

Nineteenth-century advertisement

General W. H. F. Lee (Library of Congress)

General Fitzhugh Lee (Library of Congress)

Robert E. Lee and members of his wartime staff (Library of Congress)

Richmond Confederate commemoration in 1907 (Library of Congress)

Lee monument in Richmond (Library of Congress)

Thomas Nelson Page (Library of Congress)

Lee Chapel at Washington and Lee University (Photograph by Thomas C. Bradshaw II, W & L University Public Information Service)

ACKNOWLEDGMENTS

A LARGE NUMBER of individuals provided much aid and encouragement to this project. I am particularly thankful to Professors T. Harry Williams of Louisiana State University and Frank E. Vandiver of Rice University for their assistance. Professor John Sproat of the University of South Carolina, Grady McWhiney of the University of Alabama, Archer Jones of North Dakota State University, Sara Jackson of the National Archives, and many others gave me the benefit of their insights. I am very grateful to my wife, Jan, for her steadfast support.

I owe much to many libraries and archives. Especially helpful were staff members at the National Archives, Library of Congress, Georgia Historical Society, Virginia Historical Society, Washington and Lee University, and Tulane University.

Special thanks is due to my children, Heather and Patrick, for their faithful support.

T.L.C.

PREFACE

THIS BOOK IS AN ATTEMPT to probe the image of Robert E. Lee in the American mind, from its origins among Lost Cause writers in the Reconstruction years to the era of the 1961–65 Civil War Centennial, when Lee became a hero to white middle-class America. I am also endeavoring to test the Lee image for possible distortion and to reappraise Lee himself as well. Such tasks seem sorely needed in Civil War writing. While there have been many biographies of Robert E. Lee, no one has seriously explored the process by which his image has developed since the Civil War.

My undertaking requires the examination of Lee as he was pictured in the Southern and the national mind for well over a century—beginning with his emergence from the war as only one of several major Confederate hero symbols, continuing through his elevation as the dominant historical figure of the South, and climaxing in the twentieth century with his general acceptance as a national hero.

Throughout a century of writing about Robert E. Lee, a consistent pattern is evident. In fact, this phenomenon, which one might well label the "Virginia Pattern," goes far to explain why Lee's career has received so much attention in Confederate writing, and helps us to understand why the history of the Civil War is for many Americans synonymous with the battlefields of Virginia. In every era of Civil War writing, a cult of Virginia authors has dominated Confederate letters and provided the Lee image with a base of publicity enjoyed by no other Southern hero. Moreover, Lee's great character and military prowess alone do not account for his capture of the Southern mind in the decades after Appomattox. Nor do they explain why, fifty years after helping to lead a rebellion against the United States, he became a national hero.

The Virginia writers have not only dominated the Southern viewpoint of the war, they have held up to the Southern—and national—mind an image of Lee that provided certain needed rationales and symbols. In the Reconstruction era, Lee's image offered the South explanations for both secession and defeat. In the heyday of romantic Southern letters during the 1890s, the image became the ultimate proof of the superiority of Southern life and Anglo-Saxon supremacy. To the American mind of 1900, torn between intense national pride and fear of a new value system being introduced by industrial growth, the Lee image provided a sense of nationalism and the value of individual character. During the Depression of the 1930s, Lee was the Virginia cavalier for those who sought escape in a romantic portrayal of the war. To a disillusioned generation that rejected the traditional doctrine of inevitable American progress, Lee was what Bernard De Voto termed the "Everlasting If"—the man who could have turned history's tide in a half dozen battles. And to the American mind of the 1960s, which groped for meaning and purpose in the war, Lee became the hero of the middle class.

In brief, the image of Robert Lee has prevailed so strongly because it has reflected, or represented, the Southern and national response to the meaning of the Civil War.

This book attempts to determine the degree of exaggeration and distortion in the Lee image, which has been as elusive as it has been constantly changing. Probing the mystery of Lee's personality and seeking to understand it are familiar historical exercises.

Although many biographers have failed in their efforts to fathom Lee's patterns of behavior, Lee's most eminent biographer, Douglas Southall Freeman, found no such mystery. Freeman wrote that those who sought dark currents within Lee were looking in vain. Lee was a model of simplicity, devoid of emotional problems or personality flaws. To Freeman, Lee was a Virginia gentleman, guided in life by the simple concepts of devotion to God and duty.

In truth, Lee was an extremely complex individual. Lee the man has become so intermingled with Lee the hero symbol that the real person has been obscured. Efforts to understand him, and to appraise his capabilities fairly, have been hindered by his image as a folk hero.

Lee was neither serene nor simple. His life was replete with frustration, self-doubt, and a feeling of failure. All these were hidden behind his legendary reserve and his credo of duty and self-control. He was actually a troubled man, convinced that he had failed as a prewar career officer, parent, and moral individual. He suffered the hardships of an unsatisfactory marriage, long absences from his family, and chronic homesickness for his beloved Virginia. He distrusted his own conduct. The specter of family scandals in the past, his unhappy marital situation, his strong Calvinistic obsession with sin—all united to make Lee fear for his self-control.

By the 1850s, Lee, disturbed by these inner problems, evidently made some conscious decisions about his life. He sought calm in religion, and divine providence became the unreasoning guide of his life. He grew fascinated with otherworldliness, viewing death as a happy release from a sorrowful existence. He would adopt a creed of life that later affected his generalship in the Civil War. The Lee code—duty, self-control, and self-denial—has often been described and praised.

Overlooked is the fact that the code was an almost mechanical device that suppressed his naturally strong temper and vibrant personality.

My interpretation of Robert E. Lee is not traditional, for it tries to portray him as a human being. Generations of Civil War scholarship, bent upon elucidating the Lee image, have missed his basic humanity. Much of this book, then, is not about Lee himself, but rather concerns those who constructed his image, in some cases by virtually rewriting Civil War history. Their motives were often quite different. Many were moved by a sense of devotion to Lee. Others demanded for Virginia the lion's share of credit for the war. A few desired pecuniary gain, while a handful, particularly during Reconstruction, found in their praise of Lee a vent for their own psychological pressures.

Whatever the motivations, the Lee and Virginia cults erected an image that distorted or obscured the real individual. Consequently, a man who is a great historical figure in his own right was shaped into what others wished him to be, and has become something that he never was.

Thomas Lawrence Connelly,

University of South Carolina

THE MARBLE MAN

H E BECAME A GOD FIGURE for Virginians, a saint for the white Protestant South, and a hero for the nation. To Virginians, he was the
ultimate demonstration of the superiority of their civilization. To the
postwar South, he was the rationale of the Lost Cause, the proof of the
argument that the righteous do not always prevail. And to the nation,
Robert E. Lee became the tragic hero figure, who represented all that
was good and noble in a bad cause.

The Lee image steadily gained momentum to the point where, in
the popular American mind, the Civil War became identified with
Virginia. The bloodbaths which resolved the war would be eastern
campaigns, with place names such as Malvern Hill and Chancellorsville.
Appomattox Court House, where Robert Lee surrendered a single
Rebel army, was the symbol of Confederate defeat.

Lee's image became larger than life. He was the son who never
disobeyed his mother, the perfect student, and the man of flawless
character. He was the noble Lee of 1861, who supposedly loved the
Union more than others who espoused the Confederate cause. His decision to join the Southern war effort was depicted as especially agoniz-
ing, far more difficult than the choice faced by other Southerners of the
old army in 1861.

Then Lee was shaped as the god of war, compared favorably with
Caesar, Frederick the Great, and Marlborough. He was the tactical
genius who was seldom—if ever—defeated by mistakes of his own making. Gettysburg was lost because subordinates betrayed his confidence.
He outthought Ulysses Grant in the 1864–65 Richmond campaign, only
to be engulfed by waves of men ordered to their deaths by a butcher.
Eventually he was regarded as the master strategist of the Confederacy.
He became the bridled general, whose powers to accomplish much
more—perhaps even win victory for the South—were held in check by
a jealous President Jefferson Davis.

For a century, stories reinforcing the Lee image have been repeated in biographies and histories. Lee rescuing a small bird while
under enemy fire . . . Lee the model parent and partner in an idyllic
marriage . . . Lee the epitome of reserve, humility, and self-sacrifice. His
demeanor would be likened to that of George Washington, and his code
would be compared to that of Christ.

Why has Robert E. Lee had such a hold on the American mind? For even his superb character and remarkable military feats fall short of explaining the power of his image.

During the Civil War, Lee was far from being the supreme military idol of the South. Several officers, especially Thomas "Stonewall" Jackson, rivaled—and sometimes surpassed—Lee in popularity. Jackson probably was the most popular wartime Confederate hero. From the evidence of Civil War writings prior to the 1870s, Lee did not possess the aura of the invincible military chieftain. Early biographers and historians, North and South, criticized him for major blunders. In the first years after the war, it was Lee, not his supposedly phlegmatic lieutenant, James Longstreet, who was blamed for the loss at Gettysburg.

But between 1870 and 1885 Lee emerged as the pre-eminent military idol of the South, a man described as invincible on the battlefield. He gained such a grip upon the Southern mind that by 1900 he was the great regional hero, surpassing even George Washington. By 1907 Lee's birthday had become a day of sober commemoration throughout the South, replete with religious overtones. Some state departments of education even issued manuals of instruction for teachers, to ensure that students read the proper quotations and poems of Lee admirers.

Similar questions could be raised about the progression of Robert E. Lee's image to that of a national hero. Prior to 1900, most Americans seemed to regard him as a man of lofty character and superior generalship, but not with fervent enthusiasm. However, between 1900 and World War I, Lee became a national hero. The same Lee who invaded Pennsylvania in 1863 was one of the first nominees for the new Hall of Fame in 1901. Presidents Theodore Roosevelt and Woodrow Wilson called Lee a great nationalist who helped to save the Union by his resignation to defeat after the war. President Calvin Coolidge even authorized the striking of a Lee half-dollar to help fund the Stone Mountain Memorial near Atlanta.

IF LINEAGE COUNTED FOR EVERYTHING, Lee was certainly destined for greatness. In the romantic era of the 1880s, Southern authors would dwell on the Lee ancestry, which some bolder genealogists traced back to the time of William the Conqueror. These early biographers always took care to mention Richard Lee, founder of the family dynasty in Virginia. Lee came to Virginia during its infant years, settled in the Northern Neck, and served as secretary of state for the powerful British governor, William Berkeley. Gradually the Lees separated into two clans that were prime elements of colonial Virginian aristocracy. The Stratford Lees were initially the more prominent in public life. The southeast bedroom of Stratford Hall, where Robert Lee was born in 1807, was also where two signers of the Declaration of Independence were ushered into the world.

By the end of the Revolution, the Lees of Leesylvania, already affluent in land and commerce, were active in political affairs. Lucy Grymes Lee, legendary sweetheart of George Washington, had borne Charles Lee, Attorney General for the first President, and Richard Bland Lee, the famous Virginia Federalist leader.

Yet many believed that the son most destined for greatness was that vain, ambitious romantic, Henry (Light-Horse Harry) Lee, father of Robert. Lee's cavalry exploits under George Washington in the Northern theater and under Nathanael Greene in the Carolinas provided a strong political base in Virginia for his ambitions. In 1791 he was selected as governor of Virginia; already he had served in both the Continental Congress and the first Congress under the Constitution.

Somehow, while pursuing his political fortunes, Harry Lee found time to woo his beautiful cousin Matilda Lee, heiress to Stratford Hall. Their marriage in 1782 reunited the two great Lee clans under Harry's leadership at Stratford. "Divine Matilda's" sudden death in 1790 left Harry Lee badly shaken. Still, within three years, in the best tradition of the Lee men, he again succeeded in marrying well. He became a constant visitor to Shirley, the James River plantation of Charles Carter, wealthiest man in the Commonwealth. At first he courted "King" Carter's niece, the striking Maria Farley. When she refused his advances, Lee entered quickly into a courtship with Carter's young daughter Anne. They were soon married, cementing a kinship between two of Virginia's most powerful colonial families.

But the age of the Lee dynasty was fast disappearing. Light-Horse Harry Lee had been both restless and reckless in pursuing foolish financial ventures. He had been humiliated when his first wife, on her deathbed, placed Stratford Hall and other Lee lands in trust to her children, fearful that her husband would sell them to obtain funds for some new financial schemes.

After his marriage to Robert's mother, Harry Lee suffered setbacks in both politics and finances. His political career as a Federalist declined as the power of the Jeffersonian faction grew in Virginia. He became more reckless in his investments, and was constantly hounded by creditors. In desperation he placed large chains across the doors at Stratford to keep out sheriff's officers attempting to serve papers. By 1807, when Robert was born, the huge mansion was a cheerless, barren house. Only the east wing was livable, since most of the furnishings had been sold to pay off Harry Lee's debts.

Robert Lee rarely saw his father, who served two sentences in debtor's prison before his son's second birthday. In 1811 Robert's half-brother Henry claimed his inheritance of Stratford, and Anne Lee moved with her children to a modest brick house in Alexandria. Light-Horse Harry Lee was seldom on the scene, devoting much of his time to further ventures in search of financial security. Finally, in 1813, after being badly injured during a political riot in Baltimore, he boarded a sloop for the West Indies. His self-exile became permanent, and he was never seen again by his family.

Young Robert Lee never forgot his father's disgrace. His later admonitions to his own children betrayed an underlying fear that they might have inherited their grandfather's lack of self-control. It is noteworthy that Robert Lee never named a son for his father and did not mention Light-Horse Harry in correspondence until the last ten years of his life.

There were other family problems. Shortly after the move to Alexandria, Anne Lee's fragile health worsened. By the age of twelve Robert was compelled to shoulder the burdens of being household manager and nurse for his mother. And in 1820, when Robert was only thirteen, misfortune struck the Lee clan again. His half-brother Henry became enmeshed in financial scandal and moral disgrace, and the forced sale of Stratford lost the house forever to the family.

What was Robert Lee to do? Although he loved the soil, he possessed no inheritance of land that would have made possible a planter's life. There is evidence that he was interested in a medical career, but the family could not afford the cost of a medical education. Anne Lee was already supporting Robert's older brother Carter at Harvard, and three other children in school, on a meager income of twelve hundred dollars a year.

It was obvious that Anne Lee could not sustain another child in college, though she wanted Robert to pursue a profession. Therefore, since he had long been interested in the military, in 1824 Robert accepted an appointment to the United States Military Academy. Lee's life, however, continued to be marked by sadness. His graduation from West Point in 1829, with high honors, was dampened by a call to the bedside of his ailing mother. Her death was a heavy blow to Lieutenant Lee. Forty years later he could stand in that same room and recall that "it seems but yesterday" that his beloved mother died.

Never close to his older brothers, Lee must have felt a lack of family roots as he journeyed to his first assignment at the dismal Cockspur Island post on the Savannah River. Apparently in search of a substitute for the home life he had never enjoyed, he made frequent visits to the Savannah home of his army chum Jack Mackay. The handsome, gregarious Lee delighted in the company of Mackay's beautiful sisters, and thirty years later would speak with wistful affection of those happy interludes spent on Broughton Street.

Lee's association with the Mackay family evidently kindled a strong yearning to establish his own family circle. Yet financially Lee had little to offer. Save for some three thousand dollars he had received from his mother's small estate, he had no inheritance. Previous heirs to the Lee dynasty could have anticipated considerable legacies in property and slaves. Ironically, Robert Lee, whose love for the Virginia soil was intense, never owned a square foot of land.

Yet he continued the Lee tradition of marrying well. In 1831 he wed his childhood playmate and distant cousin, Mary Custis, in the stately Arlington mansion overlooking the Potomac River. Since childhood Lee had been entranced with the Arlington house, full of relics associated with his lifetime hero, George Washington. Mary's father, George Washington Parke Custis, was Washington's adopted son. Throughout his life he extolled the virtues of the first President and made Arlington a showplace of Washington lore. Custis also doted upon his only surviving child, Mary Custis. By her late teens she was a spoiled, unpleasant woman accustomed to lavish parties and the incessant attentions of her father. In many ways she resembled Robert Lee's mother, a factor which may have attracted the young lieutenant to a woman whose personality was so unlike his own. There was a definite physical resemblance in their frail, brown-eyed appearances, and both women possessed a deep religiosity and a somber personality, which seemed foreign to Robert Lee's own buoyant nature.

Although it lasted for almost forty years, the Custis-Lee marriage was more often than not saddled with loneliness and separation, which caused Robert much frustration. From her first tour of duty with Lee at Fort Monroe, Mary Custis never blended well into nineteenth-century army life. A second lieutenant's low salary and humble quarters proved a disappointing change from the splendor of Arlington and the excitement of Washington society.

Too, Mary Lee's precarious health during the thirty years of marriage prior to the Civil War necessitated frequent and long absences from her husband. Within fifteen years she bore seven children, and she often went to Arlington for the birth of a child. Also, beginning in 1835, Mary Lee was afflicted with chronic illness which by the 1860s reduced her to an invalid. Robert Lee's correspondence for almost three decades bemoaned his absence from wife and family while on duty in Missouri, Texas, and elsewhere.

Homesickness for family and his beloved Virginia was not the only frustration of Lee's prewar army career. Except for his magnificent service on General Winfield Scott's staff during the Mexican War, Lee in 1861 appeared to have little to show for thirty-two years of military service.

His army career had involved a long series of family routine assignments which Lee often criticized in his letters home. After three years as an engineering officer at Fort Monroe, in 1834 he was transferred to the engineering department in Washington. As an assistant to General Charles Gratiot, Lee grew to dislike bureaucratic routine and petty army politics, and in 1836 even considered resigning from the army. Instead he volunteered for engineering duty on the Mississippi River. In 1837 Lee left his family at Arlington for three years of service in St. Louis. His engineering skills helped to preserve St. Louis as a port town astride unpredictable river currents. Yet the work did not test his imagination, and although the family eventually moved to St. Louis, there were more long periods of absence.

Family life became more stable in 1841. Promoted to captain three years earlier, Lee was assigned to duty at Fort Hamilton on Long Island. For five years he labored at the tedious task of modernizing the aging fortifications which overlooked the Narrows.

The outbreak of war with Mexico provided Lee with his first opportunity in field service and his only notable military role before the Civil War. At first even this duty seemed routine. In August 1846, he was ordered to report to General John E. Wool's headquarters at San Antonio. Wool's army soon advanced into northern Mexico as an adjunct to the main force commanded by General Zachary Taylor. After a disappointing autumn which involved extensive work on road construction and reconnaissance but little contact with the enemy, Lee's fortunes changed drastically. In January 1847 he was selected by General Winfield Scott to serve with other young promising officers—including Lieutenants P. G. T. Beauregard and George McClellan—on his personal staff. Lee's bold reconnaissances on the march from Veracruz to the capital at Mexico City helped to insure such victories as Cerro Gordo and won the strong admiration of Scott and other high officers.

Yet Lee's performance had little effect on his career in the next fourteen years. Between the exuberance of Chapultepec in 1847 and the ovations in Richmond in 1861, Lee's life was a mosaic of dull post assignments, long absences from family, and slow promotion.

The slowness of advancement in the regular army was no small factor in the constant depression evident in Lee's correspondence of the 1850s. Later his biographers would make much of the fact that the Lincoln government in 1861 offered him command of the army being raised for the subjugation of the Confederacy.

Despite the esteem of Scott and others, Lee's modest progress before the Civil War both discouraged him and prompted occasional considerations of resigning his commission. By 1846 he had been in the service for seventeen years, and he still was forced to support a wife and seven children on a captain's pay. Though he was breveted a full colonel during the Mexican War, only in 1855 was he promoted to lieutenant colonel, and not until 1861, after over thirty years in the service, did he attain the rank of full colonel.

A complicating factor was his service, until his transfer to the new Second Cavalry in 1855, in the engineering branch, where work and advancement were notoriously sluggish. And even after his promotion in 1861 to full colonel of a line regiment, Lee was compelled to maintain a family on an annual salary, including allowances, of scarcely four thousand dollars.

Lee was openly scornful of what seemed to be the only path to more rapid advancement, that of currying political favor. Some of his sharpest criticism in his prewar correspondence centered upon his close friend and fellow Virginian Joseph E. Johnston. More than once Lee had taken note of Johnston's politicking for his own advancement. Particularly galling was Johnston's promotion in 1860 from the rank of lieutenant colonel to quartermaster general and brigadier general, staff. Johnston's appointment had come from the desk of Secretary of War John Floyd, his cousin by marriage, who selected his kinsman over not only Lee but a regular full colonel, Albert Sidney Johnston. Bitterly Lee observed how Johnston again epitomized "the system of favoritism."

Other promising officers, weary of slow promotion and low pay, had left the regular army to seek other occupations. Captain William Tecumseh Sherman decided in 1853 to pursue a banking career in California. Captain Ulysses Grant, unhappy with garrison duty, quit the army in 1854 to attempt a farmer's life near St. Louis. Another member of Winfield Scott's Mexican War staff, Lieutenant George McClellan, resigned his commission and, as a railroad executive, by 1860 was earning almost three times the salary of Robert Lee. By the late 1850s Lee appeared to believe that a crisis of decision was approaching in his life. Beset with a sense of failure as a career soldier, Lee confided to a friend that he must soon decide the question "which I have staved off for 20 years"—that of remaining in the army or returning to Virginia. The decision was soon to be made, but not for the reasons intended. On February 13, 1861, orders reached Lieutenant Colonel Lee, acting commander of the Second Cavalry, at his headquarters at Fort Mason, north of San Antonio. He was relieved of duty with the Second Cavalry and ordered to report to Washington.

Even on the remote Texas plains, the collapse of the Union appeared inevitable. On February 1, Texas had seceded, and delegates had gone to Montgomery to participate in the organization of the Confederacy. Before Lee could collect his belongings from his quarters on the Plaza in San Antonio, the city was actually in Rebel hands, following the hasty surrender of the Texas military department to state authorities.

When Lee journeyed toward Arlington and the Potomac, he was

fifty-four years old, robust, and possessed of strikingly handsome features set off by graying hair. He was respected and well liked by his friends, admired by his fellow officers, and the favorite of General Winfield Scott, who considered him to be the service's finest product.

However, after over three decades in the regular army he was only a lieutenant colonel, had performed mainly engineering tasks, and had yet to demonstrate his ability to command in the field. And while admired by professional soldiers, he was virtually unknown outside the army. In 1861 Lee was certainly no household name, and even in Virginia he shared popular attention with other native sons such as Joseph E. Johnston and Matthew Fontaine Maury.

Most of what he was to do, and the image fashioned by his admirers upon these deeds, lay in the uncertain future.

CHAPTER I

LEE IN HIS TIME

H E HAD BEEN SITTING in his armchair by the bow window, watching the October drizzle fall on the hills around Lexington. He dozed briefly as his daughter Mildred practiced Mendelssohn's "Song Without Words" on the piano. He awoke in a few minutes, donned his frayed military cape, and walked into the parlor, where his daughter was now playing the doleful "Funeral March." He kissed her, teased her for the morbid selection, and then trudged through the cold rain to Grace Church. There, in the damp, chilly room, he presided over a long, tedious vestry meeting.

It was after dark when he returned to the house. Slowly he moved to the dining room and took his seat with his family for the evening meal. He bowed his head to say the customary grace, but the words did not come. He only muttered incoherently. His face bore a strange expression, and the family knew that Robert Lee was desperately ill.

It rained for two weeks in the Shenandoah country. The valley streams rose quickly. Just north of the Washington College campus, the North River overran its banks, and then roared southward to join the swollen James River on its rampage through the gorge of the Blue Ridge. Nearby, in the president's home on the hillside campus, they watched at his bedside. For days he lay in silence, gazing intently into the flickering coals on the hearth. Occasionally he spoke with effort, murmuring, "I am so weary." More often he could only move his head in answer to their anxious questions.

The North, South, and James rivers rose around Lexington, making it impossible for some of Lee's children to reach his bedside. By the tenth of October he had worsened, and could only stare pitifully at the watchers by the bed. His pain intensified on the eleventh, as a strong wind and rain battered the house. He wandered into delirium, babbling orders to generals long dead. By nightfall the guns had ceased, and Robert Lee lapsed into a coma. His children knelt by his bed as his former chief of artillery, the Reverend William Nelson Pendleton, read the prayers for the dead.

By morning the storm had ceased, and a bright October sun shone over the campus. He struggled for life now, and one of his daughters ran to summon a doctor. While he was on his way, Lee was observed closely by his friend William Preston Johnston, whose father had bled to death in the Shiloh peach orchard.

Suddenly it was over. At half past nine, a clock struck in Lexington village. For an odd moment, Robert Lee rallied. His clear voice demanded that his tent be struck. Then he drew one final, deep sigh.

They took his body down the gentle slope to the college chapel. He lay in state there, clad in an ordinary black suit, as the news of his death went through Virginia. Those who could do so made their way through the muddy Blue Ridge passes of the James and the Roanoke—sons Rooney and Robert, Jr., faithful staff members Charles Venable and Walter Taylor, and a smattering of state dignitaries who traveled the nearly impassable roads.

On the morning of October 15, 1870, Lee was carried in a last grand review through the narrow streets of the Scotch-Irish valley town. A battery at the Virginia Military Institute fired minute guns, and the cadet band played a funeral dirge, as the cortege moved up Washington Street. It was a hastily assembled procession—a long, weaving train of college officials, students, former Rebel soldiers, and state officials. Behind the hearse, and Lee's mount, Traveler, the column worked its way up Jefferson Street, down Main, past the Military Institute, and finally back to the college chapel.

The service was simple and brief, as he had wished it to be. A crowd of family, students, a few old war comrades, and some dignitaries overflowed the chapel onto the sloping lawn around the small building. Inside the chapel, Reverend Pendleton read the Episcopal burial service. There was no sermon. The body was lowered into a vault beneath the chapel, and the congregation sang a favorite hymn of the General's, "How Firm a Foundation." Then it was over.

THE SIMPLICITY of Lee's burial in the austere surroundings of Lexington would not long endure. On the day of his death, friends met in Lexington, organized the Lee Memorial Association, and discussed erecting a massive memorial on the college campus. Scarcely two weeks later, a call went out for a rival group, later known as the Lee Monument Association, to assemble at Richmond and initiate plans for establishing the principal memorial to Lee in that city.

Eventually these admirers of the General would gain control of Southern writing about the Civil War, and would begin to shape much of the modern image of Robert E. Lee. By the end of the Reconstruction era he would emerge as the supreme Confederate symbol. The power of these Virginia-dominated supporters would be evident shortly after 1900, when the entire nation accepted the Lee imagery and enshrined the General as an American hero of the same status as George Washington and Abraham Lincoln.

One cannot appreciate fully the development of the Lee mystique in the American mind without first examining his wartime image within the South. The writing of Confederate history has been dominated by authors dedicated to ennobling both Lee and the Virginia theater in the war. The power of these writers and the force of the Lee mystique may have distorted his actual status among contemporaries. A combination of universal respect for Lee's greatness and the enthusiasm of his more avid supporters have clouded two principal issues—what wartime Southerners thought of both the Virginia war zone and of Robert E. Lee.

In the popular mind, the war has long been synonymous with Virginia. Most Americans have believed that Virginia was the principal combat theater and that the Confederates considered it so. The assumption is that, even during the war, the clashes at Manassas and Antietam were viewed as more critical than those at Shiloh and Chickamauga. Thus the South supposedly pinned its hopes upon Virginia and Lee's army.

Certainly the eastern front, where Lee grappled with the Army of the Potomac, was always regarded as a crucial war zone. The capitals of the two contestants, Washington and Richmond, were scarcely a hundred miles apart. Lee's army not only threatened Washington but intimidated major population centers such as Philadelphia and Baltimore. Richmond itself was a vital manufacturing center. More important, Richmond held symbolic importance for a people bent upon creating a new nation. When the news reached the city of the victory at Bull Run in 1861, the editor of the *Enquirer* boasted, "This day our freedom and independence stand secure!" He was voicing the sentiments of the entire Confederacy, which always saw parallels between the revolutions of 1776 and 1861. Convinced that their cause bore both historic sanction and God's approval, Southerners naturally viewed not only Richmond but all of Virginia with pride.

They were also proud of Lee's Army of Northern Virginia, which protected the eastern front. Save for Stonewall Jackson's Shenandoah Valley campaign, the war had gone hard for the South in the winter and spring of 1861–62. Lee's successive victories in the Seven Days and Second Bull Run in the summer of 1862 rejuvenated a faltering morale. Even the disaster at Gettysburg in 1863 could be rationalized by a Southern populace weary of General Braxton Bragg's string of defeats in the West. Continual disaster in the theater between the Mississippi River and the Appalachians could be offset by Lee's tenacity in defending the country south of the Rappahannock.

The prestige associated with eastern battles became more pronounced in 1864, when General Ulysses Grant came to confront Robert E. Lee. Grant, directly or indirectly, had already achieved two of President Abraham Lincoln's three designs for victory, the opening of the Mississippi Basin and the corridor from Nashville to Atlanta. Now he would achieve the third—the seizure of Richmond.

Grant himself did not attach undue importance to the eastern front. He planned originally to establish his headquarters with the Army of the Cumberland in its push from Chattanooga to Atlanta. His comrade General Sherman begged him to remain there, warning, "Don't stay in Washington. . . . Come West; take to yourself the whole Mississippi Valley. . . . Here lies the seat of the coming empire." Grant later recalled that prior to his initial visit to Washington in March 1864, "it had been my intention before this to remain in the West."

But Grant's first view of the situation in the East quickly convinced him that "here was the point for the commanding general to be." The Army of the Potomac was wracked with command dissension. Worse, its repeated defeats by Lee had become a political issue in the presidential campaign of 1864. The Democratic party publicized the army's misfortunes, in its attempts to gain the presidency for General George McClellan. The political issue even pervaded the army's high command, where one of its few brilliant officers, General Winfield Scott Hancock, was touted by some dissidents as a possible replacement for Abraham Lincoln in the 1864 election.

Grant was aware of the problems that existed on the eastern front. Although he recalled that "I was afraid of the spirit that pervaded that army," he elected to place his headquarters with the Army of the Potomac. He was disturbed at the army's internal divisions and the political interference it suffered, and once wrote his father that Richmond would fall despite "Northern countenance and support" for the Rebels.

No doubt Lee's presence in Virginia also influenced Grant's decision. Lee seemed indomitable in the East, and officers of the Army of the Potomac warned the newcomer Grant that "you have not faced Bobby Lee yet."

When the confrontation developed in 1864, it added to the glamor of war in the East. There was Grant, who had conquered the Mississippi Valley and had opened the road to Atlanta, engaged in a struggle for the Confederate capital with its most successful general. Not without some cause did New York *Times* correspondent William Swinton describe Virginia in 1864 as the "arena" of the war.

But wartime Southerners were not as concerned about Virginia as has often been assumed. Opinion was extremely localistic regarding where the "real" war was being fought. Georgia, for example, was only mildly interested in matters on the eastern front. Georgians stressed protection of the Chattanooga–Atlanta corridor into the great munitions complex of Augusta, Atlanta, Columbus, and Macon. Tennessee reflected this same spirit, fearing the loss of some of the South's most valuable food areas, the main iron-producing region, and 90 percent of its copper. Mississippi and Louisiana were more interested in the defense of the Mississippi Basin, while Alabama feared the loss of its Gulf Coast installations and inland manufacturing areas.

A random sampling of newspapers from the western and central Confederacy reveals this intense localism. In 1862 the Augusta *Chronicle and Sentinel* scoffed at fears over the threatened seizure of Richmond by General George McClellan, noting that "the Confederate government can find a capital anywhere."[1] The Columbus, Georgia, *Daily Enquirer* also pressed for defense of the West. Shortly before the battle of Chickamauga in 1863, its editor described the impending fight as "the mightiest and most momentous battle of the war." Later, when Sherman advanced on Atlanta, the paper asserted that "within this narrow compass two of the greatest armies ever massed on the continent confront each other in a struggle for empire."[2]

In 1863, the editor of the Atlanta *Daily Intelligencer* insisted that the Federals would abandon their efforts to take Richmond and would now concentrate upon the Tennessee front. Here "the great battle of the war" would be fought. The Atlanta *Southern Confederacy* predicted that a victory on the Tennessee front would produce overtures for peace by Northern states. The Memphis *Daily Appeal* begged the government to reinforce the Tennessee front, where a Confederate victory probably "would terminate the war." And when Lee marched into Pennsylvania, bound for the fateful battle at Gettysburg, a Mississippi newspaper still claimed that "the main force of the enemy" would be concentrated in Tennessee.[3]

Another newspaper which argued for more attention for the West was the Chattanooga *Daily Rebel*. The modern view of the 1864 campaign is that the great struggle occurred between Grant and Lee, in the country from the Rapidan River to Petersburg, but westerners were more concerned with General Sherman's threat to Atlanta. The editor of the *Daily Rebel* speculated that "the great battle of 1864 will be fought in Northern Georgia," and warned that "Atlanta is of more importance in the scheme of conquest and subjugation than Richmond."[4]

A second misconception has far more importance for the steady growth of the Lee image. In the popular mind, Robert E. Lee has become the absolute symbol of the Confederacy. But it must be remembered that until the last three months of the war, Lee commanded only a single Confederate army. Lee's surrender at Appomattox Court House has become synonymous with the end of the war, but his single

army consisted of only 25,000 men, whereas some 100,000 Confederates remained under arms in major field forces in North Carolina, Alabama, and the trans-Mississippi region. Yet Lee has been depicted as
the central figure of the Rebel populace, the man to whom all looked
for salvation.

The image is one which contains both truth and distortion. Certainly by the middle of the war Lee was hailed by some as the South's
foremost military leader. Typical was a comment by the editor of the
Charleston *Mercury* in 1863, who praised Lee as "the central figure of
the war . . . beyond all question." Lee's spectacular victories against foes
such as Generals George McClellan, John Pope, Ambrose Burnside, and
Joseph Hooker were a matter of both pride and solace to the Confederacy. While the war went badly on other fronts in Mississippi and Tennessee, Lee's apparently indomitable generalship in Virginia was a
crucial morale factor. By 1865, at least to the men of his own army, Lee
was revered for both his brilliant generalship and his lofty character.
General Henry Wise summarized their feelings in a remark made to
Lee shortly before Appomattox, when he observed, "You are the country to these men. They fought for you."[5]

Yet two things must be kept in mind. The Lee of 1865, hailed by
many as the South's greatest leader, bore a completely different image
from the Lee of 1861–62, who was sometimes ignored or criticized by
Confederate newspapers. Even during the war, Lee's hero status would
develop slowly.

More important, the wartime image of Lee was not what it would
become during the Reconstruction era. By the time of Appomattox, it
remained in the future for Lost Cause authors to mold Lee into the
totally invincible leader of the Confederacy.

Lee's stature in the South was not significant until his success
against McClellan on the Peninsula in June 1862. He was a popular
career officer in the old army, a favorite of General Winfield Scott, and
was well regarded within Virginia. Yet in the first year of the war, he
was generally unknown in the South and for a time was even an unpopular figure.

His first real field command, the operations in West Virginia against
General William Rosecrans, in September–October 1861, was a disaster. Four days after his retreat from the mountains the people of the
region voted to establish the new state of West Virginia, and some
Confederate newspapers wrote scathing denunciations of Lee. He was
called a man of "a showy presence," "too tender of blood," and was
widely referred to as "Granny Lee." In 1862, the first important Confederate historian, newspaperman Edward Pollard, issued his highly
praised *First Year of the War*.

Of Lee in West Virginia, Pollard wrote:

The most remarkable circumstance of this campaign was that, it was conducted by a general who had never fought a battle, who had a pious horror of guerillas, and whose extreme tenderness of blood induced him to depend exclusively upon the resources of strategy to essay the achievement of victory without the cost of life.[6]

In November 1861, when Lee accepted a new assignment as commander of the military department of the Carolinas and Georgia, his mixed reputation went with him. Even as he left the capital, the Richmond *Examiner* editorialized that in his work on seacoast defenses, it was hoped Lee would be more successful with the spade than he had been with the sword. The news that Lee was coming to command the area created considerable uproar. Lee's devoted biographer J. William Jones recalled a round-robin letter to Jefferson Davis, allegedly signed by nearly every officer in the department, which protested the appointment. While Jones's story cannot be substantiated, it is true that Jefferson Davis was forced to take action to stifle protest. Davis recalled of Lee in 1870 that "the clamour which then arose followed him when he went to South Carolina, so that it became necessary on his departure to write a letter to Governor of that State, telling him what manner of man he was."[7]

For months Lee continued to walk in the shadow of other Confederate leaders. His appointment in March 1862 as military adviser to Jefferson Davis went virtually unnoticed in Southern newspapers, even those in Richmond. And when he took command of the Army of Northern Virginia on June 1, after Joseph E. Johnston had been wounded, Lee was still not the hope of the South. Some postwar writers later embellished the circumstances of that appointment. They claimed that the capital was near capture, because of alleged bungling by Johnston, and the placing of Lee in charge supposedly brought hope to the South.

All of this is either exaggerated or untrue. When he assumed command, the Richmond *Examiner* noted: "Evacuating Lee, who has never yet risked a single battle with the invader, is commanding general." The Macon *Daily Telegraph* asserted that when Johnston recuperated he was entitled to regain his command "or else a wound becomes a badge of disgrace." A month after Lee defeated McClellan on the Peninsula, the Savannah *Republican* would still say, "General Johnston, it is believed, is entitled to all the credit for the successful conduct of the campaign."[8]

Still, the Seven Days established Lee's reputation as a major war hero. The Macon *Daily Telegraph* now called him "our great commander" who "crowned his fame" by defeating McClellan. In its first real mention of Lee in the entire campaign, the Columbus, Georgia,

Daily Enquirer exulted on July 24 that the Peninsula success "has established the fame of General Lee as one of the great military masters."[9]

But the Confederate populace was convinced that it possessed several "great military masters." There were other men who rivaled and sometimes surpassed Lee in popularity. His main competitor for hero status among Confederates was General Thomas Stonewall Jackson. Even after his death, Jackson's popularity matched Lee's, and only in the Reconstruction era did Lee surpass him.

Before Lee assumed command of the Army of Northern Virginia, Jackson's success in the Shenandoah Valley campaign had made his name a Southern byword. His victories had come at a time when Rebel morale needed successes after the disasters at Forts Henry and Donelson, Roanoke Island, Island Number Ten, and Shiloh.

Jackson's Valley campaign in April–May 1862 dazzled the South. The Richmond *Whig* declared, "Glorious Old Stonewall is fast becoming *The Hero of the War.*" The Memphis *Daily Appeal* thought that perhaps "Stonewall Jackson is the destined deliverer of his country." On June 1, the day Lee assumed command in Virginia, the Macon *Daily Telegraph* announced that "we have found at last a military cyclops." But it was speaking of Jackson, and nine days later insisted that "the revolution has at last found a great Captain. He is Stonewall Jackson."[10]

Considerable attention was given to Jackson after his Valley army was merged as a corps into Lee's force in late June 1862. Lee's success in the Seven Days did not establish him as the South's supreme hero. Press coverage during these months more often concentrated on Jackson's activities, and some newspapers seldom mentioned Lee's name. In fact, Jackson was often credited with the victory in the Seven Days, despite his actual poor showing. His slowness at Mechanicsville and in the White Oak Swamp was not criticized until after the war.[11]

Long after the Seven Days, Jackson seemed to remain foremost in the public mind. Newspapers treated him as a separate army commander, even when he was a corps leader in Lee's army. Coverage of such battles as Antietam was more often than not centered upon Jackson's exploits. In early September a Memphis newspaper reported that Jackson had crossed the Potomac River into Maryland "with his invincible and veteran legion." After Antietam, the editor said that "it would not surprise us to hear" that Jackson was marching on Washington. An Atlanta paper saw Jackson's efforts in the Maryland campaign as "almost unparalleled in modern warfare and the work of 'a military genius.'"[12]

In October the Richmond *Examiner* spoke of how "Lee and Jackson ... won their best victory on the plains of Manassas." Later, a Chattanooga newspaper hailed Lee and Jackson as "the two great Generals of the War." In early 1863, the Jackson mystique was perhaps best summarized by journalist P. W. Alexander, in a series of articles on "Confederate Chieftains" for the *Southern Literary Messenger*. Alexander saw Jackson as "the idol of the people" and "the object of greater enthusiasm than any other military chieftain of our day."[13]

Yet nothing so revealed the hero status of Jackson as did the outpouring of grief after his death in May 1863. The Atlanta *Southern Confederacy* asked, "Who will rise to fill his place? . . . Who will be the future great and renowned chief to fill the place of Stonewall Jackson?" The Atlanta *Daily Intelligencer* called him "the idol of the people and the army." When he learned of Jackson's wound, the editor of the Richmond *Sentinel* mourned that "no life is dearer to the people." After Jackson's death, the editor asked, "Oh, who can take his place in our armies? Who can fill his place in our hearts?"[14]

Jackson's death also inspired a flurry of hastily written biographies. One such was by James Dabney McCabe, Jr., also an early biographer of Lee, who wrote martial plays, edited the *Magnolia Weekly*, and produced quickly compiled books that capitalized on current heroes. He first selected Beauregard in his 1862 novel, *Aide-de-Camp: A Romance of the War*. Then came his *Life of Thomas J. Jackson, by an Ex-Cadet*. McCabe observed of Jackson that by the time of his death "the people had learned to look upon him as the great champion of the South," and the news of his death meant "that the idol of the South was no more."[15]

Like McCabe, John Esten Cooke seemed to be something of an opportunist who fawned upon war heroes. After the war Cooke also became an early Lee biographer. But in 1863 he was a Jackson man. Already well established as a Virginia novelist, Cooke was also a freelance war correspondent, contributing articles to magazines such as the *Southern Literary Messenger*. His first biography of Jackson was published in serial form in three issues of the *Southern Illustrated News* in 1863. Entitled "Stonewall Jackson and the Old Stonewall Brigade," the articles were a paean to the man whom Cooke considered the principal Confederate hero. From his first sentence—"Greatest of Generals is General Stonewall Jackson"—Jackson was his hero, and "no soldier of the war has been more uniformly successful in his undertakings." Jackson's victories left behind "the great funeral procession of whipped Generals—dead reputations."[16]

Cooke soon found himself in the race to produce the first posthumous biography of Jackson. In his superb essay "Cooke's Lives of Jackson," Richard Harwell chronicled the ludicrous haggling. Only two weeks after Jackson's death, the *Southern Illustrated News* announced the future printing of Cooke's biography, the new "Life of Stonewall Jackson, the Hero of the Present War for Independence"!

But the Jackson family had selected one of his former staff officers, the Presbyterian minister Robert L. Dabney, as the "official" biographer. The church organ, the *Central Presbyterian,* immediately lambasted Cooke as an opportunist, "self-appointed upstart," and literary impostor.

While the Presbyterians fought with Cooke's publisher, his life of Jackson was published. It sold three thousand copies the first day, and was pirated by publishers in New York and London. Not to be outdone, the Reverend Dabney brought out in 1863 his *True Courage: A Discourse Commemorative of Lieutenant General Thomas J. Jackson.*

Harwell's research has uncovered a considerable number of other writings which strove either to eulogize Jackson or to capitalize on his reputation. For example, an Englishwoman, Catherine Cooper Hopley, offered her *"Stonewall" Jackson,* and a New York writer, under the pseudonym Markinfield Addey, produced two biographies in 1863 and 1864. Meanwhile the Virginia Military Institute issued a biography, a Georgia poet, H. M. Thompson, wrote *The Death of Jackson,* and from Richmond came a children's book on Jackson's exploits.[17]

THOUGH HE DID NOT HAVE the emotional appeal of Jackson, General P. G. T. Beauregard was another hero symbol who vied with Lee for the affection of the people of the South. Beauregard's enduring mystique was a curious business, since his war record did not match his popularity. While he frequently drew up grandiose strategic plans for friendly politicians and generals, he rarely directed any large operations. His initial command at Fort Sumter was followed by assignment to a small army at Manassas Junction, in north-central Virginia. His leadership of this force of 15,000, dubbed the Army of the Potomac, ended in July 1861, when he was superseded by Joseph E. Johnston.

In fact, only once in the war did Beauregard actually command a substantial field army. After Albert Sidney Johnston's death on the field at Shiloh, April 6, 1862, his second-in-command, Beauregard, took charge of the Army of Tennessee. Beauregard's tenure of only three months in this position was a dismal failure, embracing the loss at Shiloh and a long retreat into Mississippi. In July he was deposed by Jefferson Davis. For the remainder of the war, he occupied secondary positions, such as commanding the Charleston defenses during the 1863 siege and as a subordinate to Lee in the Petersburg operations in 1864–65.

It was this varied service which apparently lay at the heart of Beauregard's popularity. No other Rebel officer could boast the admiration of so many social and military cliques within the Confederacy. He came to Fort Sumter in 1861 with well-established political connections in Louisiana. At Fort Sumter, he was idolized by the South Carolina people. The French-educated Louisianan was an imposing figure, with his olive complexion, cropped mustache, and French accent. Women doted upon him, often engulfing his headquarters with flowers, scarves, flags, and other presents. Victory at First Manassas, which he shared with Joseph E. Johnston, reinforced Beauregard's hero status. Then came his bitter quarrel with Jefferson Davis in 1861–62.

The mutual hatred between Davis and Beauregard was an important source of the latter's wartime popularity. Like Joseph Johnston, Beauregard became a darling of the anti-administration group in the Rebel Congress, and was the hero of anti-Jefferson Davis newspapers such as the Richmond *Examiner* and Charleston *Mercury*. The theme was consistent: Beauregard was a military genius held in check by a malicious, jealous Davis. He was a general who could perhaps save the country if given a decent command; instead, Davis deliberately confined him to second-rate assignments.

Beauregard took advantage of his popularity. He often appeared more a candidate for public office than a general. No other Southerner had such a variety of contacts and avenues of publicity. Save for Lee, every important Confederate officer served under Beauregard at some time during the war. He was the only man who commanded the Virginia, Tennessee, and Carolina armies. In his background were Fort Sumter, First Manassas, and his skillful defense of Charleston in 1863.

Conscious of his image, Beauregard maintained a wide correspondence with generals, governors, congressmen, and authors. He sent pieces of the Sumter flagstaff to wounded generals, consoled officers who felt they had been badly treated by Jefferson Davis, lectured civilians on Napoleonic strategic principles, and flattered politicians. He issued bombastic, but impressive, directives, such as his appeal to Mississippi Valley planters to donate plantation bells to be melted down for artillery, and he delighted in signing orders with such gasconade as "within hearing of the enemy's guns."

The Southern people loved Beauregard. Musicians composed marches and songs in his honor, such as "The Beauregard Manassas Quick-Step." An assortment of things were named for him, including female garments, babies, and racehorses. Newspapers across the South printed turgid poems lauding his exploits.[18]

The public praise of the Creole never ceased during the war. The Atlanta *Southern Confederacy* assured all that he was "one of the greatest warriors of the age." Another Atlanta journal published a poem which proclaimed:

> *Our trust is now in thee,*
> *Beauregard,*
> *In thy hand the God of Hosts*

Hath placed the sword
And the glory of thy fame
Hath set the land aflame;
Hearts kindle at thy name,
Beauregard!

The Chattanooga *Daily Rebel* would speak of "the brilliant Beauregard," who, with Lee and Joseph Johnston, formed "the trio of the war."[19]

GENERAL JOSEPH E. JOHNSTON also rivaled Lee as a Confederate hero. Like Beauregard's, Johnston's image had roots in numerous military and political contacts. Johnston's earlier military record included the Seminole, Black Hawk, Mexican, and Mormon wars. By 1860 he held the highest office in the old army of any future Confederate soldier, that of quartermaster general.

Like Beauregard, Johnston quarreled frequently with the Richmond government and moved through several commands. His constant change of duty brought him many political connections and much local support. He and Beauregard were the only men who led both the Army of Northern Virginia and the Army of Tennessee. His service as leader of the Virginia force was ended when he was wounded at Seven Pines in May 1862. After recuperating, Johnston was sent to oversee the entire western theater, from the Appalachian Mountains to the Mississippi River. Then, in January 1864, after persistent demands by Johnston's political allies in Congress, he was appointed head of the Army of Tennessee and was sent to Georgia to face General William Sherman. After Jefferson Davis removed him in July, on the eve of the battle of Atlanta, there were continuing calls to give Johnston another field army. Finally, in February 1865, Davis restored him to the command of the Army of Tennessee.

A vital source of Johnston's popularity was his personal charm. Small and dapper with a Vandyke beard, he reminded one war correspondent of "the gamecock, the most courageous of all 'the fowls of the air.'" His public image to both troops and civilians was almost irresistible. He could win an audience, whether as a dinner guest or in review of his troops. Always paternalistic in his treatment of soldiers, "Old Joe" was beloved by them. There were fewer poignant scenes of the war than in July 1864 after Davis removed Johnston from command at Atlanta. Some troops wept openly, and regiments marched to his headquarters and lifted their hats in silent tribute.

But he could also be pedantic, quarrelsome, bitter, jealous of rank, and even paranoiac. In 1861 Johnston began a quarrel with Jefferson

Davis over his rank, First Manassas, the Peninsula campaign, and a dozen other issues. The feud, one of the great mutual hatreds of the war, served to boost Johnston's popularity in some circles.

Much of Johnston's reputation rested upon speculation. His admirers contended that he would have crushed McClellan *if* he had not been wounded at Seven Pines; he would have saved Vicksburg and Tennessee *if* Davis had given him real authority in 1863; he would have saved Atlanta *if* the President had not removed him in 1864. On the floor of Congress, Johnston's champions would accuse Davis of deliberately shelving a good officer. The anti-Davis press would portray Johnston as a martyr.

The result was a strong hero image. A Chattanooga newspaper stated that Johnston "forms unquestionably the trio of the war, with Lee and Beauregard." An Atlanta newspaper asserted that no Confederate general "has shown greater courage or more ability."[20]

ANOTHER OFFICER matched Lee, Jackson, Beauregard, and Joseph Johnston as a hero symbol. The mystique surrounding Albert Sidney Johnston was the most curious of all. No war figure had such a unique hold on the South. He represented two powerful currents of both the wartime and the postwar Confederate mind. He was a Southern Hamlet figure, the ill-starred tragic hero, doomed to fail by uncontrollable forces and destined to be struck down at the height of success. Also, more than any other Confederate, Johnston would epitomize the might-have-been situation. His death at Shiloh would be as disturbing as the "ifs" of Gettysburg.

In 1861 many saw Johnston as the potential savior of the Confederacy. He was one of the most handsome of the Confederates. Tall, muscular, and erect, with a thick mustache and a powerful head, he was the image of grace and dignity. He excited the young Confederacy with a reputation for daring. He had commanded the Army of the Texas Republic, led the famed Second Cavalry on the Plains, and headed Federal troops during the Mormon War.

Johnston had also dazzled the South in 1861 by his escape from California. Few generals could match his dramatic entrance into the Civil War. In April he had resigned as commander of the Pacific Department, determined to fight for the South. His last days in Los Angeles were in virtual captivity. His sympathies were well known in Washington, he was watched closely, and there were plans to relieve him of command even before he resigned. In June, with a small band of loyal comrades, Johnston slipped out of Los Angeles. By horseback, often on long night marches, they rode eight hundred miles to the Rio Grande. Johnston and his friends dodged Federal cavalry patrols and

Apache war parties, endured 120-degree heat, and suffered from lack of water.

By the time Johnston reached Texas, he was fast becoming a celebrity. Newspapers recounted his desert trek. Delegations of businessmen and congressmen visited the President, begging an important post for Davis's old West Point colleague. They were not disappointed. In September, Davis made Johnston a full general, outranking Lee, Beauregard, and Joe Johnston.

But Johnston's command of the Army of Tennessee was a disaster. In January–March 1862, he lost southern Kentucky and Tennessee in a series of misadventures which included the battles of Mill Springs and Forts Henry and Donelson. He was damned by the Rebel press. Newspapers that had labeled him a "genius" the previous fall now spoke of how "the blunders—perhaps the incapacity—of General Sidney Johnston" were the cause of these losses.[21]

In April 1862, Johnston attacked General U. S. Grant at Shiloh. Had he lived through that ill-organized attack in the rain-swollen creek bottoms around Shiloh Church, his reputation might have been completely destroyed. Poor planning produced an uncoordinated assault which soon disintegrated into a series of isolated skirmishes in river-bottom thickets. Badly surprised at the outset, Grant drew back his lines to the river landing, received reinforcements, and on the following day pushed the Confederates back into Mississippi. That Johnston did not live only heightened his mystique. In the early afternoon of April 6, while leading an assault in the Peach Orchard, he was felled by an arterial wound that a modern Boy Scout could have repaired.

When he died, a sense of guilt swept through the South. He became a martyr who succumbed attempting to prove his worth to doubters. A Macon newspaper mourned: "Let the Republic do justice to his memory, and repair the grievous wrongs which have of late been heaped upon him." The Savannah *Morning News* expressed the South's guilt well: "There is something painful too, in the thought that perhaps he was goaded to an imprudent exposure of his life by the unjust and illiberal criticism against him." To the editor, no Confederate general "has been more grossly assailed or unjustly blamed than the lamented Johnston." Meanwhile, an Augusta editor said that Johnston "has vindicated himself by his heroic death from the unjust and inconsiderate aspersions cast on him."[22]

Such adoration would endure long after the war. In an 1878 address, Jefferson Davis called Johnston in 1862 "the greatest soldier, the ablest man, civil or military, Confederate or Federal, then living." In his history of the war Davis depicted Johnston as the South's outstanding general and "the great pillar" of the Confederacy. Davis echoed the sentiments of Zachary Taylor's son Richard, who in his popular memoir,

Destruction and Reconstruction, described Johnston as "the foremost man of all the South."[23]

So ROBERT E. LEE lay in his coffin, in the president's home on the college slope. How far had his reputation developed?

By the end of the war many Confederates considered him their greatest general. His brilliant defense of the eastern theater was an object of pride for a struggling nation weary of disasters on other fronts. And both before and after Appomattox, Lee was cherished as a symbol of victory by a people who discovered that the American dream of inevitable success had betrayed them.

There is little question that Lee's posture during the five years after his surrender deeply impressed the South. Collections of his papers are filled with poignant letters from admirers throughout the defeated Confederacy. Lee's refusal of lucrative business offers, his acceptance of the modest position at Washington College, his counseling of moderation—all quickly became part of the legend. The deluge of funeral oratory and newspaper tributes after his death praised his efforts to help rebuild a shattered region.

Yet in two respects the Lee image in 1870 was not what it would become. Not until the 1880s would Lee be regarded as the South's invincible general, the embodiment of the Confederate cause.

By the time of Lee's death, several of the Confederate war heroes still held the deep affection of the people of the South. Eventually Stonewall Jackson's image would recede into the position of Lee's best lieutenant, but for two decades after the war his popularity was undiminished. In 1875 his statue was unveiled in Richmond—almost fifteen years before the unveiling of the Lee monument. In 1881, over 12,000 admirers crowded New Orleans's Metairie Cemetery to dedicate a huge monument to Jackson. The principal speaker, Jefferson Davis, asserted that in Europe Jackson was regarded as "the great hero of our war," and that the South "gave its whole heart to Jackson." In 1877 the New York *Times* observed that Jackson "became the greatest of all Confederate Generals with a world-wide reputation for consummate military ability."[24]

The other Southern hero symbols were still cherished in the years after Appomattox. Beauregard and Joseph Johnston commanded mass ovations wherever they traveled. Albert Sidney Johnston's bust shared prominence with those of Lee and Jackson on the elaborate monument unveiled in New Orleans in 1867. That same year, by petition from the Texas legislature, his body was removed from New Orleans for a return to his beloved Texas. His pallbearers included James Longstreet and Beauregard. The body was then sent to the port town of Galveston, where Federal military officials had forbidden a planned funeral procession. On a cold January day, thousands ignored the order and poured onto Galveston Island to file past his coffin. They came to pay tribute to the former Indian fighter who once remarked that he wanted to be buried with a handful of Texas earth over his breast.[25]

Robert E. Lee was not yet the primary hero symbol of the South. This eminence lay years ahead, with the steady development of the Lee image. But it all began on an October day in Lexington, when Lee's admirers met to plan for the future.

CHAPTER II

THE IMAGE MOLDERS

THEY WERE A CLANNISH LOT, possessed of that inbred Virginia sense of conceit, and fiercely jealous of their war hero. After his death, they gathered under the Lee standard for a variety of reasons. All admired Lee. Yet some championed him because of personal ambition, whereas others sought to cloak their own wartime mistakes. For these men of the first Lee cult, 1865–85, the General would be the only important Rebel hero, a man incapable of military or personal error. A few would even deny that Lee was defeated at Gettysburg; most would place the blame for that setback on his subordinates.

Even among Southerners, the efforts of the cult proved annoying. General Daniel Harvey Hill, one of Lee's division chiefs, spoke with disgust of "the deification of Lee" by the Virginians. He saw them as men who had "always found a scape-goat for his failure." General Dabney Maury criticized "the intimate admirers of Gen. Lee—those who have sought in their overzeal to fasten upon Longstreet all the blame" for Gettysburg. Jefferson Davis also wearied of the efforts of the Lee cult. He said that "Lee's eulogists" magnified his character by utilizing "a foundation of fiction in disparagement of others." Davis charged that Lee's reputation "needs no ornamentation," and decried its "fictitious elevation at the expense of others."[1]

Criticism of Robert Lee stimulated fierce rebuttal. Occasionally the Lee people waged war against one another when the General's image was threatened. In 1871, former cavalryman General John Imboden depicted for *Galaxy* the horror of the retreat from Gettysburg. Imboden, who had skillfully guarded that seventeen-mile wagon train of wounded men to the Potomac, was castigated by some old comrades because his vivid description made Lee's defeat appear too severe. And when novelist John Esten Cooke published a biography of Lee, the cult devoured one of its own members. To some ex-Rebels, Cooke's study contained passages in which praise of Lee was insufficient. One of Lee's former corps officers, Jubal Early, informed Cooke of his sins, while a onetime staff officer, Charles Venable, railed at the "deplorable" book as the work of one of those "good natured well meaning feeble men."[2]

This first group of Lee admirers succeeded in gaining control of

Confederate letters not long after the war. Their image of the Civil War centered upon Lee and the war in Virginia. In so doing, they raised Lee far above other war heroes, silenced his critics, and underplayed the exploits of other Confederate generals. By the 1880s the Lee cult had established him as the supreme Confederate figure of the war.

IT ALL BEGAN on an autumn day at Washington College in 1870. Classroom lectures had proceeded as usual that October morning, until a knock came at each door. A note was handed in—"General Lee died this morning. Academic exercises are suspended." Even as faculty and students filed from the red-brick buildings, town bells tolled mournfully.

Within hours after Lee's death, the organization that would publicize his image so successfully would come into being. That afternoon, at the town courthouse, college faculty joined local residents in a hasty meeting which expressed a determination "to guard his sacred dust." The powerful Lee Memorial Association was thus formed. In a matter of weeks, other organizational efforts would begin at Lexington. Lee's postwar comrades would eventually construct a mausoleum, produce the famed Edward Valentine recumbent figure, dispatch fund-raising agents throughout the South, and talk of a Lee Memorial University.

The trustees of Washington College had good reasons for these projects. The use of Lee's name by the college for fund-raising ventures had begun prior to his death. Even before Lee accepted the position in 1865, the college trustees had sensed the financial advantage of having such a prominent figure as president. After Appomattox, the trustees, led by Judge John Brockenbrough, had tried to piece together the institution's shattered fortunes. War casualties had depleted student ranks, and Federal occupation of Lexington in 1864 had left the campus a shambles. By 1865 the school had only four professors, scarcely forty students, no library or laboratories, and a handful of dilapidated buildings.

Lee's only experience in academic administration had been his term as superintendent at the United States Military Academy. Yet on August 3, the trustees offered Lee the presidency. Former governor John Letcher urged Lee to accept, and admitted that the very fact that Lee would be president would give the college "the favor and patronage of the public."[3]

Judge Brockenbrough was more direct. Visiting Lee at his temporary home on the James River below Richmond, Brockenbrough gained only a promise of serious consideration. So during his return to Lexington the Judge wrote a frank letter to Lee, admitting that "it would be uncandid to deny that the advancement of the interest of our venerable college was the primary consideration with the Board of Trustees in inducing them to solicit your acceptance of its Presidency."

After he accepted the position, Lee knew that the college was using his popularity to solicit funds. In his first week in office, the trustees issued a press release announcing the General's appointment to "the holy work," which included extensive use of the Lee name in the college's expansion program. By late 1865 the college had sent several fund-raising agents into the field. The Reverend Samuel Stuart traveled to New York and Washington, and eventually to England. Like other agents, Stuart campaigned under the banner of the "R. E. Lee Endowment." Stuart placed advertisements in the London *Times,* the Irish *Times,* and elsewhere urging donations for the "R. E. Lee Endowment Fund for Washington College." He promised that any contributor would be paying tribute to the school's endower, George Washington, and to his "worthwhile successor," Lee. Stuart's tactics aroused the anger of both sympathetic Englishmen and Confederate exiles. A number of letters reached Washington College complaining of his techniques.

The Reverend E. P. Walton barnstormed from Philadelphia to Houston for the "R. E. Lee Endowment." Like Stuart, Walton received much newspaper publicity, particularly in his appeal for funds to increase Lee's salary. Lee himself finally asked the trustees to muzzle Walton "to prevent my being presented to the country in so reprehensible a manner."[4]

Washington trustees also employed the Reverend William Nelson Pendleton as a fund-raising agent. In 1865 he canvassed Richmond, New York, and Baltimore. On one trip to New York, he ingratiated himself with Benjamin Wood of the New York *News.* Enmeshed in the postwar circulation battle among metropolitan newspapers, Wood saw the advantage of publishing articles by the former commander of the Rebel armies. He proposed to Pendleton that Lee furnish the *News* with a weekly article on any subject. The only prerequisite was "having the Genl's name and influence." Pendleton turned down this offer, knowing that Lee would refuse it. But he thought that the General might consider the proposition if the money were donated to the college. He suggested to Judge Brockenbrough that if pressure were applied, Lee might consent to a project that would bring the college "a great pecuniary benefit."[5]

Other fund-raising ventures were inaugurated while Lee was president. Faculty volunteers sought donations for endowed chairs. Lee's endorsement of a plan to enlarge the science curriculum produced another campaign by the trustees. A circular stressed that Lee had rescued a floundering college because there "he could most contribute to the resuscitation of his country." Hence, funds were needed for a program "worthy of the great man who conceived it," and any contribution would be "an enduring memorial of a Hero's patriotism."[6]

But the use of General Lee's reputation by the college had only just begun. With his death in 1870, such efforts would intensify. By the end of the Reconstruction period, the Lee identification had become a vital asset to the school, and his image in turn had received widespread advertisement.

The posthumous use of Lee's name could scarcely have been achieved without the consent of his eldest son, Custis. In October 1870, at the behest of both faculty and trustees, Custis Lee accepted the college presidency. Lee, then an engineering and mathematics professor at the Virginia Military Institute, came to a school with a new name; in late October the trustees voted to change the name to Washington and Lee University.

The career of Custis Lee as college president was a sad affair. As a friend suggested, his career involved "the constant suggestion of tragedy." For twenty-six years Custis Lee served as his father's successor in Lexington, a position he never wanted. He was often absent from the president's office, long periods when he was morose, neurotic, and disinterested in college affairs. In 1874 he submitted the first of a series of resignations, all of them rejected by the trustees. The intervals between these attempts to leave the college were filled with ill health, seclusion at home, or visits to relatives.

Under his stewardship the school floundered badly. When his father died, the enrollment had been 336 students; by the 1881–82 term, the student body had dropped to 96 and the faculty had also diminished in size. By the 1880s, most of Robert Lee's academic changes had been abandoned.

In 1896, when the trustees finally accepted his resignation, Custis Lee became a recluse. He retired to Ravensworth, the home of the widow of his brother Rooney. Only once in his remaining sixteen years did Custis Lee venture from the farm, where he busied himself happily building cisterns and studying books on engineering.

Why did Custis Lee desire seclusion? Partly because his personality was an exaggeration of Robert E. Lee's. The father's moody nature became in Custis an almost psychotic moroseness. Robert Lee's reserved manner became in Custis a dislike of people. Lee's mild hypochondria became in his eldest son a neurotic obsession with his health.

There were other tendencies, also probably derived from his father, that go far to explain Custis Lee's participation in the Lee cult. One was the sense of failure which Robert E. Lee had hammered incessantly into all of his children, and Custis, after the war most of all, seemed to consider himself a failure in life. Somehow Custis Lee had been out of the mainstream of the war. He had yearned for combat, only to see his brother Rooney become a cavalry major general at the age of twenty-five, and his cousin Fitzhugh Lee attain the same rank at twenty-six. But most of Custis's wartime service was spent as an aide to President Davis, who employed young Lee's expertise in the inspection of fortifications. It was not until the week before Appomattox that he had a taste of real field service. Then, with a motley division, he joined Dick Ewell's skeleton corps at the battle of Sailor's Creek on April 6. When Ewell surrendered, Custis Lee was captured.

Misfortune continued to beset him after the war. From the estate of his grandfather, Custis Lee hoped to receive Arlington. His younger brothers had their share of the Custis and Fitzhugh lands. Robert, Jr., inherited Romancoke, once the home of Martha Washington. Rooney took over the remains of the Custis estate at White House, and later owned Ravensworth, the manse of his mother's uncle, William Henry Fitzhugh. But Custis Lee never realized his Arlington inheritance, seized during the war by Union authorities.

Thus all he possessed lay at Lexington, and that, too, turned to ashes. After his father died in 1870, and his much-adored sister Agnes and his mother both died in 1873, Custis was alone in the president's home at Lexington with his sister Mildred. She recalled those somber days that "Custis and I spent alone in the emptied, silent house, where my room echoed with dead voices."[7]

Custis Lee seemed resigned to a life predestined to failure and unhappiness. Once he advised a student to "have all the fun you can. I never had any fun in my life." More revealing was a note written in 1887 when he spoke of his attempts to escape Lexington: "It seems to be intended that I should end my days here, and possibly it is just as well, even from my standpoint, as I am too good for nothing, now I take it, to undertake anything else."[8]

Here he displayed a trait that perhaps stemmed from his father's concept of worship of duty. Custis Lee remained as college president almost mechanically, all the time realizing that he was being used by the college because of the Lee name. On that February day when he was formally installed as president, Custis heard Judge Brockenbrough intone that "the son of General R. E. Lee was the most fit person to secure the full fruition of a policy so wisely originated and matured during the full years of a nobly spent life."[9]

Custis Lee's primary contribution to his father's image was maintaining himself in a post which he hated because he felt that the school needed the prestige of the family name. The school did not disappoint him. In 1870, the trustees announced that Lee's birthday on January 19 would be an annual commemorative event, highlighted with orations to be circulated widely. The college's chief financial agent, General R. D. Lilley, launched a campaign in 1871 for endowed chairs.

Agents visited states, lectured on Lee and the college, and collected funds. A circular pleaded for a million dollars "to carry out the plans of its lamented president." Above all, the public was reminded that the school was "presided over by General R. E. Lee during the last years of his life."[10]

A more grandiose scheme was presented in 1871 to the trustees by the commencement speaker, Colonel Joseph Taylor of Alabama. The trustees endorsed the Taylor plan, given in a fifty-two-page address to the student body and later published. The college would become the "Lee Memorial University." Taylor saw this move as a *"Final and Crowning Monument"* to Lee. His bombast carried the day with students and trustees. Was not Lexington the ideal place for "the final and crowning monument to her illustrious son," where "yon river, the queen of the valley . . . is like the fruitful moral current of his early life"? The river as well "whispers . . . of the ceaseless ongoing of his fame through the future."[11]

It was this future which interested the trustees. Taylor promised that Lee Memorial University, guided by "an enlightened and trustworthy Board of Trustees," would restore Lexington to "the days of the Egyptian Pharaohs." With Lee's body buried on the campus, the school "would form one of the most potent and valuable of all the educational agencies . . ." Thus he proposed a multimillion-dollar fund-raising drive, whereby each state would contribute a thousand dollars for every student it sent to the Confederate Valhalla at Lexington. The trustees embraced Taylor's scheme, partly because his long speech had been a diatribe against a rival Lee memorial in Richmond. Taylor urged: "I appeal to all the people of the South, to say, which of the two monuments . . . that of the supposed monumental column at Richmond or that of the supposed Memorial University at Lexington . . . will most worthily and lastingly transmit the memory of General Robert E. Lee to the future."[12]

Naturally such a venture required an agent, and naturally Taylor was available. The trustees endorsed the concept of the Lee Memorial University and Taylor joined the growing number of agents seeking funds for some Lexington project. The immediate goal was $400,000. As general agent, Taylor would keep the first $5000 raised and receive a percentage of the overall proceeds.

Such projects as the state chairs and the memorial university did not succeed during the hard financial times between 1870 and 1890. Still, the many agents and solicitations promoted the Lee image widely. But not all appreciated the college's use of Lee's name. Some educators at the University of Virginia expressed resentment. Professor Charles Venable, a member of Lee's wartime staff, groused at the "Wn College League" which "ignores entirely the fact there is a University of Virginia." Editorials in eastern Virginia newspapers accused Washington and Lee of making capital of Lee's fame. A Chicago reporter, after interviewing faculty members at the University of Virginia, described them as embittered that Lee had given the Lexington school "the fictitious advantage of his name." Even a disgusted trustee of Washington and Lee ventured to comment that the school should "cease to *ask or claim patronage for our institution* because named for General Lee."[13]

A second Lexington-based organization would also publicize Lee's reputation during Reconstruction. The Lee Memorial Association, spawned in the courthouse meeting on the day of the General's death, became a powerful lobby throughout the South. Like the college, it used fund-raising agents and massive publicity to canvass the South for funds. It sought money for three schemes related to the college: a mausoleum for Lee, a massive statue on the campus, and a projected book referred to as the "Lee Memorial Volume." Anxious for publicity, the Lexington group elected prominent ex-Confederates from sixteen states to serve as officers.[14] The organization's leader, John C. Breckinridge, former vice-president under James Buchanan, held only an honorary post. So, too, did such state vice-presidents as ex-General P. G. T. Beauregard. The real power lay in a cadre of determined Lee supporters in Lexington.

Some of these men had been touched by Lee's character in mutual association at the college. One was Professor William Preston Johnston, son of General Albert Sidney Johnston. Another was a mathematics professor and former chief of ordnance for Stonewall Jackson, Colonel William Allan. But the major figures behind this publicity campaign had other motives as well. The organizational efforts which began in Lexington after Lee's death showed a singular pattern. They were manned by leaders whose desire to commemorate Lee's memory was driven by more than admiration. While monetary considerations influenced college officials, psychological factors probably motivated the leaders of the Lee Memorial Association. This was no doubt true in the case of the General's widow.

Why did Mary Custis Lee allow the Lee Memorial Association to use, sometimes in tawdry fashion, publicity about her husband to raise funds? No doubt she felt gratitude toward the college. Even before Lee's death, the trustees had offered Mary Lee a lifetime lease on the president's home and an annual pension. And by October 28, when her son Custis was chosen as president, the Virginia General Assembly had honored the trustees' request to change the college's name to honor her husband. Above all, Mary Custis Lee's postwar mental state may explain her acquiescence. She had never been a pleasant woman and had emerged from the war sick and embittered. Though an invalid, she was titular head of the family efforts to commemorate her husband's exploits.

Mary Lee did not shrink from this idolizing of her husband, for she possessed a strong drive to enshrine his achievements. Her personality was affected by the circumstances of her last years in Lexington, and nothing embittered her so much as the loss of her beloved Arlington and its treasured George Washington relics. Within three days after she fled the mansion in 1861, Federal troops had marched across the Potomac, erected fortifications on the spacious lawns, leveled ancient trees, and turned the mansion house into officers' quarters.

As war casualties mounted, Arlington served more grim purposes. By 1862 the wounded overflowed from army hospitals in Washington, turning the Arlington grounds into a sea of tents. Some soldiers who convalesced under the massive oaks and elms did not recover, and the rising death toll brought another use for the Custis lands. Grant's 1864 campaign against Richmond resulted in heavy casualties, and the only military cemetery in Washington, Soldier's Home, overflowed with fresh graves. The government decided to turn Arlington into a military cemetery, and by the year of Lee's death almost 16,000 men were buried on its lawns.

Mary Lee lost not only the surrounding grounds but her father's house as well. An 1863 tax act required individuals who owned property in "insurrectionary districts" to pay them in person. When a Lee cousin attempted to pay the $140 required for Arlington, it was refused. In 1864 Arlington passed to the government at public auction.

Her cherished Washington heirlooms had been scattered after the flight in 1861. Some items had been stolen after the initial occupation; most had been sent by Federal officers to the Department of the Interior for safekeeping. Gone also was White House on the Virginia Peninsula, where George Washington had courted the widow Custis. The house had been gutted by fire during McClellan's invasion.

Mary Lee never attempted to hide her bitterness. Of Arlington she wrote in 1866:

> I learn that my garden laid out with so much taste by my dear Father's own hands has all been changed, the splendid forest levelled to the ground, the small enclosure allotted to his and my mother's remains . . . surrounded closely by the graves of those who aided to bring all this ruin on the children and country. They are, even planted up to the very door without any regard to common decency . . .[15]

In 1867 she wrote to a cousin: "I cannot write with any composure . . . of my own cherished Arlington. Even savages would have spared that place . . . yet they have done every thing to debase and desecrate it."[16] And when a friend asked her what she would do with the Federal graves if Arlington were recovered, Mary Lee reportedly replied, "My dear, I would smooth them off and plant my flowers."[17]

Her daughter Mildred remembered that to the end of her life "her heart was ever turned to Arlington and the fair scenes of her life's best happiness," and that "her thoughts were ever in the past at Arlington —always Arlington." Mary Lee admitted that her old home "haunts me constantly," and bemoaned: "Life is waning away, and with the exception of my own immediate family I am entirely cut off from all I have ever known and loved in my youth and my dear old Arlington I cannot bear to think of that used as it is now . . ."[18]

Mary Lee returned to Arlington scarcely five months before her death. Relatives drove her to the hill overlooking the Potomac River, where she viewed the desolate, empty house. It was now a strange place, where, save for some familiar old trees, "I could not have realized that it was Arlington." And so she sadly returned to Lexington, commenting that she never cared to see the home place again. Four months later, on the eve of the anniversary of her husband's death, Mary Lee's favorite daughter, Agnes, died at the age of thirty-two. The mother never recovered from the shock, remarking how wrong it was "that I should have outlived her." Three weeks later, on a clear November day, Mary Custis Lee died.[19]

That she expired in Lexington was another key to Mary Lee's postwar mental state. The psychological effects of the move there in 1865 were probably enormous. All but four of her fifty-seven years had been spent in the Episcopalian, eastern Virginia estates of the Custis family. From there she had entered the austere, Scotch-Irish Presbyterian aura of Lexington as a virtual refugee. The modest president's home was comfortable, but it was no Custis mansion. When Mary Lee arrived in 1865, only one room was completely outfitted. The furnishings were homemade items fashioned by a one-armed veteran.

Although treated kindly, she felt trapped in Lexington. Her chronic ill health had deteriorated completely by 1865. She was a total invalid, suffering from crippling arthritis, which kept her in constant pain. The isolated Shenandoah Valley town had few ties with eastern Virginia. She mourned her sense of being "entirely cut off from all I have ever known and loved in my youth."[20]

Four years of war had converted Mary Lee to secession, and she shared with the Lost Cause writers a need for literary justification. In 1861 she had railed against the cotton states for seceding, angrily condemning their "riotous proceedings."[21] But the hardships of war radically altered her views. In 1862, after White House was burned, she spoke of "the thievish villains," "these brave and Christian yankees who would woo us back to the Union." Indeed, "sooner than to be reunited to such a people again would I live under the despotic rule of Russia."[22]

In 1866 Mary Lee wrote "My Reminiscences of the War Waged Against the South by the United States Abolitionist Faction Immediately After the Election of Lincoln." In this unpublished account Lincoln's supporters were described as "fanatical abolitionists, unprincipled and evil." Lincoln himself had provoked a war and "has gone to render an account to the judge of all the Earth for the misery he has wrought to our unhappy country."[23]

Then came the final blow. Her view of Robert Lee's death seems vital in her relationship to the first Lee cult. After her husband died on that morning of October 12, Mary Lee retired to her room for the remainder of the day. Even while village bells tolled, she took a pen in her crippled fingers and wrote a long account of Lee's death to a cousin. The letter included minute details of times of day, statements by Lee, and similar items. It was a morbid narrative, characteristic of the family's obsession with death. Only a few hours before, she had lost the man on whom "I have leaned with perfect confidence for more than thirty years." Yet she would take the time that same afternoon to write to a cousin, because "the papers may have given you some account of his illness but rather an incorrect one, so I will commence and tell you all the details."[24]

The "details" indicated that Mary Lee already was thinking of her husband's future image. There were mentions of a life "so important to his family and country"; of a man for whom "nothing could add to his estimation in the hearts of his countrymen"; one whose memory "will be cherished in many hearts beside my own." Even that day, she could speculate that one reason she regretted his death was that it was a political loss for the South. Mary Lee acknowledged: "I was ambitious enough to hope the day might come when in a political sense at least he might again be its Deliverer from the thralldom which oppresses it."[25]

She had always been ambitious for her husband. In 1862 she had confided to a friend:

> I see by the papers that he is put in charge of the armies of the Confederacy. Now they have got into trouble, they send for him to help them out, and yet he never gets any credit for what he has done. . . . He never complains or seems to desire anything more than to perform his duty, but I may be excused for wishing him to reap the reward for his labors.[26]

Mary Lee was ever conscious of the Lee image. After his death she expressed this same pride to others. To one she wrote:

Could he have been more lamented and honoured had he obtained for our beloved South the Independence to the attainment of which he devoted his life and renounced all ease and comfort? The fame so unsought and never desired will follow his name through ages to come.[27]

To another friend she asserted that "he could not have been more lamented or his fame brighter had he lived a thousand years."[28]

Her concern for Lee's image on the very day of his death was not cold-blooded. Mary Lee meant nothing cynical when a few weeks later she told a close friend: "Had he been successful instead of the Hero of a Lost Cause he would not have been more beloved and honored. I am content and would not have him back if I could . . ."[29]

These were assertions of her belief that Lee had reached a pinnacle of fame far above others, a niche in Valhalla. Yet there was a qualifying factor. For her, Lee's ascension to this pinnacle had not come easily. She saw him as a special case of sacrifice, worthy of memorial for this reason alone. For the cause, he "had devoted his life and renounced all ease and comfort."

Somehow it always came back to Arlington. When in her 1866 reminiscence she spoke of the severest struggle of Lee's life, a struggle so intense "I will not attempt to describe it," she spoke of his 1861 decision and the loss of her home. By the time of Lee's death, all her postwar frustrations had probably come to the surface. Perhaps she sought justification not merely for him—but for herself and that place where her mind always wandered.

So, despite her failing health, Mary Lee's remaining years were devoted to projects intended to illuminate her husband's career. She assisted in preparing the "Lee Memorial Volume," helped various early biographers to obtain materials, and participated in the design of Edward Valentine's figure for the Lee chapel.[30]

Her colleague in many projects of the Lee Memorial Association was its executive director, the Reverend William Nelson Pendleton. Pendleton's devotion to preserving Lee's memory also transcended normal affection, and suggested unusual psychological motivations. For ten years after Appomattox, Pendleton ruined his already wretched health in his efforts to publicize Lee's name. While he idolized Lee, Pendleton's campaign seemed in part a search for relief from his own inner turmoil. Prior to the Civil War, his careers as an army officer and a minister had been plagued with mental depression and frequent feelings of guilt and moral inadequacy. Though he sought a career in the ministry to heal his "depraved and unsanctified heart," he experienced fits of depression and neurotic physical symptoms.[31]

The Civil War years only intensified Pendleton's consciousness of sin and search for relief. In 1861, while rector of Grace Church in Lexington, he accepted a captaincy in the Confederate army. Within hours, he was busy writing a memorandum to himself, attempting to justify his decision. In the 1830s, he had left the army for the ministry because he sought a life that would ease his sense of inadequacy. Now he strove to reconcile the inner warfare between his Gods of the Old and New Testaments. In his memorandum of 1861 he implored, "Lord Jesus go with me." Yet he never seemed totally certain that his companion was there. After Lee's defeat at Sharpsburg, Pendleton described his duties as strange for "a servant of the Prince of Peace." He sought justification in "the example of Old Abraham," but longed to find it as well in the New Testament's Jesus.

At times Pendleton buoyed himself, such as when Lee invaded Pennsylvania in 1863. Because he was certain that God marched with the Army of Northern Virginia, Pendleton was shocked by Pickett's disastrous charge and could only pray that "God has not vacated his throne." Grant's push toward Richmond, the death of his beloved son Sandie, and Appomattox only further disillusioned Pendleton. Shortly after the surrender he regretted that "I feel almost thankful that so many of our beloved have been taken from the evil here."[32]

In a sense Pendleton was an exaggeration of one element of the Lost Cause mentality which eventually turned to Lee as its supreme hero. As he would after the war, Pendleton in 1861 grappled with the question of how a righteous cause could lose. In the Civil War the fate of the South contradicted the American dogma that virtue equaled success. Confident of victory and of God's blessing, a defeated South was forced to rethink its position.

Pendleton and many other ex-Confederates were to use Robert E. Lee as a balm to soothe defeat. Lee's character served as the rebuttal to the American dream, and to the gnawing question of how a righteous cause could lose. Lee would be held up as proof that good men do not always succeed. Thus a few months after the war, Pendleton had begun to use a rationalization that spread throughout the South. He saw a parallel between the Confederacy and Jesus and his followers. Both lived "under foreign domination" in an alien society. Both were sacred causes, yet ended at Appomattox and Gethsemane. The fate of the Confederacy and first-century Christianity only proved that the race is not always won by the most sanctified.

Such comparisons demanded a Christ-like figure. Like many postwar Southerners, Pendleton found this spotless individual in Lee, whose character was adorned with "a more sacred lustre, the halo that will forever encircle his name."[33]

Shaken badly by Lee's death in 1870, Pendleton committed himself to preserving Lee's memory. For five years the "strong moving springs of his life" became an obsession with eulogizing the General.

Pendleton's tours brought much publicity to the Lee image in the South. As executive director of the Association, he endeavored to raise money for the Valentine statue and the Lee mausoleum. He also dabbled in a side project—seeking money to rebuild Grace Church, where Lee had worshipped.

These memorializing activities required funding, and in October 1870 Pendleton inaugurated a massive campaign. Circulars asked for money to be given in memory of Lee. One such pamphlet sought funds for Grace Church—now renamed the Lee Memorial Church. The church leaders regarded the project "as a sacred duty to his memory."

Pendleton also dispatched agents to raise funds for the Valentine statue. Several speakers worked the lecture circuit. General Wade Hampton spoke in Savannah on Lee's career, and then asked for donations. A Baltimore lecturer eulogized Lee's character, and assured his listeners that a donation to the Memorial Association was a means by which the average Southerner could feel some justification for defeat in the war. The Association commissioned a steel engraving of Lee by a Cincinnati firm, and sold the picture to raise money. Still another source of funds was J. William Jones's *Personal Reminiscences, Anecdotes and Letters of General Robert E. Lee,* the first influential biography of the General. Part of the proceeds of its sale went to the Association.

From Louisville to New Orleans, and from Memphis to Richmond, Pendleton toured the South for five years, delivering lectures on his idol. He enlisted local prominent ex-Rebels to publicize his efforts. Pendleton created a stock lecture, which he later published in the *Southern Magazine,* "Personal Recollections of General Lee." He preached a dual theme—that Lee's character was stainless and his generalship invincible.[34]

By 1875 such efforts had raised the funds for the Valentine statue, but not for its home. For almost two years there had been a struggle between rival factions within the Association over the location of Lee's mausoleum. Pendleton was disturbed at signs of rising Presbyterian influence on the college campus; hence, the Pendleton–Grace Church faction complained that Lee's "remains, his fame, the wealth he has secured to Washington College" were becoming Presbyterian-dominated. Pendleton's group lobbied for a separate mausoleum, while party regulars in the Memorial Association fought for the construction of the tomb in the rear of the college chapel.

Valentine informed the group in early 1875 that the statue was ready, and it was shipped by rail and canal boat to Lexington. Artillery on the Virginia Military Institute campus boomed salutes, and the gov-

ernor and ex-Rebel luminaries provided the oratory. One speaker emphasized that the Memorial Association considered it "our sacred duty
to rear to Lee the statue, the mausoleum, the memorial pile." Then the
homeless statue was committed to a storeroom.[35]

New fund-raising and publicity efforts collected funds for the
mausoleum. By 1877 the Memorial Association had agreed to attach the
mausoleum to the rear of the college chapel. The lower story would
house Lee's body, while the upper section would display the marble
statue. General R. D. Lilley, a veteran fund raiser for the college, was
borrowed to canvass for the Association. J. William Jones took to the
field under the title "general agent," and lectured on Lee's greatness.
Entertainments were organized in New Orleans, Charleston, Mobile,
and elsewhere to raise money, and circulars extolling Lee's virtues
flooded cities in the North and South.

The mausoleum was finished in 1882, but Pendleton did not live to
see his efforts come to fruition. In the winter of 1883, the man who often
boasted of his own physical resemblance to his hero, Robert Lee, died
in Lexington.

Some of Pendleton's stress may have been provoked by the competition for funds among a half dozen Lee memorial schemes. Speaker
podiums were becoming crowded. Agents for Washington and Lee
competed with professional fund raisers and raw volunteers in Southern lecture halls, seeking money for the mausoleum, the Valentine
statue, Lee Memorial Church, and other ventures.

Even in Lexington there were competitors for scarce Southern
dollars. While Pendleton hustled his agents afield, the "Lee Memorial
Volume" project also pursued donations. Within weeks after Lee's
death, his family and the college faculty began collaboration on a book
designed to raise money for several memorial undertakings.

The biography, a medley of reminiscences by military comrades
and other friends of Lee's, was a failure. The book languished because
Lee's former aide, Colonel Charles Marshall, never finished the segment on the General's military career, which was to be the cornerstone
of the project. Marshall probably became disgusted at the rising competition between rival Lee memorial groups in Lexington and Richmond.
He also was no doubt stung by the criticism of Lee's Lexington friends
by outsiders. Charles Venable berated Marshall for his involvement in
the project, and charged that the book was designed "to give greater
prominence to General Lee's connexion with Washington College than
to his fame as a great leader."[36] In 1873 Marshall announced that he
would not finish the biography, and a bewildered group of Lee devotees, anxious for funds, sought aid elsewhere.

Into the breach stepped a local Baptist preacher and Lee family
confidant, J. William Jones. The failure of the memorial volume raised

to power one of the most influential members of the Lee cult. Jones, already at work on his own biography of Lee, sensed the anxiety of the Lee family and the faculty. He proposed that he be given access to the family papers and the unfinished manuscript. In return, he would divide the profits from his biography with the Lee Memorial Association. The Association delivered the manuscript to Jones. Lee's widow, charmed by Jones's careful cultivation of her friendship, loaned him her husband's personal letters and read a rough draft of the parson's manuscript. In 1875, Jones's *Personal Reminiscences, Anecdotes and Letters of General Robert E. Lee* was published, and it became a source book for all future Lee biographers.

Had he not become so powerful a figure through his biography, Jones would have been considered humorous. He was the stereotype unreconstructed Rebel who each year began the meeting of the United Confederate Veterans with a plea for help from the "God of Israel, God of Abraham, Isaac and Jacob . . . God of Stonewall Jackson and Robert E. Lee, and Jefferson Davis." He was described as "worshipping Lee and Jackson next to God."[37]

Yet he acquired considerable influence during a career of almost forty years of writing Confederate history and praising Lee's exploits. His biography was a potpourri of anecdotes and Lee letters, and the extensive use of the letters gave the book verisimilitude, as did Jones's assertion that he was the family's handpicked biographer. A financial and literary success in the South, Jones's hodgepodge was praised by the *Southern Magazine* as "a household book in all Southern homes."

Jones joined other Lee admirers in gaining control of the faltering Southern Historical Society, and rebuilt it into one of the most powerful organizations in the United States devoted to Civil War history. From 1876 until 1887 Jones was the Society's secretary and editor of its journal. He turned this publication, the Society's *Papers,* into a magazine of carefully selected articles which praised Lee and damned his critics.

Jones built his career by fawning over the exploits of others. In 1861 he was a young preacher fresh from a Baptist seminary, whose planned missionary tour in China was interrupted by the war. His pedestrian military record involved mainly a series of chaplaincys. But in 1865 young Jones began five years of close association with Robert E. Lee. When Lee arrived in Lexington to assume the institution's presidency, Jones was minister of the local Baptist church and a college chaplain. He carefully cultivated the Lee family's friendship, and thereafter would claim an intimate acquaintance with the General.

Jones was a sycophant, a habitual name dropper who relished contact with Confederate notables. He never failed to remind his readers that his words deserved special credence. The higher the rank, the more intimate was Jones's supposed acquaintance. "It was my proud privilege to know Stonewall Jackson personally, and to see a good deal of him." His friendship with Jefferson Davis was one of "personal knowledge and intercourse."

His friendship with Lee brought Jones vicarious satisfaction. One must conclude that he capitalized upon this acquaintance and used it for almost four decades to advance his literary career. His Lee biography boasted of how he knew Lee "intimately," was "intimately associated with him," and "mingled with him in the freest social intercourse." Numerous subsequent writings, including his 1906 *Life and Letters of Robert E. Lee,* claimed such a friendship. Jones spoke "from careful personal observation," or wrote from "almost daily association" with Lee.[38]

Jones was no foppish, small-town minister. He was a cunning, ambitious man who rose to power among the cult of Lee writers at the expense of others. During his long career in the Southern Historical Society, he often attacked the reputation of such critics of Lee as General James Longstreet. On one occasion Jones arrogantly confided to a friend that "I am anxious for you to slice up what is left of Longstreet." Jones also used his position to downgrade the exploits of rival Confederate heroes such as Jackson and Beauregard.

While he assailed some individuals, he flattered others. Jones especially cultivated the friendship of Jefferson Davis. In the 1870s an embittered Davis barricaded himself in his Gulf Coast retreat at Beauvoir, preparing his memoirs. He was determined to wreak revenge upon two old Confederate enemies, Joseph Johnston and P. G. T. Beauregard, who had sharply criticized him in their postwar writings. Davis had a small army of researchers, stretching from Mississippi to Washington, D.C., who ferreted out evidence to support his claims.

Jones joined the Davis camp. As secretary of the Southern Historical Society, he had access to a rapidly growing collection of manuscripts. He secretly furnished documents to Davis which would be used to injure Johnston's and Beauregard's reputations, slanted articles in the Society's magazine against the two officers, and egged Davis on to attack them further. There was little charity in Jones's efforts. He wanted to use Davis to raise funds for the infant Southern Historical Society. Jones proposed to Davis a lecture tour from Baltimore to New Orleans, to be followed by professional agents "that . . . will raise all of the money we need."[39]

IN EARLY NOVEMBER 1870, only weeks after Lee's death, there was a full-scale revolt against the plans to enshrine Lee in Lexington. Veterans of the Army of Northern Virginia, determined that *they* would possess the General's remains, met in the Presbyterian church in Richmond.

The meeting was led by Lee's former corps leader, General Jubal Early. He and other wartime associates of Lee were irritated because they had been excluded from the funeral activities in Lexington. They were also angry that Lexington had been chosen as the site of Lee's tomb, and that the "principal" monument to Lee—the Valentine statue —was also to be located in the Shenandoah Valley town. Early considered it his "sacred duty" to overturn such decisions, and on October 25 he issued a circular letter in Virginia newspapers calling for the gathering on November 3. One private soldier set the tone for the meeting when he insisted that Lee must be reburied in Richmond so that "when the grand revilee shall sound, he will be found in the midst of his boys whom he loved so well."[40]

An emotional crowd, including many former officers who had served with Lee, jammed the Presbyterian church to hear speakers denounce the Lexington plans. Early led the assault, insisting that "an enduring monument" should be "accessible to all his boys" in Richmond.

Then came the report of Colonel Charles Venable, who headed an ad hoc "Committee on Resolutions" which reported a list of plans embodying the veterans' frustration. Venable urged that the group organize into the "Lee Monument Association." The members should dedicate themselves to erecting the main monument to Lee in Richmond, regardless of "local" statues in Lexington and elsewhere. Venable's committee also urged the reburial of Lee in Richmond. The General's remains ought to "be committed to the charge of this Association." Richmond, "founded by the companions of his knightly ancestors," should be the burial site. Lee should rest there, among the thousands of Confederate dead in the Hollywood Cemetery, so that "when the first flush of the resurrection morn tinges the skies, may their unsealed eyes behold the grand figure" of their wartime chief.

The flowery oratory had only begun. The speakers who followed Venable to the podium echoed his sentiments. General John Preston desired the monument to rest in front of the capital, and proposed the burial in Richmond, "the ground made sacred by himself." General John Gordon, one of Lee's corps leaders, declared that Lee excelled Napoleon and Marlborough. Gordon spoke lines that were later often repeated: "Lee could not be beaten: Overpowered . . . he might be, but never defeated." So let him rest here in Richmond, "here on these classic hills."[41]

There was some dissent at the meeting. The Lee Memorial Association, hearing of the Richmond gathering and determined to protect its interests, sent a delegation led by Reverend Pendleton. As soon as the group reached Richmond the lobbying began. Colonel William Allan was seconded to soothe the ruffled feelings of General Early and to attempt to squelch the rebellion. Although he heaped praise on the vain Early, somehow Allan said the wrong things. He reversed the barb fired by Colonel Venable, and described the Richmond plans for a statue as "local action." And although Allan (as did everyone) agreed that the disposition of Lee's remains was a family matter, he informed Early that there was no probability of the body being reburied in Richmond.[42]

When Allan's peace mission failed to upset Early's plans, the Lexington delegation attempted another tactic. After speeches denouncing the Washington and Lee schemes, Colonel William Preston Johnston of the college faculty came to the speaker's podium. Surely the veterans would listen to the son of the South's first revered war hero, Albert Sidney Johnston, and to his compromise offer. Johnston's proposal was simple—to divide the Lee memorabilia among the two towns. Let Lexington have Lee's body, and Richmond have "a grand statue." Both groups would then assist each other in raising money for the Lexington mausoleum and the Richmond statue.

Early's veterans were in no mood for deals, and Johnston was practically blown off the stage by more fiery oratory and resolutions. The Lexington compromise was ignored, and there was a vote to organize the Lee Monument Association and to obtain both Lee's body and his main statue.[43]

A year of guerrilla warfare now raged between the rival camps in the Shenandoah Valley and the Tidewater. Epithets were freely tossed about. The Monument Association accused the Lexington people of taking advantage of Mrs. Lee's grief to secure approval of burial there. Early's men argued that the Lexington group never intended to exchange the monument for the tomb. Eastern Virginia journalists accused Washington and Lee University of capitalizing upon Lee's reputation.

The Lexington group accused the Monument Association of "malignant and scandalous behavior." It asserted that Early's veterans were attempting to steal the officers of the Memorial Association, since its president, General John C. Breckinridge, had been named a vice-president of the rival organization. Worse, it was the Richmond bloc that was applying pressure on the General's widow. So many Richmond delegations prodded Mary Lee to rebury her husband in that city that she expressed "pain and annoyance" and asked that no more requests be made.[44]

The intense feeling that produced the Richmond group was matched by a high degree of organization, which made the Lexington efforts appear amateurish. Early's executive committee was led by men who would be familiar names in the first Lee cult, such as the General's former staff officers Charles Venable and Walter Taylor. The committee oversaw publicity efforts extending into thirteen state committees. Each state committee was headed by a vice-president, more often than not an officer whose local prominence would assist in fund-raising efforts.

The Lee Monument Association's activities had competition even within Richmond. A week before the Richmond meeting, several members of the Hollywood Memorial Association, a women's group, gathered to discuss where Lee should rest. From this meeting was organized the Ladies' Lee Monument Association, supported by Tidewater dowagers of old families such as the Randolphs. They were a determined lot, and for almost fifteen years refused to join Early's Lee Monument Association. Their plan called for Lee to be buried in Hollywood Cemetery, in a grave adorned with a massive bronze equestrian statue.

The women's group was so small that by 1884 all but two members were either dead or had moved away from Virginia. Yet they outclassed the men in fund-raising techniques. Shortly after Early's association held its first meeting, the ladies had already organized a South-wide canvass to raise funds for their Lee memorial. They sent an elaborate circular throughout the region, appealing to all churches, "Christian and Hebrew," for funds. A special collection would be taken up on November 27, all funds to be forwarded to Richmond.

This appeal caused some resentment among Southern churchmen, but it was successful. Three thousand dollars came from Savannah, Georgia, alone. The Association then hired a professional fund-raising agent to tour the South to publicize the monument. Some sixteen thousand dollars was thus raised. Early's group hired a professional agent in a competing canvass. The veterans' alliance even sent a spy to the ladies' meeting to learn their plans. Not until 1886 did Virginia governor Fitzhugh Lee convince the women to combine their efforts—and money—with Early's group.

Until that union was achieved, towns and cities in the old Confederacy were overrun by agents competing for Lee memorials. Professionals and volunteers were on the road simultaneously for the Lee Monument Association, the Ladies' Lee Monument Association, the Lee Memorial Association, the Lee Memorial Episcopal Church at Lexington, and Washington and Lee University. Further, agents employed by the Southern Historical Society raised funds by delivering lectures on Lee's campaigns.

The Lee Monument Association used devices other than professional agents. Lectures on the General's campaigns were delivered by local notables, followed by the passing of the collection plate. A lithograph of Lee astride Traveler was printed and a copy was sent to "any college, school, lodge, club, military or civic association" that would contribute ten dollars.

The sophistication of these publicity efforts was exemplified by the great campaign of 1876. That year Colonel Basset French, who directed the "Office of the Board of Managers" of the Monument Association, inaugurated a town-by-town canvass of the South on the anniversary of Lee's birthday. French asked Southern mayors to furnish lists of prominent local citizens "who would likely give an earnest support." He distributed to these notables an elaborate circular which proposed "to canvass every house in every town in the Southern States." Each mayor was urged to "lay out your city into numerous and convenient divisions, and appoint canvassers for each." The local dignitaries would "make the domiciliary visits and solicit generous contributions." French insisted that such a fund-raising drive was a "right and proper" way in which all Southerners could display "gratitude and affection" for Lee."[45]

The Richmond bloc's high degree of organization did not end with the forming of the two monument associations. On November 4, the day after Early's group was founded, that same body of veterans filled the Richmond Theatre to inaugurate the Association of the Army of Northern Virginia.

This association was the inspiration of a Harvard-educated Maryland attorney, General Bradley Johnson. Johnson, a former brigade leader under Stonewall Jackson, had envisioned the group in early 1870, intending that Robert E. Lee serve as its chief. Lee discouraged the scheme, believing that the political situation in the South made it inexpedient. But after Lee's death, Johnson proposed the organization at Early's Richmond meeting, and secured enthusiastic endorsement.

With a leadership including Early and former Lee staff members such as Walter Taylor and Charles Marshall, the Association of the Army of Northern Virginia was the most powerful veterans' group in the South prior to the advent of the United Confederate Veterans decades later. Much of its power came from its superior organization. An executive committee headed by General Bradley Johnson supervised thirteen state divisions, which in turn were controlled by thirty-nine vice-presidents and their assistants.

Johnson's penchant for organization produced a fourth group operating from Richmond—the Virginia Division. This arm of the Association grew out of Johnson's plan for a veterans' division in each state. But under the leadership of Robert E. Lee's son W. H. F. Lee and his nephew Fitzhugh Lee, the Virginia Division became a separate, powerful body.

The veterans' groups were influential in publicizing Lee's exploits. At their annual meetings there were many speeches eulogizing his career which became standard items in Lee writings. Whether issued in books, pamphlets, or the pages of the Southern Historical Society's *Papers,* these accolades enhanced Lee's reputation. Some reprinted lectures were used by the Southern Historical Society to raise funds; such was Fitzhugh Lee's address on his uncle's Chancellorsville operations, which denied to Stonewall Jackson any credit for the planning of the famous march around Joseph Hooker's right wing. W. Gordon McCabe's speech on the campaign of 1864–65 was one of the first strong assertions that Lee outgeneraled Grant, only to fail against superior numbers. Captain John Chamberlayne's examination of Lee's character, which almost placed the General among the Trinity, was to be cited repeatedly in future writings.

TWO IMPORTANT FACTORS may explain the intensity of effort in Richmond. These associations, manned by Lee's soldiers, were in part a reflection of the Confederate mind during Reconstruction. Lee, the South's most successful general, provided a rationale for a people whose emotional trauma needed some semblance of success. Ex-Confederates had to come to terms with the fact that a cause they considered righteous had been crushed. To maintain some sense of victory, they would gather in crowded veterans' halls and exaggerate the military prowess of Robert E. Lee.

But until Lee's fame was publicized far and wide, the "Northern" version of the war would be accepted by the nation. The general refusal by Federal authorities to allow Southerners access to captured Confederate records made these men wary. A speaker at the organization of the Monument Association warned that "the spoiler is now busily and rapidly taking from us, by the pen, the truth of history more precious to us than all the spoils of war which were ever captured by his sword." When the Association of the Army of Northern Virginia was organized, one speaker pointed to the Federal seizure of Confederate records and said that "the weapons of our defense, and the arguments for our complete and thorough vindication . . . are in the hands of our enemies." The only solution was to organize and to write the Confederate version of the war. Such determination should center upon Lee's army, so that Southerners could "cherish their memories" which are "fast dying away from memory, and may soon be forgotten."[46]

The structure of the Richmond leadership also explained its emotional drive. It was a small elite clique of ex-officers. Like their rivals in Lexington, the Richmond men were inspired by motives beyond their love for Robert E. Lee, to the point that their efforts often appeared to be a paranoiac defense of their hero.

The dominant military figure of the Lee cult was Jubal Early. His chief colleagues were four members of the General's wartime staff—Colonels Charles Marshall, Walter Taylor, A. L. Long, and Charles Venable. Beneath this level were more obscure figures, minor officers and private soldiers of Lee's army. Such men as General Bradley Johnson and Captain Gordon McCabe did the legwork in various associations, marshaled crowds for monument dedications, and supplied documentary evidence used by more prominent Lee devotees.

None of this group, not even Early, was a household name in the South in 1865. They stepped into a vacuum of early Civil War writing created by the absence of better-known names. They gained acclaim they had never received in their war careers. Both the Lexington and Richmond wings of the Lee cult were dominated by men whose reputations were made more by postwar enshrinement of the Lee image than by their own war records. There were only three major field officers active in the first cult, and they were among the least-known of Lee's corps leaders, all with questionable war records. Jubal Early and Fitzhugh Lee were pre-eminent in the Richmond group, while Lee's artillery chief, Reverend William Pendleton, served at Lexington. Early was the only corps general ever removed from command by Lee, Fitz Lee was the least able of Lee's cavalry commanders, and Pendleton's wartime service had evoked broad criticism.

General Bradley Johnson, a somewhat obscure brigade commander in Lee's army, made a virtual career of promoting Lee's exploits. He organized and led the Association of the Army of Northern Virginia, and was president of both the Society of Confederate States Army and Navy of Maryland and the Association of the Maryland Line. Johnson also busied himself with speechmaking and ceremonial activities. Wherever there was a monument to be unveiled—whether the Maryland shaft at Gettysburg or the Confederate monument at Fredericksburg—Bradley Johnson was the inevitable speaker. When the cornerstone for the Lee monument was laid in Richmond in 1887, Johnson headed 500 Maryland veterans in a march up Monument Avenue. Three years later at the monument's dedication, astride a white charger and surrounded by his staff, the indefatigable Johnson led 1200 Maryland veterans on parade.[47]

Yet there were also men who had had personal wartime relationships with Lee which had evoked almost fanatical love. Some of them viewed their efforts as paying a debt to the memory of one who had shown them special kindness. Others believed the mantle of Elijah had fallen upon them. Several former officers, knowing that the General had died without completing his history of the Army of Northern Virginia, believed it their destiny to complete his work.

The nature of Lee's headquarters staff encouraged close relationships. By law, Lee was allowed both a general staff and a headquarters staff. The general staff consisted of a large number of men who did not dine at Lee's mess or operate directly from his headquarters. But the headquarters staff was a closely knit cadre of young men who were in daily contact with Lee. It generally consisted of a military secretary, four aides-de-camp, and an assistant adjutant general. Several of these became strong Lee partisans. They were young, impressionable men, most of them with literary talent, placed in close proximity to a man whom they came to love fiercely. Three of these—Colonels Charles Marshall, Walter Taylor, and Charles Venable—remained with Lee until the end of the war. The fourth, Lee's secretary Colonel A. L. Long, later became an artillery officer.

Marshall, only thirty-two when he joined the staff, possessed literary abilities, which Lee had recognized. A former college professor at Indiana University and a Baltimore attorney, Marshall served as Lee's aide from the spring of 1862. From then until Appomattox, Marshall had a special role on Lee's staff. He wrote official reports of campaigns, most of Lee's correspondence to President Davis, and messages to the War Department. And it was Marshall who examined all reports sent to headquarters by Lee's subordinates.

Marshall came as close as any officer to being the General's confidant, and he forgot little. He particularly remembered the agony both men shared in the room of the McClean House at Appomattox. The only other Confederate present, Marshall recalled the events clearly and with emotion until his death in 1902.

After the war, Marshall claimed that Lee's battle reports underrated his own achievements and often had shielded erring subordinates. Marshall remarked that these reports contained "an utter forgetfulness of self, that made me lose my admiration of the great soldier in my reverence for the excellence of the man." According to Marshall, Lee struck from the original draft of his Gettysburg report statements harmful to subordinates, and "thus covered the errors and omissions of all his officers."[48]

Because he believed Lee did not do justice to himself, Marshall helped the General with his memoirs. He furnished statistical information, entreated other officers to supply documents, suggested an outline, and even gave advice on how to negotiate a book contract. Lee never completed the book, and Marshall saw himself as the General's Boswell. The Lee family regarded him as the best choice to write the official biography. By 1871 Marshall had begun work, after the family had placed Lee's papers in his custody. Though he wrote for years, the biography was incomplete when he died in 1902; not until 1927 was the unfinished narrative published by Sir Frederick Maurice.

Marshall was distracted by other Lee projects. He worked on the "Lee Memorial Volume," and was active in several groups such as the

Lee Monument Association. Because of his prominence on Lee's staff, Marshall became involved in long and frequent correspondence with other Lee defenders, supplying them testimony for use against the General's critics.

One such writer was Colonel Walter Taylor, who had his own special motives. It had been a May morning in 1861 when young Taylor first glimpsed Lee in the dining room of a Richmond hotel. A recent graduate of the Virginia Military Institute, Taylor had left a banking position in Norfolk to join the war effort. He was assigned to Lee's staff in the Provisional State Army.

The youngest of the staff, Taylor served longer than any other officer. He went with Lee into the miserable West Virginia campaign in 1861, traveled with him to the South Carolina department, and returned in the spring of 1862 when the General became the President's military adviser. Lee made good use of Taylor's capabilities as a statistician. The young banker kept the army's records and compiled the monthly returns of its strength.

Taylor was strongly devoted to his wartime "peerless and immortal leader" and was touched by Lee's postwar attitude. On one occasion in 1865, when a Federal grand jury in Norfolk had indicted Lee for treason, Taylor had written a note warning the General. Lee's unselfish response only showed concern lest Taylor and other ex-subordinates be molested.

Taylor also believed that he had inherited the task of completing Lee's work. In July 1865, Lee sent a circular request to his officers, asking their assistance in supplying data for his memoirs. Taylor was asked for his expertise in compiling statistics of the army's strength. This letter and later appeals by Lee to Taylor were explicit—the young officer must help show the world the odds that the Army of Northern Virginia had to fight against.

Thus Taylor embarked upon a career of proving "the great numerical odds" faced by Lee. When Lee died before making use of Taylor's statistics, the young aide felt charged with a special mission. He believed that "all-wise Providence" had prevented Lee from giving "a true statement of the odds against which they had to contend." Now, Taylor wrote, "the duty seemed logically to devolve upon me."[49]

Taylor's determination involved him in a number of projects. He worked on his memoir, *Four Years with General Lee*, published in 1877. He defended Lee in Southern magazines and in Northern newspapers such as the Philadelphia *Times*. He worked arduously for the Lee Monument Association, and maintained a network of correspondence with J. William Jones, Early, and Fitzhugh Lee, constantly furnishing them with statistics.

Other former members of Lee's staff pursued their own ventures.

A. L. Long, Lee's military secretary, labored in blindness for twenty-five years to write a biography, scrawling sentences upon a blackboard to be transcribed by his daughters. The General's aide Charles Venable never forgot the scene on the morning of April 9 at Appomattox Court House when Lee learned that it would be impossible to break through Grant's encircling lines. Venable heard Lee murmur his decision to meet Grant, though "I would rather die a thousand deaths." While surrounding officers talked excitedly, Venable recalled Lee's response was: "The question is, is it right to surrender this army? If it is, then I will take *all* the responsibility." Venable devoted part of his life after Appomattox to the memory of "our Great Captain," whose death he believed was caused by the heartbreak of witnessing the Southern plight during Reconstruction. Because he saw it as "a high and holy duty," Venable also joined the inner circle of Lee admirers who patiently fashioned the General's image after Appomattox.[50]

But the driving force behind the first Lee cult was Jubal Early, perhaps the most influential figure in nineteenth-century Civil War writing, North or South. Early dominated the efforts in Richmond, emerging as president of the Lee Monument Association and its companion Association of the Army of Northern Virginia. By 1873 he had solidified the rival Lee factions in Lexington and Richmond into a powerful body of partisans. He reshaped the Southern Historical Society into an organ dedicated to Lee's memory and served for years as its president.

For over three decades Early was the man most feared by both critics and admirers of Lee. Lee partisans sought his advice for their own writings, encouraged his literary assaults, and often asked his approval of their work before publication.

How Early gained so much power is a complex question, intermingled with the problem of what incessant force drove him to become what one observer described as "the fearless guardian of the fame of Lee."[51]

Early's influence and motivation existed in part because he was an exaggeration of the postbellum Southern mind. His life after Appomattox was a trek in search of justification for secession and explanation for Rebel defeat. Why and how a righteous cause could lose especially disturbed Early. Attempts to reconcile the issue led him—and other ex-Rebel writers—to irrational thinking. They denied that the South lost the war because of its own mistakes, and insisted that defeat was the product of both superior Federal numbers and chance circumstances in battle. This rationale partially explains Early's obsession with Gettysburg, where, he insisted, a few hours altered the future of the entire Western Hemisphere. Early's refusal to accept defeat also compelled him to exaggerate Lee's military prowess, until the General emerged in his mind as an invincible leader innocent of any wartime mistakes.

Early's war record held no promise of postwar eminence. He had been one of Lee's most disliked subordinates, and he understated the case when he admitted that "I was never what is called a popular man." He seemed to relish his eccentric and sour disposition, which proved repugnant to many fellow officers. Described by one friend as a "queer fish," he provoked humor and ridicule with his shabby suits, comical flopping hat, thin straggling beard, stooped appearance, and piping nasal twang.

Early never stopped talking. He was dogmatic, profane, and opinionated on every subject. His indiscreet public criticisms of other officers were well known, enough to prompt one listener to surmise that Early's habitual carping was sufficient "to have convicted him a hundred times before any court-martial."[52]

In both politics and war, Early was the Ishmael of the Confederacy, a loner often out of step with his colleagues. In the 1861 Virginia secession convention he was a staunch Union delegate who fought hard to keep his state within the Union. Only after the convention voted did Early sign the ordinance. Then he quickly adopted a position as an avid secessionist, and offered himself to Robert E. Lee's state army.

In Confederate service he eventually became an outcast. His record as one of Lee's division commanders was admirable, but his reputation collapsed in 1864. When Grant began to maneuver from the Rapidan River toward Richmond, Lee sought to duplicate the success of Stonewall Jackson's Valley campaign of 1862. He chose Early to initiate a threat against Washington, hopeful of holding back reinforcements from Grant.

Early's raid on Washington led to disaster. Unable to take the city, his small army retreated into the Shenandoah Valley. There for months he faced a vastly superior Federal force under General Philip Sheridan. By March 1865, after a string of battles, Early's force had been virtually obliterated. Violent protests by some Virginians in the area compelled Lee to remove him from command.

His subsequent conduct would not seem to have endeared him to Southerners. After Lee's surrender, Early struck westward on a quixotic flight into Texas. When he learned of the surrender of Rebel forces west of the Mississippi, he crossed the Rio Grande into Mexico, journeyed to Cuba, and then moved north to Canada. For three years he sulked in Montreal and Toronto before returning in 1869 to Virginia. Thus he bore the reputation of one who had deserted the South after Appomattox.

Early's devotion to Lee's memory was an alchemy of gratitude and guilt. Lee's praise of Early on the occasion of his 1865 removal from command was followed by other kindnesses. While Early was in exile in South America and the Caribbean, Lee furnished him with letters of recommendation, and turned aside his attempts to explain the flight from the South. Early admitted that his intense hatred of the North made his exile imperative, and Lee assured his old colleague that the question of remaining in the South after Appomattox was a personal matter.

Yet Early could not make peace with himself. His violent anti-Northern statements indicated a Cassius complex. For one who had in 1861 opposed secession, had fought for it, and then had fled the South while others remained, Early protested too much. His exile years produced a flurry of writing in defense of his flight. He always overreacted, blaming his hatred of the North for the decision. He thundered that "my motto is still 'war to the death.' "

Yet he had not fought a "war to the death," had fled after Appomattox, and now seemed driven to rationalize that decision. To fellow Southerners he explained he had chosen exile rather than submit "to the yoke of the oppressors," and begged ex-Rebels to understand the reasons why he had abandoned them.[53]

Early also believed that he had an obligation to defend his beloved Lee. Like some other ex-Rebels, Early attempted to don Lee's mantle. He believed himself destined to complete Lee's unfinished history of the army, and within weeks after the General's death, he committed his life to being the anointed successor. At the first meeting of the Lee Monument Association, Early spoke of Lee's concern that the army's history be written, and insisted it must be done "by some one competent to the task." There is no doubt that Early viewed himself as the heir "to see that the truth of history is vindicated." In the Richmond meeting he boasted of his writings which defended the Lost Cause, and produced letters from Lee urging him to write the army's history.

Many regarded him as Lee's chief guardian. By the early 1870s, Early's slashing attacks upon critics of Lee had earned him a sizable reputation. Other Lee partisans cowered before him. J. William Jones flattered Early's "skillful pen" as best able to defend Lee. The London journalist Francis Lawley exhorted him to write the army's history, and Charles Venable begged him to complete Lee's work, for "now that he is gone the duty devolves on you."[54] These men probably feared Early more than they liked him. His ability to launch a violent attack upon even mild criticism of Lee was well known. Robert Stiles mused that "no man ever took up his pen to write a line about the great conflict without the fear of Jubal Early before his eyes."[55]

No dissenter escaped Early's wrath. When a biographer of Stonewall Jackson appeared to give Lee's lieutenant too much credit for the army's victories, Early attacked him so strongly that the writer acknowledged his errors in compiling a "bungling" war history. Early asserted that John Esten Cooke, an early Lee biographer, lacked the military credentials to write such a book, and criticized Edward Pollard, another "unlicensed" Lee biographer, noting that the real threat to Rebel history came from "unjudicious" Southerners and not from the North.

Early's magazine articles reinforced his reputation as Lee's protector. A typical incident in the early 1870s was a clash with another former Lee officer, General William Mahone. Henry Dawson, editor of the New York-based *Historical Magazine,* relished Civil War controversy as a means to increase circulation. In 1870 Dawson discovered a juicy morsel that sent the Lee cult into hysterics. He printed an interview with Mahone, hero of the 1864–65 siege of Petersburg. Mahone, already unpopular in Virginia because of his pro-Republican politics, depicted Lee in an interview as an indecisive general who, on several occasions, was saved only by his advice. Early accused Mahone of being a liar and a coward. Bitter letters were exchanged, rumors were rife that the two planned a duel, and a committee of Richmond dignitaries intervened. The victor was clearly Early. Mahone printed an apology in the magazine, and reprinted the original interview with the deletion of all remarks Early saw as objectionable.[56]

Yet the ferocity of Early's rebuttals masked a significant reason for his self-assumed role. Though many cowered from his pen, it was perhaps Early who was more afraid. Early's own record was replete with errors which he tried to conceal by attacking others' reputations. His first postwar book, *Memoir of the Last Year of the War,* strongly defended his military history and exile.

Early had been criticized for his operations in 1864–65. William Swinton's *Campaigns of the Army of the Potomac* charged that the "feeble" Washington raid had cost the Rebels a great opportunity. Edward Pollard derided Early's Shenandoah Valley campaign and described him as "wandering sulkily and secretly" from Virginia after Appomattox.[57]

More important for Lee's image was the initial censure of Early for the loss at Gettysburg. Most of the first postwar histories gave a far different account from what was published in the late 1870s. The later version, which would be accepted as gospel in Civil War writing, would blame the Confederate loss on the supposed tardiness of General James Longstreet in attacking Meade's position on July 2.

But the first accounts never criticized Longstreet's conduct. Rather, blame was spread among certain individuals for their alleged mistakes on the first day, July 1—Lee, corps leader Richard Ewell, and division commander Early.

On the evening of July 1, Ewell's attack had scattered General

Oliver Howard's corps north of Gettysburg. Panic-stricken Federals fled through the town, pursued hotly by Early's division. Howard's soldiers evaporated into the ridges south of Gettysburg, while five thousand Union prisoners were herded to the rear. Ahead for the taking were the critical Culp's Hill and Cemetery Hill positions. If Early could occupy these heights, the Federal line along Cemetery Ridge would be untenable, and Meade must retreat from Gettysburg.

But Early faltered. He possessed four fresh brigades and had no orders to break off pursuit. Instead he rode aimlessly to the rear in search of Ewell. Meanwhile Ewell arrived in Gettysburg, and also hesitated. Accompanying officers begged for men to take the heights, but Ewell refused. One, General Isaac Trimble, pleaded unsuccessfully for a single regiment to scale the heights. When Ewell declined, Trimble threw down his sword and stalked away.

Ewell and Early made other mistakes that night. Lee came to Ewell's headquarters and asked their opinion of a daylight assault upon the two hills. While Ewell stood by meekly, Early argued spiritedly against such an attack, insisting that the Federals were in great strength there. If so, Lee suggested, then why not shift Ewell's corps to the far right flank during the night, and attack what Early claimed was the weak sector of the Union line? Early protested again, arguing that any thrust should be made by Longstreet's corps, then en route to a position on Lee's right wing. It was from this conversation that Lee initially made the decision that the strike on July 2 should be aimed at the right-center, not the left, and that Longstreet should carry the brunt. The result was the disasters of July 2 and 3.

One winter afternoon in 1872, at the invitation of Washington and Lee University, Early journeyed across the Blue Ridge Mountains to deliver the annual Lee birthday address at the college. The popularity of his speech—reprinted in book form and in magazines—did much to make him the leader of the Lee cult. It also probably assured his selection the following year as president of the powerful Southern Historical Society.

More important, the address marked the formal beginning of the first Lee cult. It gave notice that the rift between partisans in Lexington and eastern Virginia had been healed. The invitation was something of a peace offering to Early. It was filled with praise for that vain officer, Lee's "trusted friend and lieutenant," whose "eminent services" would give his words special merit.

Early did his part in the ceremonial love feast. His speech endorsed the Lexington group's old plan to exchange the location of Lee's chief monument for possession of the General's body. He lauded the "pious work" of constructing the tomb in Lexington, but warned his audience that in turn they must support the monument project in Richmond.[58]

The address also indicated that part of Early's enthusiasm for defending Lee involved a concern for his own discolored reputation. The speech was far less a eulogy upon Lee than a defense of Early's military career. He spoke tirelessly of his 1864–65 campaign against Phil Sheridan, explaining that the accounts of his own disaster contained "much misunderstanding and ignorant misrepresentation."

Early also delivered a long tirade on Gettysburg. He attempted to divert the blame for the defeat from the Ewell-Early failures on July 1 to Longstreet's attack on July 2. The speech was the origin of the legend of Longstreet's lateness at Gettysburg. Early said that Lee planned to crush Meade on July 2 by having Longstreet attack Cemetery Ridge at dawn. The sunrise attack was opposed by Longstreet, who lacked "that confidence and faith necessary to success." Longstreet delayed his assault until the late afternoon, allowing Meade the opportunity to reinforce his position on Cemetery Ridge. But "had the attack been made at daylight as contemplated," Early insisted, the "brilliant and decisive victory" would have been Lee's.

Early's lecture emphasized the central element that unified Lee partisans by the mid-1870s—the conviction that the General had fared badly in postwar writings. But in their campaign to eulogize his exploits, any suggestion of error by Lee became heretical.

Actually the postwar military view of Lee was not unreasonable. Most writers described him as a superb officer and the South's most distinguished general. All lauded his lofty character. But Lee was frequently charged with serious military blunders. Equally irritating to Lee partisans was the praise accorded to such generals as Joseph Johnston and Stonewall Jackson. Lee's adherents also believed that the earliest Confederate writings were weak, erroneous accounts composed by nonmilitary men who lacked proper credentials.

The criticisms of Lee's generalship, almost universal in the decade after Appomattox, cut across regional and national lines, centering upon several campaigns. Foremost was Lee's conduct at Gettysburg, which was often disparaged by Northern, Southern, and British authors. The most biting Northern criticism came from William Swinton's *Campaigns of the Army of the Potomac,* the first authoritative Union account of the war. Swinton's heavily researched book was respected by ex-belligerents from both sides. Jefferson Davis said he was "the fairest and most careful of all the Northern writers."

Swinton's *Campaigns* was extremely lenient toward the South, due mainly to the author's dislike of the generals of the Army of the Potomac. In fact, he was highly complimentary to Lee. Swinton argued that the Federal army's greatness lay in the courage of its private soldiers, who fought bravely while inept generals were checked by Lee, "the

Confederacy's foremost military leader," and "the veteran player who had checkmated many antagonists."

But Swinton's description of Gettysburg was at odds with that of Lee's adherents. In this first intensive study of the battle, Swinton fastened the blame for the defeat upon Lee, Early, and Ewell—but not upon Longstreet. Ewell and Early were condemned for their temerity on July 1 in not seizing Culp's Hill and Cemetery Hill and in seconding Lee's decision to disregard Longstreet's proposal to outflank the Federals. Lee's problem was that he was off balance. He had determined not to fight an offensive battle in Pennsylvania, but his first day's success had produced "the taste of blood." He disregarded Longstreet's wiser counsel to force Meade to retreat into Maryland by a flanking maneuver, because he had lost "the equipoise in which his faculties commonly moved." Lee thus believed he could achieve anything, and launched the fateful assaults on Cemetery Ridge, July 2 and 3.[59]

Prominent foreign observers also viewed Lee's Gettysburg conduct with a jaundiced eye. Typical was Francis Lawley, later editor of the London *Daily Telegraph*. Lawley, who witnessed the battle from Lee's own headquarters, had overwhelming admiration for the General. "I have little or no chance of ever looking on his like again," he wrote.

But Lawley appraised Lee as a mediocre offensive fighter and argued that Gettysburg alone "will forever prevent his being ranked as a great offensive general." Gettysburg exposed Lee's tendency to be overconfident, to be "admirably bold when weak." He chided Lee for "maladroit manipulation" of the army, blaming defeat upon the Ewell-Early activities on July 1 and Lee's refusal to heed Longstreet's counsel. Of Lee, Lawley observed that in Pennsylvania he was "too big for his breeches."[60]

Nor did the earliest and most prominent Confederate historians defend Lee on the Gettysburg issue. Prior to the 1874 publication of Jones's first "approved" biography, writing on Lee had been the province of journalists and novelists.

Lee's friends were incensed by these early writings. They believed that the wrong people had been describing their hero. When *A Life of Gen. Robert E. Lee,* by the Virginia novelist John Esten Cooke, was published in 1871, it was promptly attacked by men like Charles Venable and Fitzhugh Lee. William Allan praised Jubal Early for a sharp critique of Cooke's book which was printed in several newspapers. Allan wrote: "I feel like you that a crop of vultures should be frightened away from meddling with the history of our cause. They know nothing of it."[61]

Cooke irritated ardent Lee devotees for more reasons than his supposed lack of proper credentials. He was one of the three early

Confederate historians of importance, all of whom did not hesitate to criticize Lee's campaigns. Cooke's version of Gettysburg, outlined in his biography of Lee and elsewhere, varied little from other immediate postwar accounts. Lee, not Longstreet, was saddled with the blame. Lee was "carried away" by an overconfidence resembling that of men "drunk on champagne." Believing his army could achieve anything, Lee ignored Longstreet's counsel of a flanking movement and chose to assail Cemetery Ridge on July 2 and 3. Noting that "pride goes before a fall," Cooke attributed the Gettysburg loss to Lee's overconfidence. Even after the failure on July 2, Lee organized Pickett's charge on the next day because his mind "revolted" at the thought of abandoning "his great enterprise" at Gettysburg.[62]

Even more annoying to the Lee cult were the comments by Edward Pollard. Pollard was the outstanding Rebel historian of the 1860s. While an assistant editor of the Richmond *Examiner,* he had published *The First Year of the War* and *The Second Year of the War* by 1863. Pollard was so successful that he abandoned his newspaper work and moved to England to write volumes on the remaining war years. Then followed a number of other books, including *Lee and His Lieutenants* (1867) and a biography of Lee published in 1870.

Pollard had a knack for alienating people with his sarcasm, for little seemed sacred to him. The Confederate Congress was "one of the weakest and most inane bodies" that ever called itself a legislature. Jefferson Davis had little administrative or military wisdom, and Stonewall Jackson possessed "an ardent love for glory."[63]

But it was Pollard's treatment of Lee which proved unbearable to the Virginians. Though he praised Lee's character and generalship, the descriptions fell short of idolatry. Pollard's biography contained a penetrating analysis of Lee's abilities. He divided successful military leaders into three types. A born genius such as Napoleon would have done well in any career, but Lee was not a born genius. A second group did not have genius, but possessed excellence because they had developed a particular intellectual faculty; to Pollard, Lee lacked such intelligence. Rather, Lee belonged in a third category of greatness, marked not by intellect but by "a just mixture of qualities, a perfect balance of character."

This "perfect balance" did not keep Lee from committing serious blunders. Pollard especially castigated Lee for Gettysburg. He blamed Lee, Ewell, and Early for failing to occupy the two hill positions on July 1, allowing Meade to concentrate "in the strongest position that had ever been taken by either army in the war." Then Lee erred again by being overconfident on July 2 and 3, intoxicated by "the animus and inspiration of the invasion."[64]

The final member of the triumvirate of early Rebel historians would at first glance appear pleasing to Lee partisans. James McCabe, the Richmond-born novelist and editor of the *Magnolia Weekly*, possessed the proper Virginia credentials. He also admired Lee greatly, as was evidenced in his *Life and Campaigns of General Robert E. Lee* (1867). Together with Pollard and Cooke, McCabe pioneered the "bridled commander" thesis, which contended that Lee could have succeeded had he been given authority by Jefferson Davis.

But McCabe's biography of Lee also would displease the General's followers, and Gettysburg again was the crucial issue. McCabe echoed other early writers. Criticism had to be directed at Lee, not Longstreet. Defeat did not come because of any failure by Longstreet to undertake a dawn attack on July 2. Lee failed to continue pursuit of Howard's shattered corps on the evening of July 1. This "strange hesitation" was followed by the disregarding of Longstreet's plea to flank Meade from his strong position on Cemetery Ridge. Instead, an overconfident Lee ordered the disastrous strikes against the ridge on July 2 and 3.[65]

Gettysburg was certainly not the only campaign where early writers found Lee wanting. Most took the General to task for his command in the Seven Days against McClellan, especially for the final, near-suicidal assault at Malvern Hill. Northern writer John William Draper praised Lee's character and abilities as a defensive combatant in his prestigious multivolume *History of the American Civil War*. But Draper considered Lee a mediocre offensive tactician and cited the Malvern Hill attack as evidence. William Swinton's *Campaigns of the Army of the Potomac* offered the same criticism, viewing the attack at Malvern Hill as a foolish affair in which "never before nor since" did Lee deliver a battle "so ill-judged in conception or so faulty in its details of execution."

Southern authors also condemned Lee's conduct at Malvern Hill. John Esten Cooke regarded Lee's attack as a total failure, describing it as "halting" and "bungling." James McCabe looked upon Lee's entire conduct of the Seven Days operations with a critical eye. In the Seven Days, Lee's "feeble and spiritless" pursuit of the retreating McClellan cost "the best opportunity Lee had for destroying the Army of the Potomac."

Lee's handling of the 1862 Maryland campaign also drew early criticism. Swinton asserted that the Antietam campaign exhibited some crucial weaknesses in Lee, including political naïveté and a contemptuous view of the Federal leadership. Only McClellan's temerity saved Lee from destruction in an invasion which "degenerated into a raid." And McCabe speculated that here Lee "was not . . . so visionary as the press at the time reported him," as he chose to invade the North "when his army was totally unprepared for an offensive."

Even Lee's famous repulse of General Ambrose Burnside's army at

Fredericksburg in 1862 drew barbed comments from the early Rebel historians. Like Pollard and Cooke, McCabe believed that Lee fumbled badly. After Burnside's attack across the Rappahannock River had been turned back with frightful losses, Stonewall Jackson had urged a counterattack to drive the Federals into the river. Of Lee's refusal to do so, McCabe wrote that "it is a pity that General Lee did not take General Jackson's advice," for "had he done so, he could not have failed to destroy the Army of the Potomac."[66]

Equally vexing to Lee partisans was the amount of praise given by these historians to other Confederate hero figures. Two cases in particular could only anger them.

By the 1880s, Lee's admirers would shape the image of General Joseph Johnston into that of a veritable bungler. These authors would take pains to depict the Army of Northern Virginia under Johnston's command as near collapse when Lee took charge in June 1862. But this was not the verdict of the earliest historians, Southern or Northern. Edward Pollard wrote that "not a few military critics have considered Johnston superior to Lee in the highest qualities of generalship." He also asserted that "the best judgement of the enemy" considered Johnston "the master military mind of the Confederacy." Meanwhile, Swinton praised Johnston for his handling of the army prior to Lee's arrival. Swinton rejected the theory that the army was near disaster when Lee took charge.[67]

More annoying to the Lee cult was the praise accorded to Jackson by early writers who often gave him credit for critical battle victories. Prior to writing his biography of Lee, John Esten Cooke had enjoyed a successful career in eulogizing Jackson. As a wartime cavalry officer, Cooke published sketches and poetry about Jackson in the popular *Southern Illustrated News*. Like some other popular writers, Cooke capitalized on the death of a war hero. Within two weeks of Jackson's death, advertisements heralded Cooke's forthcoming biography of Stonewall Jackson. When issued in August 1863, Cooke's volume sold 3000 copies the first day, and was pirated by a New York publisher. Three years later, Appleton of New York released a much larger version, *Stonewall Jackson: A Military Biography*.

Cooke believed that Jackson, not Lee, was the "Man of Fate" and "the idol of the popular heart" in 1862 as McClellan's army neared the outskirts of Richmond. Cooke praised Jackson for the famed flanking march at Chancellorsville. It was Jackson who fashioned the plan to which Lee "speedily assented." Indeed, Cooke wrote of Jackson that "few human beings equalled him in the great art of making war."[68]

Before he switched attention to Lee's career, James McCabe also sang Jackson's praises. In his hastily written *Life of Thomas J. Jackson, by an Ex-Cadet*, McCabe gave Jackson a quality of wisdom not possessed by Lee. Again the Chancellorsville victory was due to Jackson's genius, and when he was killed, "the idol" and "great champion" of the South was dead.[69]

Edward Pollard pursued the same themes. Unlike later Lee writers, Pollard gave the General no credit for Jackson's Shenandoah Valley campaign. Nor was Lee responsible for "the great stroke of genius" at Chancellorsville, which "originated with Jackson and not with General Lee." Pollard also criticized those who regarded Jackson merely as Lee's subordinate. Indeed, "the war produced no military genius more complete" than Jackson, one of "the greatest characters of history."[70]

THIS WAS NOT the image of Lee his partisans desired, and their determination to recast his career became an obsession by the mid-1870s. Goaded by criticism, overcome by devotion to Lee's memory, friends resolved to turn the tide of Civil War history, to make Lee not simply superb but invincible.

The signs of this determination were everywhere. They were present in the crowded Richmond hall when General John Gordon shouted that "Lee was never really beaten. Lee could not be beaten. Overpowered, foiled in his efforts, he might be, but never defeated." General Jubal Early pleaded with Lee's friends to make certain that his career was "vindicated" and that "crude histories compiled by mercenary writers" were suppressed. Colonel Charles Marshall swore that one Lee critic must "make amends for his grievous faults."

Above all, the determination was there at Lexington in 1872, when Early's speech marked the commitment of the Lee cult to control Confederate letters. His call for "truthful history" marked a new era. Once again Lee's veterans were mounting an offensive, and the image of the invincible General was emerging.

CHAPTER III

THE MAKING
OF A SOUTHERN IDOL

H E WAS PAST SEVENTY and wielded an ear trumpet to aid his deafness. Once a muscular 240 pounds, his frail body now weighed
a hundred pounds less. At his side dangled a limp arm, a bitter memory
of the accidental wounding by his own men in the Wilderness. Now,
thirty years later, on an April day in 1893, a special excursion train was
carrying General James Longstreet back to Gettysburg.

He had come up from his lonely turkey farm in northern Georgia
to be a guest of honor at a Union League dinner in Philadelphia, where
he paid tribute to the man who had married his cousin Julia Dent, his
old West Point friend Ulysses Grant. Then, accompanied by a cortege
of other veteran officers, and newsmen from eastern cities, Longstreet
went back to Gettysburg.

Two trains roared through the Susquehanna country, carrying a
sentimental band of outcasts. They were men who had clung together
because they shared, if nothing else, some onus of error in battle. For
years, Longstreet had been castigated by the Virginians as the villain
of Gettysburg. With him was his friend little Billy Mahone, a comical
cut in his ruffled shirt, baggy pants, and old brigadier's white hat, an
outcast in his own right. Like Longstreet, he had been a Republican
during Reconstruction; like the Georgian, Mahone had criticized Lee.

Also present were two former Union corps leaders whose return to
Gettysburg was no less poignant. One-armed Oliver Howard came back
to relive that grim dusk of July 1, when his corps, pummeled by Ewell's
onslaught, dissolved into a panic-stricken mob in Gettysburg's narrow
streets. On another train was Dan Sickles, the flamboyant one-legged
connoisseur of women and politics, whose memories were also bitter.
It was Sickles who on the second day of the battle led his corps on an
unauthorized advance to an isolated patch of high ground at the Peach
Orchard. There, Longstreet's violent afternoon attack had caught Sickles's men badly exposed. Sickles's corps was wrecked, his leg was shattered, and his military reputation was tarnished.

There were lesser figures in the entourage. Colonel Porter Alexander, Longstreet's artillery chief, had supervised the tremendous cannonade that preceded Pickett's advance on the third day of the battle. General Charles Howard could remember his frustrating journey to Two Taverns on the afternoon of July 1, when he had pleaded with General Henry Slocum to send reinforcements to his brother.

The old soldiers arrived at Gettysburg on a Friday afternoon, settled into a train of barouches, and rode through the fields. There were some occasional scenes of comedy such as when the carriages halted at Oak Hill to hear a local guide eulogize the action of July 1. His bluster was suddenly interrupted, and he was carefully positioned beside Pete Longstreet's good ear.

Porter Alexander pointed out where he and Lee watered their horses by Willoughby Run before Pickett's attack. Longstreet's staff officer, Colonel Osman Latrobe, showed the reporters the woods road and where Pickett's men loaded their guns before the attack.

Old men of scarred reputations sought almost childlike reassurance from one another. Longstreet sat in his barouche on Oak Hill with Oliver Howard. As the reporters pressed closely to listen, Howard patted the knee of his former enemy, and begged him to assure the onlookers that his deployments against Lee on July 1 had been judicious. Roused from his deafness, Longstreet told the crowd that Howard had not erred.

In the drizzle of the next day, Longstreet rode out to Little Round Top with his adversary of that fight, Dan Sickles. The party scrambled up the muddy hill, with Sickles trailing behind on his crutches. They halted near the top, rested on a rock shelf, and looked back toward the Peach Orchard. Sickles asked Longstreet to tell the crowd that his advance there had been wise. Longstreet, roused again, assured the assembly, and then the group moved slowly back to Gettysburg.

There was much irony in the attention given to Longstreet during the 1893 excursion. In that era of reunionism, he was always a welcome guest at Northern commemorative ceremonies. When Grant's Tomb in New York was dedicated, Longstreet was in the party of Vice-President Adlai Stevenson, was a conspicuous part of the parade down Broadway, and was a guest of honor at the reception given by President William McKinley. In 1901, when McKinley was inaugurated for a second term, Longstreet was a guest of honor. Three months later, he was invited by Theodore Roosevelt and Dan Sickles to review the Memorial Day parade of the Army of the Potomac's old Third Corps.

Toward the end of 1901, only two years before his death, Longstreet attended the centennial observance of West Point. He still suffered badly from his Wilderness wounds, wore curious goggles to aid his eyesight, and was failing from cancer. He sat in near darkness at the alumni luncheon, armed with his ear trumpet. When a speaker's remarks about Longstreet brought a thunder of applause, the aging general did not hear.

HE WOULD NOT SURVIVE to hear the charges of J. William Jones's second Lee biography, that Longstreet's conduct at Gettysburg cost the South victory in the Civil War. Nor would he know that after his death the United Daughters of the Confederacy in Savannah, Georgia, would refuse to send flowers to his funeral. Or that in Wilmington, North Carolina, the United Confederate Veterans would vote not to send condolences to his family.

Nor would Longstreet know that in the heydey of the erection of Confederate memorials, from 1895 to 1910, he would be left wanting. When the Virginians commemorated their war heroes on Monument Avenue and elsewhere in Richmond, there would be elaborate monuments to Lee's other chief lieutenants, but none to Longstreet. No cemetery, courthouse, or battlefield statue was erected in Longstreet's honor, although thousands were dedicated to more obscure figures. By the 1950s, only an obscure river bridge in Georgia memorialized the man Lee once dubbed his "war horse."

Longstreet's sin was not against the Southern people, but against the organizers of the South's historical writing. If there is a monument to Longstreet, it was in the fate of one who criticized the Lee image. For in the 1870s, when Longstreet dared to question Lee's generalship, Civil War writing was so dominated by a clique of Virginians that they were able to destroy much of his reputation.

These historians and biographers had assumed control of the history of the war from the Southern side. The earlier criticisms of Lee were replaced by accounts that made him the invincible general defeated only when subordinates failed him. The exploits of other major Rebel heroes were downplayed. Generals such as Jackson, once either Lee's superior or at least equal in the estimation of historians, were reassigned subordinate positions. The likes of Beauregard and Joseph Johnston were no longer on the same level as Lee.

Certainly the early Lee cult did not *create* the General's fame. Given his charisma, military reputation, and character, Lee would have emerged from the war as a major hero, even without any devotees. His military greatness alone would have assured his niche as a major national figure. But Lee's admirers went further, and by exaggeration fashioned him into something inviolable. They elevated their hero by silencing his critics or comparing him favorably with the other Confederate officers.

Their avenues of publicity were widespread. The memorial organization created after Lee's death and the efforts of fund raisers at Washington and Lee University helped eulogize his exploits. At Washington and Lee there always seemed to be some ceremony afoot. During the Reconstruction the college never hesitated to capitalize on Lee's name to raise funds. There were campaigns throughout the South to endow chairs. A million-dollar drive sought funds for a project Lee had supposedly endorsed before his death; promotional material pleaded for money "to carry out the plans of its lamented president."

Memorial projects in Richmond and Lexington also brought wide publicity to Lee. The Lee Monument Association sponsored a twenty-year fund-raising campaign which used professional agents, church donations, lectures by prominent Confederates, sales of Lee lithographs, and other schemes. The Board of Managers of the Association underwrote a contest with $3000 in prize money for the artist who could design the best statue of Lee for Richmond. Advertisements in leading American and European art journals bore fruit in 1887, when Jubal Early's group accepted the entry of the French sculptor Antonin Mercié. While Mercié labored at his Paris studio with Lee's daughter Mary as his adviser, the Association celebrated the laying of the monument's cornerstone. A band played "We'll Be Gay and Happy Still," and marchers gathered to hear a round of speeches from Lee's old comrades.

While the Richmond group raised funds for Lee's statue, the Memorial Association in Lexington collected money to build his tomb. The climax of the Lexington campaign was the dedication in 1883 of the Valentine figure in the Lee chapel. Jefferson Davis's daughter Winnie, who managed for fifty years to hold the title of the "Child of the Confederacy," sent a battle flag of flowers to master of ceremonies Jubal Early. Major John Daniel delivered a three-hour speech so popular that it was distributed throughout the South in book form.

The Northern press gave the Lee mystique another important avenue of publicity. The two decades after 1870 were the golden age of American magazines. In 1865 some 700 publications were issued in the United States; within the next twenty years over 8000 magazines satisfied the new American thirst for cheaply printed reading matter. A rising middle-class establishment and a population increase of 20 million between 1860 and 1880 encouraged the magazine market.

In 1883 Cyrus Curtis unveiled *The Ladies' Home Journal,* which had 400,000 readers within four years. By the 1870s, *Harper's Weekly* had tripled its wartime subscription list. Older literary magazines like *The Atlantic Monthly* found themselves hard-pressed by new rivals such as *The Nation, Galaxy,* and *Lippincott's.*

Competition was even keener among daily newspapers. Within twenty years of Robert Lee's death the number of American newspapers would double to 9000. Much of this was made possible by technological changes after the Civil War. The New York *World* pioneered in the use of wood-pulp paper, far cheaper than rag paper. By 1877 a telephone was broadcasting news from the Bell laboratory to a Massachusetts newspaper, and in the next decade journals were using such new devices as linotype machines and halftone etchings.

The postwar years also saw the advent of Sunday newspapers replete with articles on literature and history. Before 1861 only four American newspapers printed Sunday editions, but the thirst for war news overcame the religious taboo, and by 1890 there were 200 Sunday newspapers.

Competition among newspapers was fierce. In New York, James Gordon Bennett's *Herald* underwrote the expedition of Henry Stanley to find missionary-explorer David Livingstone. Bennett was hard-pressed by Joseph Pulitzer's *World,* Whitelaw Reid's *Tribune,* and Charles Dana's *Sun.* The *Herald* promoted a fraudulent "escape" in 1874 of animals from the Central Park Zoo, while the *World* sponsored Nellie Bly's race via train, sampan, and burro to best the round-the-world time of characters in Jules Verne's novel.

Americans also were turning to history as a hobby of escape. Some were bored with the drabness of industrial society. Others sought a sense of national purpose in an era of political corruption, sectional hate, and foreign immigration. The American mind of this age was almost schizophrenic. There was pride in the Civil War's outcome and in industrial development, but there was also fear of rising Eastern European migration and the anonymity of a factory society.

American interest in history was also stimulated by the 1876 Centennial, which fixed the national mood on the past. This mood may have been expressed best by a minister's prayer at the dedication of the Philadelphia exposition grounds in 1876, when he implored, "May the new century be better than the last."

What did the American think of his progress in 1876? His mind, like the Centennial itself, reflected a contrast of rural values and industrial might, of searchers for a national purpose and the tawdry political scandals, of seekers of reunion and lingering sectional hatred. The Centennial was a quest that drew many back not only to Boston and Yorktown but to Gettysburg as well.

In 1876 this was an America where Jay Gould and his associates built the New York elevated railroad, while slums flourished in Philadelphia's St. Mary's district. It was a year when tourists still took the waters at old spas such as White Sulphur Springs, while in Florida the venerable Harriet Beecher Stowe raised oranges and wrote tourist guides for northeastern visitors. The National League enjoyed its first no-hit baseball game, and Custer was defeated at the Little Bighorn. Medicine man Dan Pinkham flooded Brooklyn with handbills promoting his 18 percent alcohol cureall for a woman's miseries, while in Savannah 1500 citizens perished from yellow fever.

The Philadelphia exposition itself reflected the nation's shifting values and aspirations. It was a contrast of pride in country amidst the displays of wild men of Borneo and shooting galleries. Charles Hire's root-beer exhibit vied with Queen Victoria's handwoven furnishings. The same building that displayed hydraulic rams and automatic switches contained Ben Franklin's hand press.

It was a gaudy pageant of a nation whose pride in technology was dimmed by shame at industrial-political corruption. Talk of a reunited people rang hollow amidst postwar "bloody shirt" journalism. Confidence in the slide rule was matched by bewilderment at the anonymity of factory existence. While crowds applauded in Machinery Hall for the Pyramid Pen Company's straight-pen packer, the Dakota Sioux remained triumphant on the Tongue, Bighorn, and Rosebud.

LEE'S HERO IMAGE grew as a result of this new national interest in history. The popularity of colonial history in the Centennial years evoked curiosity and admiration for Virginia's culture. Interest in the Civil War increased among the reading public of large eastern cities. Earlier, readers had been still war-weary and hostile to Southern culture. In the five years after 1868 *Harper's* printed only two articles on the Civil War, and in the eight years after 1868 the *North American Review* published a single piece on the conflict.

But rising historical interest after 1870 made the South—especially Virginia—a popular topic. The new *Scribner's Monthly* stole a march on its older competitors in 1873 by featuring the "Great South" series. Its young editor, Roswell Smith, had discerned a new fascination with Southern culture, and sent journalist Edward King on a 25,000-mile tour which resulted in fifteen articles on the old Confederate states. The popularity of the King series inspired competing articles in other magazines. *Harper's,* in 1874, inaugurated the "New South" series, while *The Atlantic Monthly* featured a serialized "Studies of the South."

The several hundred articles published on the South in the 1870s in part reflected increasing sympathy with the Southern plight in Reconstruction. *Harper's* praised efforts to rebuild "from the evils, political, social, industrial, and financial, that have stifled and oppressed" the region. More important was the national fascination with Virginia culture. Virginia was becoming a special place in American letters, with a peculiar charm, a colonial legacy, and a breed of people whose values excelled those of the cotton South.

The Philadelphia celebration symbolized the growing Virginia mystique. The highlight was a massive July 4 parade. While warships fired salutes in the Navy Yard, a parade of military units included the Centennial Legion, led by General Henry Heth, the Virginia general who had threatened Philadelphia thirteen years before as a division commander under Lee. Then Richard Henry Lee II, grandson of the man who had offered the resolution for independence and a distant cousin of Robert E. Lee, read the Declaration of Independence.

The national stereotype of Virginia as the center of antebellum Southern culture gradually became established. The Virginia plantation was regarded as a humane, almost idyllic affair, festooned with faithful slaves and gentle masters whose honor was unexcelled. Virginia life was pictured in a variety of ways, from florid descriptions of the lush Shenandoah Valley to tales of the elegance of Tidewater society in the days of George Washington.

For *Lippincott's,* a Virginia authoress, Jennie Stabler, wrote nine articles on life in her state, bearing such titles as "Mammy" and "How Ham Was Cured." Virginia novelist Thomas Nelson Page made his national debut in *Scribner's* with articles called "Uncle Gab's White Folks" and "Old Yorktown." *Harper's New Monthly* engaged Page to publish some of his best stories such as "Ole 'Stracted," used later in his book *In Ole Virginia* (1887). *The Atlantic Monthly* commissioned Virginia novelist George Cary Eggleston to write the serialized "A Rebel's Recollections," which readers found so charming that it was issued in book form.[1]

There was great interest in Robert E. Lee's operations on the eastern front. Lee had been the most ominous threat to the metropolitan Northeast, particularly Philadelphia. Likewise, though state allotments were scattered throughout the Federal army, the bulk of soldiers from the Northeast had fought in the Army of the Potomac against Lee.

Thus major Northern magazines and newspapers emphasized the theater that seemed most appealing—war on the Virginia front. Henry Dawson's *Historical Magazine* recognized reader interest in such battlefields as Chancellorsville and Gettysburg. Dawson took charge of the magazine in 1866, and liked to print historical controversy which would boost his circulation.

Many articles helped to bolster the growing image of Lee as the invincible Southern general. Dawson printed material furnished by Lee's admirers. J. William Jones first received national exposure in an 1873 issue with his article on Lee at Appomattox. Jones provided a composite of the Appomattox segment of the Lee image which would become standard issue. Lee was not defeated by Grant, only overwhelmed by superior Federal numbers. Appomattox also became Lee's greatest victory, a mixture of devotion to duty, resignation to defeat, and determination to help rebuild the South.

Dawson claimed that his magazine would "fearlessly expose and condemn" untruth in history. He welcomed the writings of Jubal Early and unknowingly helped to establish Early's reputation as Lee's prime defender. Early assailed Grant biographer Adam Badeau for questioning whether Lee had been badly outnumbered by Grant in 1864. The most prominent biographer of Stonewall Jackson, Robert Dabney, was attacked for what Early considered to be excessive praise of Jackson. Early condemned criticism of Lee in the writings of Edward Pollard. He was infuriated by many of Pollard's statements, including his assertion that Lee was guilty at Fredericksburg of "unpardonable negligence" in not heeding Jackson's plea for a counterattack against Burnside's defeated army. As mentioned previously, General William Mahone's comments on Lee's generalship sparked a long argument in the magazine which almost ended in a duel between Early and Mahone.[2]

Dawson's counterpart in capitalizing on the eastern theater of war in Northern newspapers was Colonel Alexander McClure. Lawyer, politician, and medicine man, McClure created the Philadelphia *Times* in 1877, and competed strongly with more established city presses such as the *Public Ledger* and the *Evening Item*. McClure quickly developed his newspaper into Philadelphia's second-largest daily, and his exploitation of interest in the Civil War was a decisive factor. He initiated the "Annals of the Civil War" series, which promised "chapters of the unwritten *History of the Late Civil War* from leading actors."

McClure was chasing circulation, and many of his "leading actors" were officers in Lee's army. He sought articles that would romanticize the war, and thus printed many sagas of Lee's cavalry. One former officer of Mosby's Rangers gave a rousing description of the "Black Horse Cavalry," while ex-cavalryman General John Imboden related his days of war in the Shenandoah Valley in "Fire, Sword, and Halter." Especially popular were the vignettes of John Esten Cooke, who portrayed Lee's army as a band of romantic cavaliers. General Turner Ashby was "the type of chevalier as much as Bayard was." Mosby became "a wild cat ready to spring," and in "Stuart and the Lady Prisoners," Jeb Stuart emerged as "the knight errant of the middle ages," a man for whom "romance and adventure made up the everyday staple of his life."[3]

Yet the organization of Lee's image in memorial associations and the national media was not as influential as the dominance by Lee's adherents of postwar Confederate writing.

The Reconstruction South boasted few literary outlets, and the Virginians controlled them all. The intense, homogeneous nature of Lee's Virginia admirers produced a flood of books praising their hero, books eagerly accepted by national publishers trying to capitalize on Civil War interest.

The Virginians also were most prominent in the publication of postwar literary and historical magazines. After the war, Southern literary talent was centered in the Virginia-Maryland region. Charleston's power in Southern letters had been shattered by the war. The era of Paul Hamilton Hayne, Henry Timrod, and William Gilmore Simms had disappeared, while in Virginia there emerged John Esten Cooke, George Cary Eggleston, and Thomas Nelson Page. Baltimore and Richmond alone issued thirty-one literary magazines during Reconstruction.

Magazines which did not court the Virginia mystique were usually short-lived. Save for *De Bow's Review* in New Orleans, chiefly a commercial magazine, literary and historical publications outside Virginia had a high death rate. *The Annals of the Army of Tennessee,* which celebrated the battles in the western theater, died in its infancy. *Our Living and Our Dead,* an attempt to glorify North Carolina's war achievements, lasted only three years.

Those magazines—and writers—who endured were centered in the Atlantic South. The *Southern Magazine,* published first in Richmond and later in Baltimore, was the official organ of the Southern Historical Society until that group began its own magazine in 1876. It was dedicated to praising Lee's exploits as the victory symbol of the Lost Cause.

The desire to use Lee as the symbol of Confederate arms filled the pages of the powerful *Southern Review* of Baltimore, edited by a former University of Virginia professor, Albert Bledsoe. Once a colleague of Abraham Lincoln's, in Illinois law practice, Bledsoe committed his magazine to the task of justifying the Lost Cause. To Bledsoe, Robert Lee was the epitome of the Southern rationale. Bledsoe preached the standard Lost Cause argument that might did not make right. Northern victory proved nothing, and Southerners were still the better people. Bledsoe railed at Northerners as a people: "Mammon is its god, and nowhere has he more devout and abject worshippers, or has set up a more polluted civilization than in the North." In contrast, the South, boasting "every element of purity, stability and greatness," was best represented by Robert Lee. The *Review* constantly extolled Lee's character—how could a cause which had produced such a man be wrong?

Bledsoe's magazine viewed the war as a saga in which the South, particularly Lee, was not defeated but overwhelmed by Federal numbers. Lee was a military genius whose skills were "unsurpassed in the annals of war." Striving to pull some semblance of victory out of Appomattox, the magazine, as did others, made Lee the South's symbolic winner. The Lost Cause became a war in Virginia, and Lee became unbeatable. He was even victorious at Gettysburg. Only the repulse of Pickett's troops on July 3 "neutralized the success of the first two days and rendered a withdrawal into Virginia necessary." Even then, the Federals "had suffered too severely to follow."[4]

Given the paltry number of Southern magazines available, it was natural that Lee's followers looked for other audiences. Many of the articles on Virginia life which appeared in Northern magazines after 1875 were highly partisan defenses of Lee's military career. Colonel McClure's series in the Philadelphia *Times* provided an outlet for Colonel A. L. Long, in his "After Seven Pines," to popularize the theory that when Lee took command in 1862 the Army of Northern Virginia was on the verge of destruction because of General Joseph Johnston's poor generalship. Colonel Walter Taylor's "The Campaign in Pennsylvania . . . Who Was Responsible?", which absolved Lee of error for the defeat, was also printed in the *Times*.

Lee's wartime friends were joined in these efforts by a growing body of Virginia journalists. George Cary Eggleston was a former Indiana schoolteacher who would make his chief contribution to the Lee image later in the nineteenth century, when such romantic novels as *The Warrens of Virginia* would influence national opinion of Southern culture. Yet even during the Reconstruction, Eggleston wrote about "the dear old days" of Virginia in order to "change some people's views of the South and Southerners." Eggleston's account of life in Lee's army, "A Rebel's Recollections," first serialized by *The Atlantic Monthly* in 1874, became an early Civil War classic. It was the first important statement of a theme that Virginia writers would steadily develop in later years. Virginians were superior to other ex-Rebels because they possessed a code of duty, honor, and love for country not found in the cotton South.

Eggleston's friend John Esten Cooke also did his part. Although his biography of Lee was criticized by other Lee admirers, Cooke and his tireless pen did much to publicize the General's image. He wrote many of the tales of Lee's cavalry that were printed in the Detroit *Free Press,* the Philadelphia *Times,* and elsewhere. *Surry of Eagle's-Nest,* the first important Civil War novel, romanticized the cavalier image; of his hero Cooke wrote: "In every movement of his person, every tone of his voice . . . was the perfect grace, the sweet and yet stately courtesy of the old Virginia gentlemen."[5]

Cooke's writings helped establish the Northern—and Southern— view of the war as primarily a contest that took place in Virginia. His popular reminiscence of his war service, *Wearing of the Gray* (1867), was dedicated to his old chief, Jeb Stuart, the "Flower of Cavaliers." As a story of life in Lee's army, it praised "the fresh life of the forest—the wandering existence which brings back the days of old romance."[6] In 1869 two of his novels on the war in Virginia, *Hilt to Hilt* and *Mohun: Or the Last Days of Lee and His Paladins,* were highly popular, and

in 1870 he followed with *Hammer and Rapier,* a novel of the Lee-Grant
struggle of 1864–65. It was a classic assertion of the Lost Cause rationale
that Lee had outfought Grant, only to be overcome by greater numbers. Grant was the hammer, who sought with "the sledge-hammer in
both hands" to pound to bits the brilliant General Lee, "that great
swordsman," who "had parried every lunge" by Federal generals.[7]

After his biography, Cooke wrote widely on Lee's fame and Virginia's superiority in Northern journals and newspapers. Within five years
after Lee's death, Cooke published thirty-one articles in *Appleton's*
alone. None was more influential than "The Personal Character of General Lee" (1875), a concise statement of the image of Lee held by his
admirers. Cooke spoke of Lee as godlike, describing his "personal
beauty," "simplicity, naturalness and virtue," great moral character,
devotion to his mother, piety, reserve, and a dozen other traits.[8]

LEE'S ADMIRERS began to control the Southern Historical Society in the
1870s. During the next four decades, the Society was the most powerful
historical organization in the South, and its *Papers* the most influential
outlet of the "Confederate" viewpoint. Even in the Reconstruction era,
the *New England Historical Register* observed of the *Papers* that "no
library, public or private, which pretends to historic fullness, *Can
Afford To Be Without These Volumes."* The *London Saturday Review*
reported that "they contain a mass of information relative to the late
War, *Without A Careful Study Of Which No Librarian, However Limited His Scope Should Venture To Treat Any Engagement Of That Most
Interesting Story."*[9]

The Southern Historical Society had been conceived as a South-
wide organization, to defend secession and Confederate conduct in the
war. It had originated one April night in 1869, when a cadre of ex-Rebel
officers gathered in New Orleans. The initial group, which included
such notables as former generals Braxton Bragg and P. G. T. Beauregard, had decided to form a center in New Orleans, with local branches
throughout the South.

The Society's aims were to collect, preserve, and eventually print
manuscripts which explained the Confederate version of the war. In the
Reconstruction years, when captured Rebel archives in Washington
were initially closed to most Southerners, there was widespread fear
that unless ex-Confederates gathered and published their own material,
their version of the war would remain unwritten.

The Society's first president, Dr. Benjamin Palmer, was a Louisianan. Vice-presidents were elected from each ex-Rebel state and the
District of Columbia. By such, "it was hoped that State Societies would
speedily be organized as articulated members of the parent Society;

and that branching out from these, local and affiliated Societies would be formed, covering like a net the entire Southern country."[10]

But the original dream of a network of local organizations, cemented by a core at New Orleans, soon collapsed. In a region struggling to recover from the war, historical societies were a luxury. Membership remained small, and few local groups developed. Lacking funds for a magazine, the Society had to be content with sporadic publication of its materials in newspapers and magazines. The Society's treasury shrank to $172 and its officers admitted in 1872 that their expectations of South-wide support had been in vain.

It was during its general convention in 1873 at White Sulphur Springs that the Society was reshaped. Because their efforts had not "received the cooperation of our people to the extent that they deserve," the Society's leaders sought aid from Jubal Early. Early's reputation as a Confederate exhorter was considerable, and he was asked not only to select the delegates from Virginia but to make the convention's keynote speech. Beauregard and others of the original executive committee had lamented the lack of Lee partisans in the group.

At the White Sulphur Springs meeting in August, Early and other followers of Lee took control. Instead of picking a maximum of five delegates as suggested, Early brought twenty-one. Thus almost half of the fifty-four delegates were from Virginia, many of them adherents of Lee—his nephew Fitzhugh Lee, his former aide Charles Venable, and ex-generals such as Early, Eppa Hunton, and Henry Heth.

These men cast the Society into a Virginia-dominated institution. Early was made permanent president, while other Virginians were elected as secretary and treasurer. Later, in 1875, J. William Jones became secretary-treasurer, and in 1876, when the Society began publication of its *Papers,* Jones was chosen as editor. He would continue to edit the influential *Papers* until 1887, when he was succeeded by Robert Brock, a veteran of Lee's army and secretary of the Virginia Historical Society. And at the White Sulphur Springs meeting, Early and his colleagues succeeded in having the Society's headquarters transferred to Richmond, where the state legislature provided a room in the capitol. The Lee people also revamped the Society's executive committee, requiring that all its officers be residents of Virginia. When the meeting adjourned, the most influential Civil War history association in the South was under the control of a select group.[11]

SEVERAL TECHNIQUES were employed to establish Lee as the pre-eminent Southern war hero. Although the Southern Historical Society purported to be a South-wide body, its *Papers* were devoted to the idolization of Lee and his army. In its first year, the *Papers* printed twenty-nine articles on Lee and the Virginia army, and five on military affairs elsewhere. The 1877 volume contained forty-four articles on the Virginia theater, and only five on other military events. By 1878 there were rumblings of displeasure in other parts of the South over this imbalance. Veterans of the western campaigns, angry at the Society's pro-Virginia stance, began publishing a rival journal, *The Annals of the Army of Tennessee.*

Early and Jones were worried. The Southern Historical Society was conducting a drive across the South to raise money for a building in Richmond and a $100,000 "endowment fund." For almost a decade the Society would use Lee's name for fund-raising purposes, just as the Lee memorial organizations were doing. General George Johnston was hired as a professional agent to tour the South. Johnston and others arranged lectures and meetings, extolling Lee's exploits and seeking funds for "the vindication of the name and fame of our Confederate leaders and people."

The western organization would cut into the Society's sources of funds. Jones suggested to Early that they undercut the new group's aspirations by printing more articles on non-Virginia topics, since "it is especially important just now that we should propitiate our friends in the West, as our agent [General Johnston] is making a fine canvas [*sic*] there." Jones promised his readers that western military operations "will now claim a good share of our attention." But in the next issue 80 percent of the articles praised the Army of Northern Virginia.[12]

Lee's adherents corresponded with each other exhaustively, suggested rebuttal arguments against criticisms of their hero, and praised one another's literary achievements. They were determined to elevate Lee and to stifle criticism of him. In 1867 Jones suggested to Early:

> I do wish you would write for us a paper on *General Lee as an Offensive Commander,* or some title, refuting the idea so often advanced that while he was very good on the *Defensive,* he failed when he took the *Offensive.*[13]

When Early was displeased at an article written by Porter Alexander, General James Longstreet's former chief of artillery, Jones explained that "if you will send me a correction of the errors . . . I will put them in our next issue with great pleasure." Here Jones defined the basic policy of the Lee cult—counterattack any criticism of Lee. He explained:

> When a paper containing grave errors is sent us, and quietly filed, the errors are simply *put away* to turn up at some future time when, perhaps, those capable of correcting it have passed off the

stage. But where the papers are published some vigilant sentinel, like yourself, detects the errors, and makes the corrections and the antidote goes down with the poison.[14]

Such planning was designed to offset the criticisms of Lee by men such as General Joseph Johnston. Jones advised Early:

> Suppose General Johnston had sent us a paper on Seven Pines . . . and we had quietly filed it—Col. Marshall and yourself would then have had no opportunity of correcting the errors and it would have some day turned up bearing all of the authority of his great name.[15]

When in 1877 the multivolume war history by Louis Philippe d'Orléans, Comte de Paris, seemed to threaten Lee's invincibility, Jones urged Early to "give us at least one article on his blunders in the *military* history." When a Kentucky newspaper printed an article on Lee's conduct by Longstreet, Jones suggested to Early, "Would it not be well to get them to copy your reply or for you to write another?"[16]

The methods had been developed years before. In 1871 Colonel Charles Venable had exhorted Early to "defeat the deplorable efforts" of John Esten Cooke's biography of Lee. The same year Colonel William Preston Johnston delighted in Early's efforts to rebut statements in the London *Times* by Grant's biographer Adam Badeau, terming it an "annihilation." After Joseph Johnston's memoirs criticized Lee and Early wrote a fierce reply, Colonel Charles Marshall applauded the assault, one "I could not undertake to do, and what I could not have done half as well," since Early had "routed him beyond the power of explanation." When an article on Gettysburg displeased Fitzhugh Lee, the general's nephew, he advised the Society's leaders: "I think it is best to offset all such communications that they may not go down to posterity uncontradicted." One of Lee's Lexington followers, William Allan, took note of an article in an English journal critical of Lee, and was delighted that Early was composing a reply, for "it is our duty as far as we are able to correct these things . . ."[17]

The campaign to defend Lee was carried to every front. When Emily Mason's biography was issued, Allan implored Early to "correct the errors" in the military section because "she is not the person to relate that part of General Lee's life." In 1873, when working on his biography of Lee, Marshall desired to meet with Early and Custis Lee "because there are one or two things about my sketch of General Lee's life that I want to consult some judicious friends about." After reading a Longstreet article on Gettysburg, Colonel Walter Taylor wrote exultantly to Early, "Give General Longstreet rope enough, and he will soon hang himself." And when Marshall read an attack by Early upon Joseph

Johnston's criticisms of Lee, he offered to provide Early more ammuni-
tion regarding Seven Pines and Gettysburg: ". . . wait until I can send
you a more careful review of these great matters, a full knowledge of
which will make Gettysburg as well understood as you and I understand
Seven Pines, General Johnston to the contrary."[18]

Lee's supporters also cooperated in the 1870s with Jefferson Davis's
followers. While Lee's lobby was the strongest, friends of other Confederate heroes were active. Stonewall Jackson's circle included his wife,
family biographer Robert Dabney, and two brothers-in-law, ex-Confederate generals Daniel Harvey Hill and Rufus Barringer. Among Beauregard's backers were his former chief of staff, Thomas Jordan, and the
handpicked biographer Alfred Roman.

But next to Lee, Jefferson Davis had the largest following during
the Reconstruction. When the embittered Davis was released from
prison in 1867, he was obsessed with two goals as he methodically
prepared his memoirs for publication. Secession must be justified, and
two old wartime enemies, who attacked Davis after 1865, must be
answered. Criticisms from the camps of Beauregard and Johnston had
stung Davis severely. An article by Beauregard's former aide Jordan
appeared in an 1865 issue of *Harper's*, blaming Davis for the Rebel
defeat. In Johnston's *Narrative of Military Operations* (1874), the general's last two chapters, an analysis of the defeat, castigated Davis's
administration.

From his residence on the Mississippi Gulf Coast, Davis commanded a loyal band of supporters who unearthed material for his
rebuttal. His "field general" was Major W. T. Walthall, responsible
chiefly for approaching ex-Confederates to obtain documents damaging
to Beauregard and Johnston. General Marcus Wright was Davis's man
in Washington. Now head of the division of captured Confederate
records in the War Department, Wright continually advised Davis concerning what records were available.

The Lee circle also gave Davis assistance—partly out of a common
dislike of Johnston and Beauregard, but more importantly because the
Lee cult feared the Davis group. They knew that Davis held several
grudges against Lee.

Davis believed that equal attention was not being paid to men
whom he considered to be Lee's equals. In 1882 he complained that
"we do not wish to wholly appropriate the glory of Lee but will willingly
share it with those who have an equal right to it." Davis thought that
Albert Sidney Johnston and Stonewall Jackson were Lee's equals, and
always spoke of them as the South's "three great soldiers." Johnston he
termed "the greatest soldier, the ablest man" living in the United States
in 1861. And in 1881, in a speech at the unveiling of a statue of Jackson,
he said the general "was regarded as the great hero of our war . . ."

Later he spoke of how Lee and Jackson "supplemented each other, and together, with any fair opportunity, they were absolutely invincible."[19]

Davis naturally resented what he considered to be excessive praise of Lee. When he read an article in the Southern Historical Society's *Papers* that appeared to criticize Sidney Johnston and extol Lee, Davis wrote a strong retort, arguing that Lee's reputation needed no "fictitious elevation at the expense of others." To a friend he complained that "if Lee's eulogists could better comprehend his character they would not seek to build for it a foundation of fiction in disparagement of others." Another time Davis protested in a letter to a Louisville newspaper that Lee "needs no pedestal constructed of the wrecks of his associates' reputations."[20]

Davis was even more angered when it appeared that Lee's reputation was being exalted at his own expense. By the early 1870s Davis's imprisonment had made him a martyr, and there was resentment in the South at any disparagement of his career. Yet an essential element of the postwar Lee image preached by his admirers involved criticism of Davis. Beginning with the earliest writings on Lee by Edward Pollard and James McCabe, the Virginians had advanced the "bridled commander" thesis. Lee was the master strategist never given enough power by a Confederate President jealous of his prerogatives. The tendency to make Davis the scapegoat was particularly applied to operations in 1864–65. Davis was portrayed as the man who stubbornly insisted that Richmond and Petersburg be held, refusing to allow Lee —who knew better—to withdraw in time to save his army. Then Davis bungled in the last hours of the Richmond siege by not making certain that supplies were sent to Lee's army retreating toward Amelia Courthouse; had Lee had the supplies in hand, he would not have had to stop and forage, and would have escaped surrender at Appomattox.

Until his last years, Davis bitterly assailed this version of Lee. After the publication of Colonel A. L. Long's *Memoirs of Robert E. Lee,* he openly attacked the book in print. Davis complained that Lee's admirers attributed his misfortunes to "a policy of the Civil Administration overruling the wished military opinions" of Lee. He was infuriated by the Amelia Courthouse charge. A desire to refute this "unfounded accusation" moved him in 1873 to request of former commissary general I. M. St. John data to prove that ample supplies were on hand. Even as late as 1890, in an article for the *North American Review,* Davis refought the controversy, insisting that Lee had never actually ordered supplies to be deposited there.[21]

To placate Davis, Fitzhugh Lee and Jubal Early provided Davis with material on the sins of Beauregard and Joseph Johnston, such as the latter's weak leadership on the Peninsula in 1862. Early even journeyed to Mississippi for a conference with the Davis camp.

Another visitor to the Gulf Coast was J. William Jones, who sought
to take advantage of Davis's new postwar popularity. He thought that
a Southern lecture tour by the ex-President could net the Southern
Historical Society a healthy $100,000. With his characteristic charm,
Jones promised the vain Davis that such a tour would provide the
Southern people the opportunity of giving "a grand ovation to their
President whom they still cherish." Naturally, "the President of Our
Society, General Early, and the members of the Executive Committee
generally are your warm admirers." Jones wrote articles praising Davis
and begged permission to write his biography, but "only on the condi-
tion that your family should have an equal share in the profits."[22]

The Society's Richmond headquarters became a clearing house of
information needed by Davis. When a typical plea for aid came in 1879
from the Davis camp, Jones wrote:

> Yes! We have many of the letters of Generals Beauregard and
> Johnston to the Department for 1861 . . . and will take pleasure in
> finding for you any you may designate . . .

Jones promised that he was "keeping my ears and eyes open" for other
material.[23]

Jones was no more enthusiastic than Colonel William Preston John-
ston, who was strongly active in the Lee Memorial Association and the
"Lee Memorial Volume." Later the president of the Tulane University,
Johnston was an important bridge between the Lee and Davis camps.
He detested Beauregard, "the 'defender of pig chitterlings' " and the
"Babbler." Johnston's resentment grew out of the controversy that had
arisen during the war over his dead father, Albert Sidney Johnston, and
Beauregard after the battle of Shiloh. For years Beauregard's supporters took credit for the planning at Shiloh and criticized Johnston's
generalship as inept. In turn, Johnston's followers, as in his son's 1878
biography, blamed Beauregard's halting of the attack on the first day
of the battle, after Johnston's death, for costing the Confederates not
only victory on the field but perhaps success in the war.

William Preston Johnston collected materials for Davis on a wide
range of subjects, such as Joseph Johnston's conduct in the Vicksburg
campaign and Beauregard's generalship at First Manassas. He made
several trips from Lexington to Washington, spending weeks copying
documents which the Davis camp wished to use against both Beauregard and Johnston.[24]

LEE'S ACHIEVEMENTS were deliberately magnified at the expense of the
reputations of others. This involved both minimizing the exploits of

other officers and attempts to destroy the credibility of Lee's critics.

Not all of Lee's rivals required such treatment. Beauregard's decline as a hero may have shown that a Civil War figure was better off having died without publishing his reminiscences. Beauregard and his entourage probably wore out readers with their boasting and criticism of others. For almost two decades after Appomattox, books and articles praised Beauregard excessively, damned Jefferson Davis, and were even critical of an old friend, Joseph Johnston.

The climax was the two-volume *Military Operations of General Beauregard* (1884), supposedly composed by a long-time friend, Louisiana attorney Alfred Roman. The book was actually written by Beauregard. Moved by the knowledge that his hated enemy Jefferson Davis was preparing his memoirs, Beauregard enlisted Roman's aid. Roman was to receive half the profits, and was "to take Beauregard's notes and smooth out the writing ... and prepare attacks on Davis and other enemies." Roman admitted that he did not write the book. To Beauregard he wrote, "It is your book and not mine. It was from your notes that I wrote it. . . . I submitted to you line after line of everything I had done."[25]

The publication of *Military Operations* damaged Beauregard's reputation. The Louisianan had failed to understand that Davis's imprisonment had made him a martyr. He did not grasp the meaning of a letter to Davis in 1866 by a Georgia Baptist preacher, who wrote that "the South ... feels that your fate should be, and is, her fate," or the comment of another that Davis was "a martyr for our cause."[26]

Military Operations and Beauregard's subsequent articles in *Century* magazine caused even his friend Roman to complain, "Why attack, always attack Mr. Davis?" A Northern reviewer observed of his biography that "the chief sufferer from its publication is likely to be General Beauregard himself."[27]

The postwar conduct of Joseph Johnston also played squarely into the hands of those who sought to diminish his reputation. Like Beauregard, Johnston failed to perceive Davis's martyrdom. In 1874 Appleton and Company issued Johnston's famous *Narrative of Military Operations*. It was the climax of a hatred of Jefferson Davis which he had harbored since 1861. Johnston's *Narrative* criticized Davis's wartime leadership, and blamed him for the loss of the war.

Johnston also made foolish statements. In an interview for a Philadelphia newspaper in 1881, Johnston practically called Davis a thief, charging him with failing to account for two million dollars in gold held by the Confederate government at the time of surrender. One ex-soldier remarked that the Confederate gold story astonished Johnston's friends, for "he had inflicted upon his own reputation a wound that cannot be effaced." A former cavalry officer described Johnston's treat-

ment of Davis as "unjust, wanton, outrageous, and cowardly," while the
Memphis *Appeal* described it as a "mean and dastardly assault."[28]

Lee's supporters helped create a "new" Johnston who was a far cry
from the man described in wartime newspapers and in postwar history
books. He was no longer a brilliant officer who was frequently given
second-rate commands by Jefferson Davis, but a bumbling, quarrelsome
general whose failures in the field justified the President's opinions. Nor
was Johnston now an efficient leader whose operations against McClellan in 1862 were meritorious and who helped design Jackson's Valley
campaign. He became an indecisive, careless officer whose generalship
before he was wounded at Seven Pines was incompetent. Only Lee's
wisdom (which now also shaped Jackson's Valley campaign) saved the
demoralized Army of Northern Virginia from destruction.

This reversal of imagery was achieved by means of dozens of Lee
biographies, articles, and speeches. Typical was the attack upon Johnston after the publication of his *Narrative* in 1874. Lee's circle was
particularly outraged by Johnston's version of the Peninsula campaign.
Johnston suggested that the government did not support his desire to
concentrate on the Peninsula against McClellan, but when Lee replaced him, the new commander was given troops from other areas
which Davis and Lee had previously held back from Johnston. Johnston
was believed to have blamed Lee for the failure to crush McClellan on
the Peninsula, the assumption being that had Lee resumed the attack
on June 1, shortly after Johnston was wounded, the war's decisive battle
would have been won by the Rebels.

When Colonel Charles Marshall addressed the Virginia Division of
the Association of the Army of Northern Virginia, he in effect called
Johnston a liar, noting that future historians would be hard put "to
reconcile 'Johnston's narrative' with the official reports."[29] When Johnston wrote a reply, Jubal Early criticized him for his attack on Marshall.
In newspapers and the Society's *Papers,* Early virtually accused Johnston of lying in his memoirs, and Marshall praised Early for speaking out
against Johnston.

While Beauregard and Johnston were downgraded through a combination of their own statements and criticism by the Lee people, the
case of Stonewall Jackson was different. Jackson's wartime and immediate postwar image as a "co-worker" with Lee was radically altered
between 1870 and 1885. He eventually emerged as an able but eccentric subordinate whose successes were due mainly to his ability to carry
out Lee's plans.

Lee himself had unwittingly helped initiate the rewriting of Jackson's image. In late 1865, Jackson's widow requested Lee's help in the
preparation of Robert Dabney's forthcoming biography. She asked that

Lee read the manuscript and give "your candid opinion" of the book. After perusing the manuscript, Lee replied that the book would be better "had questions and topics, calculated to excite unpleasant discussion" been omitted. He spoke cryptically of "some errors into which the author has no doubt inadvertently fallen." In early 1866 Mrs. Jackson appealed to Lee to provide a memorandum of the "errors" so that Dabney could correct them.[30]

Lee agreed to point out the "errors," and it was obvious that he believed Jackson was being given too much credit for the army's success. He explained that officers of the army's other corps "might reasonably think, that less weight than was due had been given to the effect they produce" in battle.

Lee was obviously unhappy with Dabney's account of the Seven Days, which did not fault Jackson's performance. Dabney claimed that Jackson's arrival on the Peninsula brought a strength "beyond that of his numbers." Indeed:

> His fame as a warrior had just risen to the zenith; while all the other armies of the Confederacy had been retreating before the enemy, or at least holding the defensive with difficulty, his alone had marched, and attacked, and conquered.

When Richmond learned that Jackson had joined Lee, the citizens allegedly "were filled with unbounded joy" and the Federals were "struck with a corresponding panic."

Dabney criticized Lee's management of Malvern Hill and the failure to pursue McClellan to his base on the James River at Harrison's Landing. Dabney intimated that Lee moved slowly while Jackson was "chafing as a lion at the delay."[31] Like others, Dabney gave Jackson the credit for the flanking march around Hooker at Chancellorsville. He described Lee as somewhat unsure where the attack should be made.

In his reply to Mrs. Jackson, Lee strove to correct these matters. Later, in 1867, he was plainly irritated over the Chancellorsville story. After an article on the battle had appeared in the *Southern Review*, the editor, Albert Bledsoe, asked Lee whether he or Jackson fashioned the flanking march. Lee responded:

> I have . . . learned from others that the various authors of the life of Jackson award to him the credit of the success gained by the Army of Northern Virginia where he was present and describe the movements of his corps or command as independent of the general plan of operations and undertaken at his own suggestion and upon his own responsibility.[32]

While Lee did not wish to detract from Jackson's fame, he insisted "this could not have been so." Lee pointed out that every move of an army must be properly ordered," so "there was no question as to who was responsible for the operations of the Confederates, or to whom any failure would have been charged."[33]

Thus there was precedent for the revision of the Jackson image, and for restoring it to what it was in Lee's mind when he wrote the letter to Bledsoe. These efforts especially hinged on Chancellorsville, a battle for which Jackson had been given most of the credit for victory. An initial salvo was Jubal Early's address at Washington and Lee, when he said that Lee was responsible for Chancellorsville. Then in his *Personal Reminiscences* (1874), J. William Jones reprinted the Bledsoe letter because "it is due alike to General Lee and to the truth of history." Three years later, Colonel Walter Taylor in his *Four Years with General Lee* agreed that Lee contrived the strategy for Jackson's flank attack.

But the culmination of the efforts to recast the history of Chancellorsville came with Fitzhugh Lee's "Southern Tours." In 1879 he delivered a flowery address on Chancellorsville before a meeting of the Army of Northern Virginia Association. Lee admitted that he was determined to settle the question of who originated the famed flanking movement. He denied that his uncle had been fooled by Hooker's march across the Rappahannock River above Fredericksburg, as earlier writers had charged, and praised instead Robert Lee's "almost superhuman intelligence."

Fitz Lee described Jackson as overconfident and convinced that Hooker would retreat. Robert Lee was "the only one" who wisely knew that a battle must be fought at Chancellorsville. Consequently, Lee ordered Jackson to make the flanking march around Hooker's right wing. For good measure, Fitz Lee quoted passages that he believed would support his argument, including his uncle's letter to Albert Bledsoe.

By the late 1870s the revamped Southern Historical Society had fallen upon hard times. Money was sorely needed to pay for the printing of its *Papers,* and the Society wanted a fireproof building in which to store the growing collections of Confederate papers. Just as he had courted Jefferson Davis to lecture for the Society, J. William Jones approached Fitz Lee. Would he consent to a series of fund-raising lectures in Southern cities and towns repeating his "true" version of Chancellorsville?

The vain Fitz Lee, no doubt anxious to bolster his rising prestige in postwar Virginia politics, readily agreed. For two years he barnstormed through the South, in what were publicized as Fitzhugh Lee's "Southern Tours." Through 1881 and 1882 he spread the new gospel

—that underlying Jackson's success was the genius of Lee. Southern audiences, weary of years of economic and political hardship, welcomed the dashing Virginia cavalryman who provided them with a strong victory symbol in Robert Lee. The Charleston city council escorted him to a packed hall; an overflowing opera house applauded his lecture in Montgomery; there were artillery salutes in Mobile and receptions in New Orleans, Galveston, and deep into Texas.[34]

Jones attacked Jackson's performance in the Seven Days in a series of articles in the Society's *Papers*. He revised Jackson's wartime image as being largely responsible for McClellan's defeat on the Peninsula. According to the new version, at the battle of Mechanicsville, Jackson's men "were too late . . . to get into the fight or help their comrades." At Gaines' Mill, other Rebel units had to bear the brunt because "Jackson had been delayed." At Frazier's Farm, Jackson "made a great blunder" by his "feeble effort" to cross White Oak Swamp, and remained "an idle spectator of the gallant fight." For the Atlanta *Constitution,* Jones wrote a long rehash of the Chancellorsville campaign, arguing that the flanking movement "originated with Lee, and not (as has been popularly supposed) with Jackson." Jones's second biography of Lee (1906) contained a half dozen pages of documentation to prove his case. That same year, a former Lee aide, Major T. M. R. Talcott, published a twenty-six-page article in the Society's *Papers* arguing that Jackson should be denied credit for the flanking move.[35]

To Lee's admirers, Gettysburg was the most prominent blemish on Robert E. Lee's reputation. It was far more dangerous than any rival such as Jackson or any critic such as Johnston.

The concern with Gettysburg reflected again the Lost Cause mentality. The Reconstruction South sought to rationalize defeat by assertions of its military prowess, and Lee's followers were determined that the needed victory symbolism rested in a portrayal of their hero as invincible on the battlefield.

But this image of Lee was threatened by Gettysburg. As mentioned, until the early 1870s, many war writers had regarded his performance as poor. It was one thing to revise the Jackson image, and it was not too difficult to use Joseph Johnston's rising postwar unpopularity against him to rewrite the story of the 1862 Peninsula campaign.

But reconstructing Gettysburg was another matter. By 1870 William Swinton's *Campaigns of the Army of the Potomac* was still the accepted version of the battle. However, within the decade blame had shifted from Lee and the Ewell-Early failures of July 1, so that General James Longstreet was the scapegoat for Lee's alleged misdeeds of July 2.

Longstreet had made himself a target by his alliance with the Republican party in Louisiana. Charles Marshall called Longstreet a traitor for his conversion to the Republicans, asserting that he had chosen "to consort with such infamous villains . . . to take part against his own people with the vile gang that was robbing and insulting them." Marshall believed that Longstreet's postwar criticisms of Lee were designed to cull favor with Northern Republicans. For all of these sins, Marshall saw only one solution—Longstreet must "make mends for his grievous faults."[36]

Swinton's *Campaigns* documented "a full and free conversation" with Longstreet in 1865. Exactly how much of the Swinton version of Gettysburg came from Longstreet is uncertain, but evidently the general did supply material on several crucial issues: that prior to the campaign Lee promised he would not fight an offensive battle and later went back on his word; and that Lee lost his sense of perspective after the success on July 1, and was so afire with battle that he rejected any flanking proposal and ordered the assaults of July 2–3.

The campaign to blame Longstreet for the defeat began with the publication of a battle report in Dawson's *Historical Magazine* months after the battle. The existence of the paper, far more critical of Longstreet than Lee's initial Gettysburg report, surprised Lee himself, who thought it had been destroyed during the retreat from Richmond. Actually the report had been furnished to the magazine by Marshall, and Jubal Early took pains to have it reprinted in the influential *Southern Magazine* in 1872. Early claimed its publication should silence criticisms of Lee by "persons not well acquainted with the facts."[37]

Early's 1872 commemorative address was the first formal attempt to blame Longstreet for Gettysburg. It transferred emphasis from any misfortunes on July 1, and devised the notion that Lee planned an early assault against Meade's position on Cemetery Ridge on July 2. Longstreet's corps was to begin the attack on the right wing, but that officer opposed the plan, disobeyed orders, and delayed his assault until 4 P.M. "Had the attack been made at daylight, as contemplated," Lee would have won a "brilliant and decisive victory."

William Pendleton embellished Early's version and contended that on the night of July 1 Lee had ordered Longstreet to attack Meade at dawn. Pendleton wrote that he made a reconnaissance of Meade's left wing on Cemetery Ridge, and Lee had personally told him of the order for Longstreet to attack at dawn, but it was pure fabrication, even embarrassing some members of Lee's staff. Charles Venable admitted the statement was due to Pendleton's obvious emotional illness, "to an absolute loss of memory said to be brought on by frequent attacks resembling paralysis." Other Lee staff members—A. L. Long, Walter Taylor, and Charles Marshall—however much they hated Longstreet, denied that any sunrise order had been given. Venable even lamented, "It is a pity, it ever got into print."

Yet it was published and became an influential document, and the legend of the sunrise attack was becoming the standard version in war writings. For two years Pendleton had toured the South on the lecture circuit, raising funds for several Lee memorial projects in Lexington. Even the Northern press was interested, and there were inquiries about publication. At first Pendleton resisted, insisting that his anti-Longstreet document was more useful as a fund-raising device. Finally, in late 1874, he allowed it to appear in the *Southern Magazine*.[38]

But by 1877, partly because of his Republican leanings, Longstreet was becoming a popular figure in the North. For several years after Pendleton's speech in 1873, he fought the Gettysburg issue with Lee partisans in the national press. Then Colonel Alexander McClure of the Philadelphia *Times* saw some promise in articles by Longstreet for the "Annals of the Civil War" series. Although Longstreet at first hesitated, McClure was determined to obtain them. A *Times* editor, George Morgan, later recalled that McClure went so far as to plant articles uncomplimentary to Longstreet in Virginia newspapers in order to goad him. Certainly McClure did enlist the later celebrated editor, then a *Times* correspondent in Atlanta, Henry Grady, to assist Longstreet. When Longstreet consented, Grady edited the articles and may have written them.[39]

The announcement that the *Times* would soon publish articles by Longstreet worried the Lee cult. J. William Jones had already been warned by a New York book agent that "the Philadelphia *Times* seems to be encroaching upon your ground" by securing good articles from ex-Rebels. Jones wrote Jubal Early that "Longstreet is said to have 'an elaborate article with maps' on Gettysburg in the *Times*. I have written to know whether they will admit of a reply."[40]

IN 1875 THE FIRST VOLUME of the English translation of the Comte de Paris's *History of the Civil War in America* was released. It attracted wide notice as one of the first serious war studies, composed by a French nobleman who had served on McClellan's staff during the Peninsula campaign.

Both the first volume and the second, published in 1877, infuriated Lee's supporters. The Comte criticized Lee for exerting poor generalship in the Seven Days and Maryland operations, and credited much of his success at Second Manassas to either luck or Stonewall Jackson. One Virginian said the work was filled with errors "which a stupid schoolboy would be ashamed to commit," while Early advised the Frenchman that if he wanted to produce anything worthwhile, "he had better consign to the flames all that he has so far published."[41]

The Comte de Paris hastily tried to mend his Southern fences. He joined the Southern Historical Society. He flattered Jones, praised Lee as a great general, and promised to work to help the South "obtain that fair hearing at the bar of history." By 1877 he was researching his volume on the third year of the war, and needed the help of the Lee people in assembling material on the battle of Gettysburg. In January of that year, he sent a letter to editor J. William Jones that was to ignite the Gettysburg controversy.

It was obvious from his letter that the Comte's version of Gettysburg would be based heavily upon Swinton's writing. He sent Jones a list of five mistakes which he believed Lee had committed in the battle, including his failure to heed Longstreet's advice for the flanking movement and his order for Pickett's charge. He asked Jones to circulate the list "to some of the Confederate leaders who are still alive" for their comments.

What followed may be fairly called the most cynical manipulation that ever occurred in the writing of Civil War history, as the Lee cult strove to blame Longstreet for the loss of Gettysburg. The intrigue, which slowly developed over a two-year span, took two closely knit approaches—discredit the Comte's version even before it appeared in print, and destroy Longstreet's Gettysburg reputation.

J. William Jones confided to Early that "it really seems a fine opportunity" to give the Comte "the true story of Gettysburg." A flurry of correspondence and meetings followed among Early, Jones, Fitz Lee, Charles Marshall, and others. Jones arranged for some of them to write "revised" versions of the battle to be mailed to the Frenchman. In addition, Early began to prepare an article for the Society's *Papers* blaming Gettysburg on Longstreet, while Walter Taylor wrote a similar piece for the Philadelphia *Times*. While Marshall was composing his paper for the Comte, he requested a meeting with Early to obtain his opinions before completing it. Jones was openly cordial to the Frenchman, but he secretly attempted to destroy his credibility as a historian. He wrote Early: "Now that your hand is in can you not give us a paper or two on the Count of Paris' Second Vol. If you have not the book I can loan it to you." Marshall warned against Jones's desire to expose the Comte's "blunders," since "I fear that if he be severely criticized it will give an importance to his statements that they do not really deserve."[42] Taylor's article in the Philadelphia *Times* not only repeated the charge that Longstreet disobeyed orders on July 2, but somehow even managed to blame him for Pickett's disastrous charge.[43]

At the same time a European writer who might rival the Comte de Paris in prestige was found. Major Justus Scheibert had been an official observer for the Prussian army and had been at Lee's headquarters during Pickett's charge. He had published two books on the war in German, praising Lee as a "rare man" and "one of the first Generals of his century."[44] Lee's former staff officer Charles Venable recognized Scheibert's value. He urged Early to furnish him with friendly documentary evidence, so that the cause would "find us a strong interpreter in Prussian military circles." Venable felt that Scheibert's writings were coming "at a most opportune time," "just after the issue of the work of the Comte de Paris . . ." He admitted that the Prussian's efforts would supply a good counterpoise to the Frenchman, and hoped his writings would provide "a complete refutation . . . of the Comte's slip-shod misrepresentations."[45]

LEE'S FOLLOWERS were determined to settle the matter in their famed "Gettysburg Series," printed in the Society's *Papers,* which was a total assault upon Longstreet's reputation. It began in August 1877, when Jones published the first of twenty replies to the list of Lee's mistakes suggested earlier by the Comte de Paris. Jones and Early selected the authors, and Longstreet was not consulted.

The first issue was typical of what would follow. Early wrote a long tirade exonerating himself and damning Longstreet. Fitzhugh Lee, William Allan, and Walter Taylor echoed the new theme. Up to the December issue, a succession of Lee admirers offered their testimony, shifting the blame to Longstreet.

But Early was not satisfied, and his fear for his own reputation was obvious. He believed that some of the nineteen other writers had neither condemned Longstreet severely enough nor sufficiently absolved Early. So in the December issue he printed a forty-page article which summarized and often rebutted his comrades. It was an impassioned defense of his conduct on July 1, which, to his surprise, some of Lee's friends had criticized. Early pleaded with his readers that "it is a little remarkable" that men even attempted to discuss the reasons for defeat, "when there is an all-sufficient cause staring us in the face . . . which fully explains and accounts for that failure"—Longstreet's conduct.

Early displayed his fear in that same issue with a second article attacking Longstreet's writings. Longstreet's first piece for the Philadelphia *Times* had appeared in November. It was a familiar restatement of the original version of Gettysburg—an indictment of Ewell and Early, and a critique of Lee's failure to outflank Meade. Although he did not print Longstreet's article, J. William Jones published Early's violent rebuttal. The editor explained that this curious procedure was followed "due to fairness and a proper desire to aid the search for truth."

More and more, it was apparent that the shifting of blame to Longstreet was less a search for truth or a rehabilitation of Lee than an attempt to salvage Early's reputation. But Early and his friends were soon caught in a lie which threatened to destroy his efforts to avoid blame for Gettysburg.

The threat came from General J. E. B. Stuart's former adjutant, Major Henry McClellan. Like Longstreet, Stuart had escaped much of the initial criticism for the defeat at Gettysburg. Eventually Walter Taylor and Harry Heth began labeling Stuart a secondary culprit. Articles by Lee partisans charged that Stuart's failure to keep in touch with the army during the march and his tardiness in arriving at Gettysburg deprived Lee of needed information. In turn, friends of Stuart such as McClellan and Colonel John Mosby defended him in the Philadelphia *Times*.

McClellan frightened Early so badly that he attempted to make a deal with the ex-cavalryman. In a September article in the *Times*, McClellan pointed out that Stuart had expected to join up with Lee's infantry advance near York, and "had Stuart received that cooperation from the infantry officers commanding the advance," he would have reached Lee a day earlier.

McClellan was convinced that Early was the infantry commander who had primarily failed Stuart, and was determined to prove it. He asked J. William Jones for copies of Early's reports, but was refused. Then McClellan requested the information from Early, and cryptically reminded him that Stuart had been ordered to communicate with him, and "how anxiously Stuart looked for any trace . . . from you."

Early offered to drop his indictment of Stuart if McClellan would let him alone. He wrote an article for the *Papers* which he urged McClellan to read, as it "vindicated Stuart and exempted him from responsibility for the loss of the battle of Gettysburg." Early now said that Stuart's absence was "no real harm," for Lee "did find out where the enemy was."[46]

But Early was in a trap. In 1876 the Society's *Papers* had published a copy of Stuart's Gettysburg report. When Jones and Early printed it, a key paragraph was omitted in which Stuart blamed Early for his failure to make contact with Lee's army. Stuart charged that Early had been directed by Lee to watch for the cavalry, but failed to do so, even though "he had reason to expect me, and had been directed to look out for me."[47]

McClellan had not seen a copy of Stuart's original report. When he finally compared it with the printed Jones-Early version, and noted that it had been doctored, he protested to Early in a tough letter which promised to expose the matter in another article for the Philadelphia *Times*.

Early first attempted to bully McClellan:

I caution you, therefore, to beware, for I cannot remain silent. I do not want to write what I will be compelled to write, when the omitted portions of Stuart's report and your comments in connection therewith appear in print.[48]

Early offered to shift the blame for Gettysburg entirely from Stuart to Longstreet. He admitted that McClellan's upcoming article would criticize his own conduct, and pleaded that Gettysburg was not lost because he and Stuart failed to communicate. Early capped his bargain with an incredible statement—that had Stuart been on time at Gettysburg, armed with the best intelligence of Meade's army, Lee would have been no better off. Even then, Lee would never have been in a better situation than he was to be on July 2, the time of Longstreet's failure.[49]

In effect a bargain was struck between admirers of Lee and Stuart. Later in 1878, McClellan's article in defense of Stuart appeared in the *Times,* avoiding any outright criticism of Early and making no mention of the omitted paragraph in Stuart's report. McClellan was warmly congratulated by Fitz Lee, who stated:

I have only said that it was unfortunate Stuart was *not* in General Lee's front on the 1st of July, but *the* responsibility of the loss of the *battle* is irrecoverably fastened upon Longstreet.

In turn, Fitz Lee wrote an article for the Society's *Papers.* His "A Reply to General Longstreet" only reflected the hypocrisy of the Lee cult. Before he published the article, Fitz Lee confided to Early what he would do. "You need not worry about my abusing Ewell" for the mistakes of July 1. Nor would Stuart be blamed, for "I am going to take Stuart and his affairs up . . . with an affectionate hand." Naturally Longstreet would be the culprit. Lee promised Early that "I am going to clinch your effort in fixing the responsibility of the 2nd where it properly belongs . . ."[50]

In 1878 the Society's *Papers* finally reprinted two articles by Longstreet in defense of his own conduct. Early, encouraged by Jones, came out against Longstreet in a long, brutal article piously dedicated "to vindicate the fame of the great commander of the Army of Northern Virginia and the truth of history."[51]

Lee's partisans doggedly pursued Longstreet. Any article he composed was followed by an automatic rebuttal in the Society's *Papers* or elsewhere. In 1885, when Longstreet wrote on the Seven Days for *Century,* Jubal Early provided a fiery retort which used a fable to intimate that Longstreet was an ass. In 1886 Longstreet published an article in *Century* on the Maryland campaign. William Allan produced a long "Review of General Longstreet" in the Society's *Papers* which accused him of various sins, including "distorted vision upon Lee and his deeds." In 1878 the Society's *Papers* printed excerpts from General Richard Taylor's forthcoming *Destruction and Reconstruction*. Jones smugly commented that he personally would not express an opinion "as to the keen thrusts of the distinguished author." One such thrust was a repetition of the new Gettysburg story, in which Taylor compared Lee and Longstreet to the Biblical characters of Balaam and his ass."[52]

In 1904, deaf, pain-ridden by his Wilderness wound, and half blind from cancer, the outcast Longstreet died in Georgia. Two years later, the aging Jones could still berate him in his second biography of Lee. Jones hooted at Longstreet's "ludicrously inaccurate" statements, and, perhaps symbolically, accused him of "criticizing with unsparing severity the conduct of Lee, Jackson, and Early."[53]

How LEE'S FOLLOWERS dealt with the images of his rivals and critics is obvious. How did they deal with the image of their hero?

In the Reconstruction years Lee's admirers held up to the South an irresistible, consistent image. There was little variance in the depiction of Lee by Emily Mason, J. William Jones, George Cary Eggleston, John Esten Cooke, and a score of other members of the cult. It resounded through the pages of Southern Lost Cause magazines and popular Northern journals, through the publicity leaflets of Washington and Lee, and in the fund-raising campaigns of a half dozen Lee memorial projects.

The image of Lee advanced by his early admirers would actually change little in future times. Lee was born of a family steeped in both English nobility and a Revolutionary heritage. His family ties were strong with his own idol, George Washington. His boyhood was a model of devotion to his mother and to the principles of duty and self-denial which she taught him. After a stainless record at West Point, Lee entered into an idyllic marriage to the "Child of Arlington," Mary Custis.

When the war came in 1861, Lee was faced with an agony endured by no other Southerner. He hated both slavery and secession, and loved the Union more deeply than most. Yet his sense of duty to Virginia prevailed. He shunned potential military eminence in the Federal army, gave up his beloved Arlington, and chose to fight for Virginia.

He became the strategic and tactical genius of the war. He was so brilliant that, had Jefferson Davis allowed him real authority, the Confederates might have won the war. Instead, he remained the contained commander, hampered by Davis's jealousy of his own prerogatives.

Still, Lee had no equal. In 1862 he took charge of the Army of

Northern Virginia when McClellan stood at Richmond's gates and when the Southern army was on the verge of demoralization due to Joseph Johnston's bungling. Lee's victory in the Seven Days immediately made him the central war hero to whom the South looked for salvation.

Lee rarely—if ever—made a command error. Defeats were due to the sins of subordinates. At Gettysburg, where Lee would have defeated Meade and probably have won the war, his lieutenants failed him. Typical of Lee's charity and Christ-like spirit was his refusal to blame his lieutenants for their failures.

Eventually Lee would be defeated, but not because of his own mistakes. Grant did not outgeneral Lee in the 1864–65 campaign, for he was not the Virginian's equal. Rather, he overpowered Lee by his superior numbers.

After Appomattox, Lee further displayed traits superior to other Rebels. His surrender to Grant eventually helped to restore the Union because Lee believed that guerrilla warfare would prevent a rebuilding of the South. More than other Confederate leaders, Lee exhibited self-sacrifice. He avoided lucrative business offers, and went instead to tiny Washington College. The entire South looked to him for guidance.

Two things must be kept in mind when observing the postwar South's reaction to this image of Lee. Heroes are not made of nothing, and Robert Lee was a man of more substance than many others. While Lee's military record will be discussed later, it is important here that he was a superb general, and was regarded as such by many of his contemporaries. They also saw him as a man of lofty character, whose demeanor transcended the pettiness of many other men. Lee did not require a cult of admirers to establish his reputation.

But the cult existed, and transformed Lee into a virtual demigod. And because such men as Jubal Early and J. William Jones were themselves possessed of the Lost Cause mentality, the exaggerated image of Lee which they constructed provided needed rationales for a defeated South.

THE PSYCHOLOGICAL TRAUMA of the South's defeat was enormous. The economic collapse was total. Two billion dollars of human slavery had been eliminated. Banks and insurance firms had collapsed, while hundreds of millions of dollars in investments ranging from railroads to farm machinery had evaporated.

More important were the losses in human resources. The war had cost the Confederates over a quarter of a million dead, plus hundreds of thousands physically or mentally maimed. Leadership had also been swept away in a region that had always placed faith in political and military personalities. Hundreds of military and civilian leaders were dead. Many more prominent citizens had deserted the South after Appomattox. Thousands had fled across the Rio Grande to Mexico, Brazil, and Venezuela. Others were exiled in Canada, searched for exotic military commands in the Middle East, or took advantage of enduring pro-Confederate sympathies in England and France.

The Southern problem was compounded by a Puritan ethic that in 1865 was still a strong force, holding that there was a direct link between God's grace and success in any realm. But the South had learned that hard work coupled with a belief in God's grace did not guarantee success. The belief that God was on the side of the Confederacy had been universal in the South. An Atlanta newspaper editor in 1862 boasted: "Our cause is sacred. Our ultimate triumph is certain." After the victory at Second Manassas in 1862, a war correspondent for the Savannah *Republican* observed that "never since Adam was planted in the garden of Eden, did a holier cause engage the hearts and arms of any nation." Jefferson Davis explained the victory as an event in which "our armies have been blessed by the Lord of Hosts."[54]

But after Appomattox, the South had to grapple with the question of why God had not saved the South. Equally difficult was the task of explaining why Southern arms had not won. Southerners had faith in their military prowess. Even during Grant's drive on Richmond in 1864, an editor could ask how the Union could hope for victory "when their armies are thus annually defeated and driven back ..." The editor gloated that "a few more days" would bring "full deliverance."[55]

But when "full deliverance" did not come, many Southerners were stunned. One recalled that he had no "foresight of the cataclysm," and believed that "the Day of Judgement could come" before Richmond could be captured.[56]

The Reconstruction South compensated for defeat by justifying its military prowess. That the South would turn to Lee was logical. He was by far the most successful Confederate general, and his Army of Northern Virginia had menaced populous eastern cities.

Essential to the image of Lee as the South's symbol was the claim that he was never defeated in battle. How could a man thought by Jubal Early to be a better general than "Caesar, Napoleon, Marlborough or Wellington" lose? General John Gordon well expressed the position when he said that "Lee was never really beaten. Lee could not be beaten."[57]

So the Lee cult—and the entire South—groped for other reasons for Lee's defeat. Some maintained that his loss was due to chance. Some claimed that Lee would have destroyed Grant in the Wilderness had not Longstreet been accidentally wounded by his own men. This "devil theory" held that only some unforeseen chance stymied his generalship. One writer said that so many chance circumstances wrecked the Rebel effort that "we almost seem to be struggling against destiny itself . . . capricious Fortune snatches the victory from their grasp."[58]

It was widely claimed that Lee was overwhelmed by superior odds. It became a matter of faith in Rebel letters to contend that Lee was the better general, but that Grant had the superior numbers. Grant realized this, and resorted to bullish slaughter tactics which eventually wore down his opponent. Scarcely any book, article, or speech on Lee during the Reconstruction failed to make this assertion. Typical was a postwar address in Richmond in which it was claimed that Lee in 1864–65 fought alone against "the whole resources of the United States."[59]

Such explanations represent the Lee cult's attitude toward his critics and rivals in the postwar years. Any notion that Lee had made mistakes jeopardized the Reconstruction image of the victorious Lee. The blaming of Stonewall Jackson and others for failures in the Seven Days . . . the crucifixion of Longstreet for Gettysburg . . . the violent assaults upon Joseph E. Johnston—all had common sources: devotion to Lee's memory and a hostility toward any who would tamper with an image of victory sought by the postwar South.

IT WAS IRONIC that the same admirers who cast Lee as a victory symbol also made him a symbol of defeat.

Lee was a symbol of poverty, one with whom a distraught people could identify. The stories of how Lee shunned attractive postwar offers and accepted the presidency at Washington College became legendary in the years after Appomattox. One might contend that others as well were interested in rebuilding the South, men such as Beauregard in his New Orleans business ventures, or Joseph Johnston in Virginia politics. Yet many Southerners viewed Lee as a symbol of sacrifice and poverty. Jones's *Personal Reminiscences* devoted an entire chapter to this theme. In 1884, when the Lee monument was unveiled in New Orleans, the speaker, Charles Fenner, summarized what scores of other books and speeches had said, that Lee was the example of

> . . . that gracious and beautiful life to which he retired as college president . . . and in which he labored, to the moment of his death, in repairing the neglected education of the Southern youth, and in teaching his people . . .[60]

The postwar South was hard-pressed to explain its defeat amidst a rising tide of pragmatism in American life. Even before the pragmatic approach—that whatever succeeds is the true course—became an intellectual topic, it was deeply embedded in the national mind. Basic to the American doctrine of progress was the conviction that the nation was successful because its precepts were noble. During the Reconstruction, Northern authors emphasized this theme.

Southern writers argued that the North's success did not prove its worthiness, insisting that good causes often lose. As one speaker observed in 1868, "It is only the atheist who adopts success as the *criterion* of right," that often God designed that "the brave and true" would fail.[61]

Thus it was necessary first to prove that the North was not right, but was itself an evil force. Southerners questioned how a generation that produced the likes of Washington and Lee could be inferior "to Yankees, negroes, Germans, and Irish." Northern armies were accused of a wide range of sins—cowardice, cruelty to Southern women, barbaric treatment of prisoners, profanity and drunkenness, immorality, and even the use of poison bullets. An Atlanta editor described the North as "a swindling race," while the editor of the *Southern Literary Messenger* announced that "the Southern man is now, as he has always been . . . superior to the Northern man . . ."[62]

That was only one side of the proverbial coin. The South had to magnify its own sense of purity. General Daniel Harvey Hill's magazine, *The Land We Love,* displayed a verse on its masthead, a line which had been written by an English admirer of Lee, which asserted: "No nation rose so white and fair, or fell so pure of crimes."

The ultimate rationale of this pure nation was the character of Lee. The Lost Cause argument stated that any society which produced a man of such splendid character must be right.

The Lee cult—and the entire South—emphasized this use of Lee as an example of the righteous loser. Senator Ben Hill of Georgia described Lee as "a private citizen without wrong . . . a man without guile." To an orator at a veterans' meeting in Richmond in 1876, Lee was "so blameless as might become a Saint." Perhaps the editor of the Lost Cause organ, the *Southern Magazine,* best summarized this symbolism in 1872 when he urged that Lee's character be held up to the South, for "we consider Robert Edward Lee as . . . the noblest type of manhood that this age has produced."[63]

ROBERT LEE served well also as a religious explanation for Southern defeat. The Confederate faith in the aid of Divine Providence had been strong. Lee himself believed that God intervened in the war. Often when his tactics failed to crush an opponent, as at Cheat Mountain and Chancellorsville, he considered that it was because "God ordered otherwise."[64]

When deliverance did not come, a religious explanation seemed needed for the Lost Cause. How could so fine a society, guided by God, lose? The appeal was to a Christian interpretation of history. Man was an instrument of divine providence, and often had to endure travail as part of God's discipline. A catastrophe to one's society did not prove lack of merit; it only showed God's hand at work.

Lee's character was almost deified as he became a Christ symbol. If Christ had his Gethsemane, Lee had his Appomattox. Writers turned to Lee as an example of the better man who could lose, and honed his character to perfection.

The groundwork for this image was prepared by the first Lee cult. Many comparisons were made between Lee and Christ. Lee's decision at Arlington in 1861 was often compared to Christ's three temptations in the wilderness. The three temptations of Lee in 1861—fame, power, and riches—were a central element in the pageantry of the unveiling of the Valentine statue in 1883 at Lexington. The principal orator, Major John Daniel, imagined Lee on that fateful April day, gazing across the Potomac River from an upstairs room at Arlington. He thought about the offer from Winfield Scott to command the army that would conquer the South. If Lee accepted, he would be "the foremost man" of the nation, "with all honor and glory that riches and office and power and public applause can supply."

Instead, Lee's response was Christ-like; he shunned the offer. In Daniel's words:

Since the Son of Man stood upon the Mount, and saw "all the kingdoms of the world and the glory of them" stretched before him, and turned away . . . to the Cross of Calvary beyond, no follower of the meek and lowly Saviour can have undergone more trying ordeal.[65]

There were other Christ symbols in the Lee image. His life was frequently described as "spotless." Some saw Lee's postwar conduct as resembling Christ's walk to Calvary. Here was the man without blemish, bearing without a murmur the punishment for his people, and advising them to love their enemy. Others stressed his fondness for children, consideration for animals, and spirit of forgiveness to erring subordinates—especially to Longstreet.

Lee's biographer Marshall Fishwick was close to the mark when he suggested that the General was the closest thing to a saint in the Protestant South. He was canonized not only as the South's military hero but also as its supreme religious symbol.

.   .   .

THE ATTEMPT to connect secession with the forefathers of the Revolutionary War was not new. In February 1861, on the day he arrived at the new government seat in Montgomery, Jefferson Davis prayed "that Southern valor still shines as brightly as in the days of '76." In his inaugural address as President, Davis's words foreshadowed an idea that sprang up after the war—that the causes were comparable. He spoke of how the Revolutionary fathers had designed a government based on the principle of a compact of states, with the inherent right to withdraw if the government violated the compact. The South had been true to the Constitution, while the North had violated it by attacks upon the expansion of slavery and other issues. So in 1861 it was the South, steeped in the traditions of Washington and Jefferson, that was the real preserver of the Constitution.

In the first volume of his memoir, *The Rise and Fall of the Confederate Government,* Davis spent 200 pages asserting that the Confederates had been the preservers of the Revolutionary heritage. This argument was the centerpiece of Alexander Stephens's famous 1868–70 apology, *A Constitutional View of the Late War Between the States,* Albert Bledsoe's *Is Davis a Traitor?,* and scores of other writings.

Gradually Lost Cause authors put forward Virginia as the showpiece of the Confederacy. To a nation under the influence of the 1876 Centennial of independence, the Virginia that produced Washington, Jefferson, Yorktown, Light-Horse Harry Lee, and other symbols seemed to represent the best in American history.

Lost Cause advocates beat a constant drum—that Virginia almost single-handedly won the Revolution and established the American government. In one postwar address, General Daniel Harvey Hill reminded his hearers that "the Southern-born Washington" had success in such battles as Trenton and Saratoga primarily because of Virginia troops. The oceanographer Matthew Fontaine Maury took the argument a step further and saw Virginia as the Republic's foundation stone. "Virginia was the leader in the war . . . and *her* sons were the masterspirits of it." When the Republic was organized, "four of her sons . . . were called, one after the other, to preside." Thus Virginia "had laid the corner-stone of the Union, *Her* sons were its chief architects."[66]

Southern apologists viewed Robert Lee as the essential link between the Revolutionary and Confederate heritage. Lee's image contained all the necessary ingredients. The Washington and Lee families possessed ties of family and friendship. Lee's father had been a close friend and favorite general of George Washington. His son Robert had married the daughter of Washington's stepson.

Such symbolism proved irrepressible. The Lee cult emphasized his colonial background, the family relationship, and the personality likenesses of the two Virginia heroes. In his biography of Lee, John Esten

Cooke wrote four chapters on the General's English and Revolutionary backgrounds. In Emily Mason's *Popular Life of Robert Edward Lee,* she described Lee's acceptance of the presidency of Washington College:

> It is remarkable that the institution which enjoyed the munificence and inherited the name of the hero of the first American Revolution, should have opened its arms to receive . . . the foremost man of the second.[67]

All of this imagery came together on a clear June afternoon in 1883, on the gentle slope below the president's home at Washington and Lee University. Thousands came to Lexington by train, carriage, and horseback, to witness the unveiling of the Valentine recumbent figure in the college chapel. Special trains brought veterans of the war. Parades wound from the depot up steep Washington Street, and past the courthouse where the Lee Memorial Association had been conceived in the autumn of 1870. Among the Confederate celebrities were Governor Wade Hampton of South Carolina, the poet Father Abram Ryan, and the widows of Pickett, Stuart, and Stonewall Jackson. Some eight thousand people surrounded the small college chapel for the dedication ceremonies.

No doubt Lee's followers on the reviewing platform, men like Custis Lee and Jubal Early, saw the event as the culmination of years of devotion. Their labors since Lee's death had been an alchemy of devotion to a hero and their own personal motivations. They had worked the image of a man of exceptional character into a godlike figure.

The main ceremonial address summarized the defeated Confederacy's view of Lee. Even the speaker was symbolic. Major John Daniel represented a growing trend of Southern politicians who, deliberately or otherwise, found it politically profitable to invoke the name of Robert Lee.

Until this speech, Daniel was by all measurements a political loser. The wartime chief of staff for Early, he had been active in the struggle between ex-Confederate, conservative Virginia Democrats against a coalition of Republican-Readjuster factions. Twice Daniel had failed to win the Democratic nomination for Congress. In 1877 he lost the nomination for governor. In 1881 he won the Democratic nomination, but was defeated by one of Lee's critics, General William Mahone, who headed the Republican-Readjuster coalition.

At the time of the Lexington convocation, Daniel was engaged in another campaign for Congress. His biographer called Daniel's speech the most important of his life, and it revitalized his political career. Newspapers across the country printed the three-hour address; the

Washington *Post* devoted its entire first page to the text, and it was published in book form. The following year John Daniel finally won an election.[68]

Daniel's description of Lee was a correct analysis of the Southern mind. He concentrated, perhaps unknowingly, upon the four symbols of the Southern apologia for secession and defeat, and described Lee as the cornerstone of all four. Lee was the Christ symbol whose anguish in his decision of 1861 was likened by Daniel to "the agony and bloody sweat of Gethsemane, and to the Cross of Calvary beyond . . ." He was the symbol of defeat, an object lesson that right does not always prevail and that success was no test of virtue. Lee was the symbol of victory, the man who could not be matched in generalship. Lee was also the likeness of George Washington, and the historic tie of secession with the Revolutionary generation. In Virginia, "there has sprung from the loins of her heroic race" two men of exception. Each, Washington and Lee, "fought for liberty and independence."[69]

So Daniel spoke for an epoch, a time when Lee's image had been restructured by those who had the power to do so. The marble man of Edward Valentine's genius had been dedicated, and Lee had been consecrated as the Confederacy's supreme war hero.

Lee was not yet what he would become, the almost godlike hero of the South. Nor was he yet considered a national symbol of the nobility of the Southern experience.

It remained for a new group of Lee admirers to achieve this. Some of these people were in the audience when Daniel finished his speech and applause resounded across the narrow valley. The crowds who had come to bear witness departed slowly from the shrine in the Shenandoah country, and a new generation of Southern writers looked toward the future.

CHAPTER IV

BIRTH OF A
NATIONAL HERO

E ARLY IN THE SUMMER OF 1890, elaborate ceremonies marked the dedication of the Robert E. Lee statue in Richmond. But the response of the national press was either hostile or bored. The Minneapolis *Tribune* suggested that Lee "lacked the stuff that the highest type of hero is made of "; the Indianapolis *Journal* saw the statue as "sculptured treason"; and the Philadelphia *North American* suggested that Benedict Arnold had more justification for such honors than did Lee.[1]

Even more moderate Northern accounts of the Richmond ceremonies were unenthusiastic. While Lee's character and military ability were complimented, he was viewed as a regional figure. *Harper's Weekly* said Lee "personified what was best of a bad cause." The magazine did not oppose such ceremonies, but suggested that the South needed heroes to remember an "epic" in their lives. But to *Harper's*, Lee seemed outdated. Wearily, the magazine hoped that the Richmond dedication would prove the last act "of the war of secession," and that the nation could return to its business.[2]

A generation later, the national attitude toward Lee had changed sharply. By 1910 he was a national hero. A mania for Lee swept the country as if America could not praise him enough, or read enough of his army's exploits. *Harper's* now called him "the pride of the whole country," and a writer in the *Chautauquan* termed him a member "of the first triumvirate of greatness" with Abraham Lincoln and George Washington.[3]

President Theodore Roosevelt said he was a "matter of pride to all our countrymen" and proposed that a permanent memorial be established. Woodrow Wilson concluded that Lee was so great that he could not "be lifted to any new place of distinction by any man's words of praise." *The Ladies' Home Journal* eulogized Lee's love "for his old gray horse," while *Literary Digest* described a pet hen kept at his headquarters.[4]

Anything or anyone associated with the Virginian seemed to possess market value after 1900. *Cosmopolitan* published Mrs. George

Pickett's reminiscences in ten installments, and *Scribner's* chose the recollections of General John Gordon. In addition to a barrage of new biographies of Lee, numerous reminiscences appeared by former Lee associates such as Jubal Early, Robert Stiles, and John Gordon.[5]

HOW DOES ONE EXPLAIN this change in attitude after 1900? The answer probably is found in another application of the "Virginia pattern" in Civil War writing. The image of Lee held up by a new cult of Confederate writers meshed well with the national mood. Confederate heroes were more acceptable to the nation, and Lee perhaps best symbolized the general attitude toward the meaning of the war. While there was an optimistic national fervor toward imperialism and Anglo-Saxon racial conceit, there was also a more tolerant attitude toward former Confederates and a Darwinian faith in progress.

Beneath this optimism lay a strong current of uneasiness. The mechanization of American life had engendered bewilderment in an agrarian society caught in the throes of a readjustment of values. There was a loss of personal values amid changing ethical standards. Natural man seemed to be losing a battle with industrial society. Too, there was nostalgia at the passing of the nineteenth century and the approaching fifty-year commemoration of the Civil War. There were also some unresolved questions: whether the South had been too harshly treated in the Reconstruction; whether the new society forged by war, beset with industrial blight and immigration, had not destroyed a finer life.

Robert E. Lee's image would have a tremendous impact upon these national moods after 1900. To appreciate this influence requires an understanding of his status in the Southern mind by the turn of the century. By then, he had become the South's central hero symbol, surpassing even George Washington. His enshrinement reached its zenith in the 1907 celebration of his birthday, an event that was almost a religious holiday in the South.

Much of Lee's new hero status was due to the efforts of a cult of historians who were prominent in Civil War writing during the romantic age, between 1885 and 1915. These admirers of Lee created an image that had a special appeal to the Southern—and eventually to the national—mind.

Lee's image in the late nineteenth century was tied closely to the enduring Southern search for justification. For two decades after Appomattox, Southerners had sought to explain away military defeat, and their explanations were always tinged with bitterness. Ex-Confederates either denied that Lee had been defeated or blamed one another for Rebel misfortune.

The apologias were altered radically in the romantic era after 1885.

Gradually, the passing of time motivated ex-Rebels to look upon the war as a great, heroic epic. It was a nostalgic looking backward by aging men, many of whom were strapped to a drab New South existence. For them, battles became less matters of winner and loser and more a case of heroic deeds by men such as Lee.

Confederate writings were saturated with the epic syndrome. A survivor of J. E. B. Stuart's cavalry could recall that "the memory of those days seems like a beautiful dream—seen through the mists of the rolling years." An ex-Tennessee infantryman mused that "as I write, I place my hand in Memory's and retrace with her the paths that trailing years have worn."[6]

This romantic outlook blended well with the Southern notion of chivalry. The idea of chivalry in part reflected the nation's rising feelings of Anglo-Saxon superiority in an age threatened by unsettling forces such as immigration from Eastern Europe. It was a holdover from the antebellum planter fascination with the code of Sir Walter Scott's novels. Defeat in the war had driven Southerners to exaggerate their military prowess. Southern novelists expanded the image of chivalry with romanticized novels of prewar plantation life.

Jousting tournaments were staged throughout the South, in which "knights received the trophies upon their lances" and rode away to offer them to their favorite ladies.[7] One tournament on the North Anna River in Virginia featured a group of knights who were ex-Rebel cavalrymen, wearing "plumed hats that had covered their heads in real cavalry charges."[8] In her novel *The Valiants of Virginia,* Hallie Rives quoted the "charge to the knights" given before each tournament, in which they were implored to uphold the manly principles "of the knighthood of Virginia."[9]

Given such a mentality, it was natural that many ex-Confederates, as time produced more nostalgia, regarded their war effort as a knightly crusade. One speaker in 1898 saw the war as a fight to protect Southern womanhood, for "true chivalry means the protecting of the weak by the strong." An orator at a veterans' reunion in Georgia could without blushing depict the men who fought Sherman as knights reincarnate, "symbol of a past, consecrated by aspiration the purest, impulses the most patriotic . . . examples of valor, chivalry."[10]

Quite naturally Robert Lee became the centerpiece of this symbolism. He could supply all the needed ingredients. His military prowess was matched by his alleged credentials of knightly ancestry. Many early Lee biographers had waxed long on his English origins. Lee's new biographers embellished the story. A Louisville professor strove hard to prove that the General descended from "King Robert the Bruce, of Scotland" and argued that the General was a man "in whose veins coursed the mingled blood of . . . heroes of the middle ages." Another writer, in the *South Atlantic Quarterly*, found that he was of "pure Norman blood" and that his ancestry could be traced "to Launcelot Lee ... who accompanied William the Conqueror." J. William Jones was ecstatic over such "findings" and published articles on Lee's ancestry in the Southern Historical Society's *Papers*, so that everyone would know that "*our* 'King of Men' was descended from the noble King Robert Bruce of Scotland."[11]

THE END OF RECONSTRUCTION did not extinguish the Southern desire to justify secession and defeat. Southern apologists only shifted their defense to a new argument, which, like the old, was dependent upon the Lee image.

The new rationale of the 1880s represented a skillful picking and choosing among certain ideals of Social Darwinism. The romantics denied the Darwinian theory that the stronger institution invariably survives, and attacked the notion that success always equals right. But the new Lost Cause approach was keyed to another Darwinian concept—that man is shaped by his environment. The South had fought to protect its environment, to defend a finer society. Southern writers focused on the issue to explain why they fought and why they were defeated—not by military prowess, but by the essential weaknesses of an agrarian life, lack of manpower and machinery.

The Civil War was seen as a fight for the homeland and its finer principles. Typical was a speech in 1891 by General Bradley Johnson, dedicating a Confederate monument in Virginia. Johnson freely used the new Southern weapon—Charles Darwin. Environmental factors had forced North and South to develop contrasting societies. The North, "invigorated" by constant struggle with nature, became materialistic, grasping for wealth and power. The South's "more generous climate" had wrought a life-style based upon non-materialism and adherence to a finer code of "veracity and honor in man, chastity and fidelity in women."[12]

General Daniel Harvey Hill, speaking to an 1887 Confederate reunion in Baltimore, argued that the Southern climate was responsible for a superior civilization "of pure women and brave men; the South of Washington and Jefferson ... of Andrew Jackson and Winfield Scott." Southern journalist Henry Watterson saw the downfall of the South in like terms. Because of the nature of its agrarian society, "the Confederacy was doomed in its cradle."[13]

The Lost Cause apologia was difficult to refute because it contained built-in escape mechanisms. Honed carefully by a generation of novelists and historians, it was a two-pronged argument. The South's conduct in secession had been caused by environmental influences. Southerners had fought to defend their rights because of honest convictions and concern for their homeland. Defeat came not because they were wrong or because of any military failure on the part of Lee. Rather, the agrarian life that infused them with virtue also provided them with too few guns and too little manpower to overcome an industrial society. The honest convictions for which they had fought, such as duty and honor, only illustrated a superior code of life conditioned by the Southern environment.

The new Lost Cause rationale was difficult to refute because the writers who described this civilization related it, not to the entire South, but to romantic Virginia. Virginia came to epitomize in secession a society that fought for finer virtues. In defeat, Virginia only taught that a finer civilization could lose.

It was no surprise that Virginia became the "best face" put forward by the romantic South. Reconstruction Virginia writers had already depicted their state as a special, more noble society. Northern magazines examining Southern culture in the 1870s had concentrated on the unique charm and Revolutionary heritage of Virginia.

Virginia's place on a pedestal became more celebrated after 1885. From then until World War I, Virginians dominated the writing of both history and fiction in the South. Virginia authors wistfully portrayed a vanquished civilization, which was contrasted with the crude industrial society that had destroyed it.

Virginians who wrote novels or their war reminiscences usually recalled the enchantment of this finer life. Until his death in 1886, John Esten Cooke never ceased to idolize Virginia. Between 1870 and his passing, he published fifteen more books, and forty-nine articles for *Harper's* and *Appleton's* alone. Such books as *Stories of the Old Dominion* praised the vanished, happy Virginia plantation life, where the field slave "was a merry, jovial being; and when his day's work was over, played his banjo in front of his cabin, and laughed and jested and danced by the light of the moon."[14]

By the late 1880s, Thomas Nelson Page had replaced Cooke as the leading fiction writer of Virginia culture. Page gradually helped to change the national image of the Confederacy by identifying it with Virginia civilization. His compilation of short stories *In Ole Virginia* (1887) and novels such as *Red Rock* (1898) stressed the uniqueness of Virginia.

Page's charm was not lost upon Northern audiences. When *Red Rock* was published, a reviewer in *The Atlantic Monthly* lauded the Virginia life, and lamented: "We have reason to blush, as Americans, for the fact that the contemptible persecution of the vanquished, which went on ... should have received the sanction of the central government at Washington."[15]

Page's most prominent work was *The Old Dominion* (1908), a popular history of the Commonwealth from Jamestown through Reconstruction. The Lost Cause theme was evident: once there was a superior culture, and it produced men of better values. Indeed, "it was by no mere accident" that men such as Washington, Jefferson, and Madison came from Virginia. They were only "the proper product of her distinctive Civilization." The war swept away much of the society which had given America men who "entertained like a gentleman whoever came within his gates . . . fox hunted in winter, and at Christmas gathered his children, his relatives and his friends about his hearth."

Yet the war had not destroyed the inner values produced by this life. To Page, Virginians still based their conduct "on the old foundations," and "the old standards of gentility and righteousness of life still stand."[16]

Cooke and Page were only two of many writers who offered justifications for the South and eventually charmed the nation. There were Page's kinswoman Mary McClelland, whose novels were published intact in *Lippincott's,* and her cousin Amélie Rives, who wrote such novelettes in *Harper's* as "Virginia of Virginia." And there were many others—Jennie Woodville, Molly Seawell, Lucy Thompson, Phoebe Yates Pember, William Pope Dabney—who wrote of the glories of a destroyed past.

A number of reminiscences of Virginia life during the war were published. These writings helped gain a national sympathy for the South. None was more moving than the works of Sara Pryor. In her *Reminiscences of Peace and War* and its sequel, *My Day,* Mrs. Pryor wrote of the life of a young Virginia girl reared in the elegance of Cedar Grove and Shrubbery Hill; through her marriage to Virginia congressman Roger Pryor and the social elegance of Washington in the 1850s; the toll of the war; and her husband's courageous struggle from a Brooklyn slum apartment to rebuild his career as an attorney in postwar New York.

Sara Pryor's theme was constant—that something better had been lost by the downfall of Virginia society. She spoke of a childhood morning, when "from my bed I ran out in my bare feet to a lovely veranda shaded by roses . . . gardens everywhere; abloom with roses, lilies, violets, jonquils. . . . I can see myself in the early hot summer, sent forth to breathe the cool air of the morning." But her young childhood had been swept away by war. "Alas! neither you nor I can ever again—except in fancy—cool our lips with the dew-washed fruits of an 'old Virginia' garden."[17]

It was a proverbial wonderland, where the aged Mrs. Pryor could look back and recall a Christmas dress of her youth, "blue silk, opening over white . . . laced from throat to hem with narrow black velvet," of horseback rides, bedecked with "green cloth habit, green velvet turban, and long green feather, fastened with a diamond buckle." But this era passed too, and "I must linger no longer in this enchanted valley among the mountains. A long road lies before me."[18]

This road took her to Washington as the wife of Pryor, co-editor of the Washington *Union*, the influential organ of the Democratic party. She remembered the Southern power structure in the Washington of President James Buchanan, "a garden of delights, over which the spring trailed an early robe of green." It was a nostalgic picture of elegant Southern men and women. She remembered the spring of 1860, when on Saturdays the Marine Band would play while she sat on the veranda of the White House, or "visited Mr. and Mrs. Robert E. Lee at Arlington." Always there was the elegance of the Southern-dominated social set, in lavish White House parties where "there were glittering haystacks of spun sugar; wonderful Roman Chariots drawn by swans . . . pyramids of costly bonbons; dolphins in a sea of rock candy; and ices in every form from a pair of turtle doves to a pillared temple." But secession, war, and the destruction of Virginia came. The dream ended, and Sara Pryor lamented the passing of an era: "Alas, alas! Whom the gods destroy they first infatuate." Her descriptions of Virginia's devastation during the war were some of the most forceful in late-nineteenth-century Southern letters. Particularly striking was her account of a romantic boat trip down the James River, contrasting the good life in Virginia with the rude advent of Federal armies. She floated past Bermuda Hundred, where pretty Mary Isham—ancestor of Jefferson, John Marshall, and Lee—once "played on her 'citern' to the soothing accompaniment of the lapping waves of the river." She passed historic Westover, now "fallen into decay" after McClellan's gunboats "would shell the old mansion and level it to the ground."

Now it was all gone, and the river became dark. She stood on the deck and mused that in 1861 few Virginians had dreamed that "the man who was now drilling a small company of volunteers in Galena would be in these waters . . . destined to overwhelm us in the end."[19]

A reviewer in the Boston *Herald* lauded Sara Pryor's "charming side" of the South, while the Philadelphia *Public Ledger* described her writings on Virginia as "essential to the true understanding of history."[20] Yet they were more than exaggerated accounts of a gallant Virginia society. Otherwise a skeptical Northern public might have hooted them.

Virginia writers also contended that the state's splendid environment had produced superior men, grounded in duty, honor, and patriotism. As the new century approached, the question whether the Confederates were justified became a secondary issue. What was important was devotion to principle, an exhibition of character which defeat could not obliterate.

Just as Virginia was the example of a better society, so its leaders, especially Lee, became the supreme examples of men who possessed finer traits. And the South seemed to sense that its best national image rested in Virginia. During these years Southern writers emphasized the "Virginia argument."

This rationale has been repeated through every era of Civil War writing. With Robert Lee as its central theme, it preached that Virginia was unlike the cotton South. Virginia (and Lee) hated slavery and secession. Virginia (and Lee) possessed a unique love for the Union born out of the Revolutionary heritage. Thus secession was a more difficult task for Virginians than for other Southerners because they cherished the Union more.

Yet Virginia was forced to secede because of its devotion to principle. After Abraham Lincoln issued his call for troops to crush the rebellion, Virginia sorrowfully left the Union. Men like Lee were aware that secession involved probable defeat, but devotion to principle was the higher ground. Virginians felt that it was wrong for the Federal government to coerce a seceding state. Thus, out of belief in duty, Virginia—and Lee—withdrew from the Union.

Both the concept of a finer life and the peculiar Virginia argument began as abstract arguments involving all Virginians. Yet by 1900 the apologia centered totally upon Lee as the prime example of the good society.

The South had no stronger voice in the Virginia argument than the novelist George Cary Eggleston. The young Indiana schoolteacher had come to the state at the age of seventeen to inherit a family plantation in Amelia County. Thus:

> I quitted the rapidly developing, cosmopolitan, kaleidoscopic West, and became a dweller upon the old family plantation . . . where my race had been bred and nurtured ever since 1635.

Eggleston was soon enraptured with what he saw as the ideal life of Virginia:

> . . . its repose, the absence of stress or strain or anxious anticipation, the appreciation of tomorrow as the equal of today in the doing of things. . . . The restful leisureliness of life in Virginia was borne in upon me at every hand.

Eggleston made a decision: "I shall write of the old Virginia life as I remember it," because "the greatest joy I have known in life . . . has come from my efforts to depict it." To his friend John Esten Cooke, Eggleston admitted that he wrote in the hope that his books "may change some people's views of the South and Southerners."[21]

It was Eggleston who first offered to the nation the Virginia argument in concise form. In 1874, *The Atlantic Monthly* serialized his "A Rebel's Recollections," which was printed that same year by a New York publisher. Eggleston contended that the leaders of the cotton South "were types of a class" which brought upon the South odium with "their bragging, their intolerance, their contempt for the North, their arrogance." In contrast, Virginia felt that secession was unwise, and was indignant toward those Southerners who were "endangering the peace of the land."[22]

Why then did Virginia secede? She was an innocent victim of circumstances and "without cowardice and dishonor" could not have done otherwise. When Lincoln called for troops to put down the rebellion, Virginians were faced with a heartrending choice: should Virginia seek safety in dishonor, or should she meet destruction in doing that which she believed to be right? Sadly, then, Lee's people "freely offered themselves upon the altar of an abstract principle of right" and chose to fight a war "which they knew must work hopeless ruin to themselves."[23]

Eggleston's literary career was devoted to publicizing this theme. *The Master of Warlock* (1902) explained Virginia's secession. *The Warrens of Virginia* described Colonel Warren as the flower of Virginia manhood. Warren was "first of all and above all, an American," and "his love for the American Union was intense." After Lincoln's call for troops, "there was but one honorable choice."[24]

It was a powerful appeal that became standard in Confederate writings of the romantic age. Virginia had stood between North and South, pleading, "with one hand reaching northward and the other southward," for calm reason to prevail. When calm did not prevail, a Virginia minister in 1884 insisted, "their sole aim was to protect their altars, their families and their rights under the Constitution."[25]

By 1900 ROBERT E. LEE had become the symbol of both the finer society and the character traits it had produced. Major John Daniel's address at Lexington in 1883 was the opening statement of an evolving process which eventually made Lee the total justification of the Southern cause. Daniel's argument—that Lee loved the Union more, hated slavery, disliked secession and seceded out of a sense of honor—was reiterated in the works of other partisans, such as A. L. Long's *Memoirs of Robert E. Lee* (1886), Fitzhugh Lee's *General Lee* (1894), and Henry White's *Robert E. Lee and the Southern Confederacy* (1897). The production of such works increased markedly after 1900. In scores of books, and hundreds of speeches and articles, the South made Lee's character the climax of the Lost Cause argument. To justify Lee was to justify the Southern cause.

Three ideas were emphasized in this new spurt of writing on Lee. First of all, he was a product of his environment; what he did in 1861 was his answer to principles instilled by Virginia society. Lee was thus responding as any good American would—following his life's principles. Second, the writings now stressed Lee's character, and emphasis on his military feats receded noticeably. Finally, Lee's partisans accentuated his nationalism. Lee's decision in 1861 involved sacrifice experienced by no other Southerner, for he loved the Union more. Then, in the postwar days, Lee helped to lead the South back into the Union by refusing to prolong the war, advising moderation, and attempting to educate Southern youth.

In 1904 Robert E. Lee, Jr., published his *Recollections and Letters of General Robert E. Lee*. This work, actually a piecemeal publication of his father's letters, had a tremendous effect upon the national view of Lee. The younger Lee stressed the themes of character, environment, and nationalism. In his *Life of Robert Edward Lee* (1906), Henry Shepherd deemed Lee "the whole world's darling" and admitted that "an essential feature of my task" was "to vindicate the cause of the South." Shepherd attacked "our uncultured and unreflecting contemporary life," beset with evils such as "the greed of wealth, the quest of material power, the expansion of corporate interests . . ."[26]

The historian William P. Trent issued his *Robert E. Lee* (1899) in the Beacon Biographies of Eminent Americans series. Trent also wrote about Lee's character and nationalism. He felt that "Lee's noble genius and character lift him, by quite unanimous consent, above all other Confederates." Thus, "I learned to see him as he is—not merely a great son of my own native State, not merely a great Southern general, not merely a great American . . . but better than all of these, a supremely great and good man."[27]

The environmental argument was the core of John Deering's *Lee and His Cause: Or, the Why and the How of the War Between the States* (1907). A former Rebel soldier, Deering mixed the elements of environmentalism and character, viewing the Southern cause as doomed to failure because of the agrarian environment:

> The war was hopeless for want of revenue, credit and a sound currency; for want of mines and manufactories . . . It was hopeless for want of materials, of skilled mechanics, suitable ships, blankets, clothing, shoes, medicine, salt, lead, iron, copper, leather, sulphur, saltpetre and anesthetics. . . . We had pride and patriotism to spare, but we couldn't feed the living, or raise again our dead!

Yet Deering claimed that the same background which failed the South produced men of superior principles, of whom Lee was the epitome. Deering not only paid service to the usual elements of Lee's character, but insisted that Lee was a supreme nationalist. Lee declined to prolong the war by guerrilla fighting. He shunned lucrative business offers and devoted his life to training Southern youth. And he preached moderation, "dying without saying a word or leaving a line to vindicate his conduct or enhance his fame."[28]

An even more exaggerated depiction was Robert Stiles's *Four Years Under Marse Robert* (1903). Like Eggleston, Stiles showed that the most professional of Virginians could be non-Virginians. A Georgia native, Stiles had lived in Richmond for four years as a child while his father was a Presbyterian minister. "Charmed with everything I saw and every one I met," he never forgot his enchantment with Virginia. After graduating from Yale, he was a student at Columbia University Law School when the war broke out.

Once he overheard some New York businessmen discussing Virginia:

> It made my heart glow to hear how these great financier and merchant princes spoke of my adopted State. They said in effect, that it had always been so; that Virginia was undoubtedly the greatest and most influential of all the States; that she had been the nursing mother of the Union . . . that Virginians had really made the United States in the olden days—Washington, Jefferson, Madison, Marshall . . .[29]

When the war came, Stiles, denied a pass by Federal authorities, made a daring sailing expedition down the east coast to Virginia, where he joined Lee's army. Stiles's book was dedicated to Lee, "that Great Captain to Whom the World Today Attributes More of the Loftiest Virtues and Powers of Humanity, with less of its grossness and littleness, than to any other military leader in history."[30]

These themes in books about Lee—environment, character, and nationalism—were stressed by the Virginia historian Philip Alexander Bruce in two important compositions. In 1907, the "American Crisis Biography" series issued his *Robert E. Lee;* four years later, his "The National Spirit of General Lee" appeared in the *South Atlantic Quarterly.*

Bruce emphasized Lee's character and love of country, and his constant theme was that they represented the flower of a better life. Bruce never ceased to mourn the obliteration of antebellum Virginia life. In a speech in 1881, he lamented the loss of the "proud, sensitive, kindly and leisurely past," in which existed "all that is great in the annals of the colony and the state."[31]

In 1906, Walter Taylor, one of the original admirers of Lee, published his *General Lee*. It contained all of the new imagery: the peculiarity of the Virginia culture, Lee as the center of its greatness, and his postwar help in saving the nation. Novelist Thomas Nelson Page's *Robert E. Lee: The Southerner* (1909), and its revision, *Robert E. Lee: Man and Soldier* (1911), stressed the new themes. In a journal article, "Lee in Defeat," Page hailed him as "the leader of the New South." J. William Jones's *Life and Letters of Robert Edward Lee* contained chapter titles such as "After the War—Promoting Peace" and "Analysis of His Character."[32]

LEE'S ADHERENTS also continued to control the Southern Historical Society and its *Papers*, which remained the South's chief organ of war history. In 1887, Robert Brock, a veteran of Lee's army, succeeded J. William Jones as editor of the *Papers;* in turn, Brock was followed by James Power Smith, who had been on Ewell's staff. Brock and Smith perpetuated the dynasty established by Jubal Early and Jones. The magazine remained devoted to the Lee image, and constantly dredged up old issues, such as how Longstreet lost the battle of Gettysburg.[33]

But most organizational efforts reflected the South's desire after 1890 to commemorate the war dead. Clearly by then the South viewed the war as an epic of valor, and the sentimentalism inspired by an aging generation of veterans prompted a great number of memorial projects.

The Confederate monuments raised between 1890 and 1910 reflected the commemorative spirit. Even by 1892, Richmond citizens had expended, according to one observer, $750,000 for such projects as monuments to Lee, Jackson, J. E. B. Stuart, and others. In a single New Orleans cemetery, four monuments, including one to Lee, represented an investment of $150,000. Yet the monument fever was not confined to large cities. Helena, Arkansas, imported a sculptured memorial from Italy to commemorate its war dead. Tiny Hardeman County in Tennessee spent nearly $3000 on a marble shaft; in the poverty-stricken South Carolina Piedmont, the women of Newberry raised $1300 for the shaft on the courthouse square.

Simultaneously there was a rise of Confederate memorial associations. In 1889–90, the United Confederate Veterans was organized. By 1903 there were 80,000 members lodged in 1523 organizational camps throughout the South. The annual encampment of the veterans was much sought after by cities like Atlanta, Nashville, and Richmond. Chambers of commerce and railroad lines discovered potential profits in the efforts to commemorate a nonbusiness society's demise. When the veterans gathered in Nashville in 1897, a local jeweler took an

*Robert E. Lee at thirty-one, painted in 1838 by the noted
American artist William E. West.*

Mary Custis Lee, also painted in 1838 by West.

Arlington in 1864.

*Washington College as it looked shortly after the Civil War,
when Lee assumed the presidency.*

ABOVE LEFT: *A rarely reproduced postwar photograph of Lee*
by Michael Miley, a Lexington, Virginia, photographer.

ABOVE RIGHT: *Lee at his residence in Richmond shortly after Appomattox,*
flanked by his son General Custis Lee (left) and by Colonel Walter Taylor,
one of Lee's most avid defenders. Photograph by Mathew Brady.

The Lee funeral cortege turning onto Lexington's Main Street.
Already, in the courthouse to the right, the powerful Lee Memorial
Association had begun organizational efforts.

ABOVE LEFT: *General Jubal Early, leader of the first Lee cult.*

ABOVE RIGHT: *A typical late-nineteenth-century attempt to capitalize upon Lee's reputation.*

OPPOSITE, TOP TO BOTTOM:

Washington College chapel during Lee's funeral.

A rarely reproduced photograph of Washington College students guarding Lee's coffin prior to his funeral.

View from the parlor of Lee's home into the dining room where he died.

TOP LEFT: *General W. H. F. ("Rooney") Lee, active during postwar years in commemorating his father's memory.*

TOP RIGHT: *General Fitzhugh Lee, Robert E. Lee's nephew and at one time his chief of cavalry.*

BOTTOM: *Lee and members of his wartime staff, including several of his staunchest postwar defenders: Walter Taylor, Charles Marshall, and William Pendleton.*

Fitzhugh Lee (center) at a 1907 Confederate commemoration in Richmond.

The Lee monument in Richmond, shortly after 1900.

Thomas Nelson Page, Lee biographer and Virginia novelist.

The interior of the Lee Chapel at Washington and Lee University, showing the recumbent figure of Lee by Edward Valentine.

entire page in the society's organ, the *Confederate Veteran,* to advertise such items as "The Official Reunion Badge." Not to be outdone, Colonel E. Daniel Boone, identified as an ex-Rebel officer, soldier of fortune in Cuba, and military instructor to the Peruvian army, urged veterans to visit his "Gorman and Boone's Wild Animal Exhibit," which boasted a "Troupe of Performing Seals—and many other attractions." A cyclorama of Gettysburg was designed to lure veterans at Nashville:

> The vividness of the scene beggars the description of a Roman orator. General Armistead, who led the forlorn hopes of the Confederates, is seen falling from his horse desperately wounded, his horse rearing and plunging, mad with terror. ... The fate of a nation hanging on the issue of the struggle; men falling on every side, amid screams of the wounded. Dead horses gashed and bleeding lie scattered around. ... Don't fail to see it. Admission 50 cents. All Confederate veterans will be given half rate of admission.[34]

By the last decade of the century Southern leaders of memorial organizations and reunions were utilizing the same techniques of a corporate society which they frequently deplored in their reunion orations—organization and commercialism. As the fifty-year anniversary of the war neared, interest in the Civil War heightened in both North and South.

When the Federal Army of the Cumberland met for an 1889 reunion in Chattanooga, the W. C. Green Real Estate Company responded with: "Welcome comrades in blue and gray—offered for sale long leaf yellow pine and hardwood lumber, mineral lands, city and suburban property, farms," and the Lookout Photograph and View Gallery hawked fifteen-cent views of the town as "War Photographs. Historic Scenes! Heroic Deeds." The Manassas Panorama Company unveiled a massive painting of the battle of Second Bull Run by a dozen French artists. The panorama drew accolades from the Washington *Post* and other newspapers. One reporter praised its realism:

> The construction of the piece is such that the spectator seems to stand in the center of the field; at his feet is a dark pool of clotted blood, a musket, an old haversack, or a soldier's cap; over yonder a dead man, his glassy eyes looking at you with a ghastly stare.[35]

In 1900, a large number of women's memorial groups throughout the South were combined into the Confederated Memorial Association of the South. Whether it was the Ladies' Memorial Association of Sandersville, Georgia, or the Confederate Cemetery Memorial Association of Vicksburg, the women joined in the desire "to perpetuate the memories and deeds of Southern heroes."[36]

In 1896 the Confederate Memorial Association was founded. Perhaps no other effort so reflected the Southern mentality. The group was created in Atlanta to lead a fund-raising drive to erect a Valhalla of Confederate heroes. This dream of what was called the "Battle Abbey," one speaker compared to "what Melrose Abbey is to Scotland, Westminster to England, and the glorious Pantheon to France." It would be a place "to pay deserved tribute" to "heroic deeds."[37]

But the Battle Abbey scheme became less a monument to Southern valor than an object lesson in how Virginians could dominate the Confederate past. For over a decade Southern cities vied for the memorial, and bloodlettings among the United Daughters of the Confederacy at their national conventions were not uncommon. Finally in 1908, after Richmond's city fathers had offered a $50,000 bonus, the Virginians carried the day at the annual United Daughters convention. The meeting was replete with typical statements of Virginianism such as

God's acres of Confederate blood and bones, which lie under the soil along the Chickahominy, at Cold Harbor, Malvern Hill . . . all speak eloquently for Virginia to be chosen . . . Virginia has an inalienable right to be selected.[38]

Battle Abbey, financed South-wide and intended as a memorial for all Southerners, became another symbol of Virginia pride. At the 1921 dedication, the main address was by Snowden Marshall, son of Lee's aide, Colonel Charles Marshall. Marshall asked:

Why is it that, when we arrange the places at the table of that Valhalla of our history where sit our heroes, we put the place of General Lee at the head, and rank below him even such commanding figures as George Washington?[39]

By 1946 Battle Abbey would no longer make any pretense of representing a South-wide association. That year, the owners of the Abbey, the Confederate Memorial Association, merged with the Virginia Historical Society, which took charge of the museum.

VIRGINIA'S CONTROL of the new United Confederate Veterans was assured when, from 1889 to 1904, Lee's old corps leader, General John Gordon, was its commander. In 1899, when the Veterans began issuing their twelve-volume *Confederate Military History,* the editor was one of Lee's former division commanders, General Clement Evans. In 1895, the Veterans Historical Committee, desirous of having "true" history texts in the schools, recommended the *School History of the United*

States, by Susan Pendleton Lee. Susan Lee, daughter of Lee's artillery chief, William Pendleton, had married a kinsman of Robert Lee. Her book, designed to supply "an *Unprejudiced and Truthful* history," repeated the old themes—Virginians were superior people and the Civil War was fought mainly in the commonwealth.[40]

An even better example of juvenile brainwashing was a supplementary school text by Mary Williamson entitled *The Life of General Robert E. Lee* (1895). Her book, designed to "lay the foundation for sound historical knowledge," was a classic in the organization of an image. Her chapter on Lee's youth stressed his knightly ancestry in England, his model childhood, and his unblemished West Point career. Of Lee's 1861 decision: "His only wish was to do his duty ... His soul was wrung with grief but he obeyed the call of duty." Of Gettysburg: "Lee's orders had not been carried out and, for the first time, he had been foiled." At Appomattox, Lee had 8000 troops, while Grant commanded 200,000. Hence "in all of these battles of which you have been told, General Lee had not been really defeated; but he had to give up at last because he had no more men and no more food." Lee's character emerged as unsurpassed: "Perhaps no man ever lived that was so great, so good, and so unselfish as Lee."[41]

Student indoctrination was obviously the goal of the *Memorial Day Annual* issued to Virginia schoolteachers by the state government. This compilation of articles on Virginia's role in the secession crisis was little more than propaganda. Stating that "no child should be allowed to grow up without a clear understanding of the issues," the booklet emphasized that Virginians loved the Union and hated secession in 1861, and joined the Confederacy out of a sense of duty. A pageant was suggested in which girls representing each Southern state would contemplate secession. As poor "Virginia" muses on her past Revolutionary greatness, including "my Jefferson who penned the Declaration, my Washington who broke the power of Great Britain," her temptors come out of the wings. Students representing a variety of evils—"Centralized Government, Victory, Wealth and Worldly Honors"—try to lure Virginia into remaining within the Union. But temptation is averted, for "True Honor" is "dearer to me." Who will lead the quest for "True Honor"? "Enter Robert E. Lee, who comes and kneels beside Virginia," while "True Honor" stands by proudly.[42]

The commemoration of the General's birthday became the main event in the homage to Lee. Massive birthday celebrations would become almost a religious ritual in the South. The culmination was the 1907 centennial of Lee's birth.

The centennial was the product of a surging tide of emotionalism. In a nostalgic era, Southerners now saw Lee as a veritable saint. Even in 1890 some 100,000 people lined Richmond's streets to witness the dedication of the Lee monument. A huge parade by Lee's veterans, a sham battle, and other festivities preceded an outpouring of oratory praising the Southern idol.

The Virginia General Assembly proclaimed Lee's birthday, January 19, as a legal holiday. The ceremonies included numerous orations which praised the "new" Lee-Virginia image. One Richmond speaker showed how far the Lee mystique had developed in the Southern mind. He declared that Lee's name would be inscribed "beside that of Washington himself—on the roll of those immortal few 'that were not born to die.' "[43]

In the new century the Lee birthday celebration became a carefully organized effort throughout the South. Even in Los Angeles, Rebel veterans met in 1900 to hear a speaker tell them that "it is your duty to look into the books your children read . . . and see that they know the truth" of the old South.[44]

There were many who were determined that all Southerners should "know the truth." At the Lee birthdays the same poems, anecdotes, and other material were used year after year. In 1905 the state school commissioner of Georgia issued his *Selections for the Observance . . . of the Birth of Robert E. Lee in the Schools of Georgia*. The commissioner instructed the teachers that "it is our duty to teach to the youth under our supervision and care the great lesson of his personality and his principles." The Georgia booklet contained stock comments on Lee's character by Lord Garnet Wolseley, Father Abram Ryan's poem "The Sword of Robert E. Lee," and quotations from Lee devotees such as General John Gordon and J. William Jones.[45] The Alabama Department of Education issued a similar booklet of instructions in 1907. The state superintendent of education explained that the program was designed so "that the children of Alabama may learn to emulate the example of the hero of the Southern Confederacy."[46] The Confederate Association of New Orleans issued its *Suggestions for the Celebration of the One Hundredth Anniversary*. It suggested use of Senator Ben Hill's tribute to Lee's character; the remark of Lord Wolseley that Lee "was cast in a grander mold and made of different and finer metal than other men"; and Father Ryan's poem.[47]

No element of the image was overlooked. One author even wrote a manual of instructions for pantomiming and reciting Father Ryan's poem. The student was told, for example, that when the phrase "Flashed the Sword of Lee" was recited, he should:

Sway weight of body forward to R. foot as R. arm swings out to R. oblique at shoulder-level, then swing straight above head; head tilted back; face up. Pleased expression.[48]

.   .   .

WHAT PRODUCED this deluge of Lee memorialism by Southerners after 1900? Certainly admiration for Lee was strong. Also, to a nostalgic generation of aging veterans, the Civil War was their life's great experience, and Lee symbolized its romance and valor. Perhaps as well, the South was becoming consciously proud of Lee as he gradually emerged as a national hero symbol.

The national image after 1900 was not new, but there was a noticeable shift in emphasis. Gone were dogmatic portrayals of Lee's military invincibility. Southern writers often pictured him as flailing helplessly against the power of an Industrial Revolution far beyond his control. The emphasis was upon those segments of Lee's career which illuminated his character and love for the Union. But the old material was still used. In fact, only one new element had been added to the image. By his postwar demeanor, Lee was portrayed as helping to save the Union by leading his people in a temperate fashion. By 1900, Southerners were skillfully describing Lee as a nationalist.

This image was accepted almost wholesale by the nation. Two events gave an indication of what was to come. One was the national reception of the publication in 1904 of *Recollections and Letters of Robert E. Lee*, by Robert E. Lee, Jr. This work exemplified the question of whether a book molds the opinions of its readers or merely reflects existing social currents. In the matter of Lee's *Recollections*, the process was retroactive. By the twentieth century, the American mind could accept Lee as a national hero.

Lee's *Recollections* was a charming tale of a son's relationship with his father, and it quoted freely from the General's personal letters. Scarcely one third of the book dealt with Lee's military service. Most of it emphasized his superb character, sense of duty, and nationalism, in chapters such as "An Ideal Father" and "An Adviser of Young Men."

Of Robert E. Lee, the New York *Times* observed:

His true character was not fully understood until after the publication of Captain Robert E. Lee's, his son, *Recollections*. ... The modesty, the courage, the humility and the grandeur of soul ... were brought out in that record so beautifully that scorners were subdued to contrition.[49]

In *The Atlantic Monthly*, DeWolfe Howe stated:

... the dignity and beauty of the individual life in which the lost cause was chiefly embodied receive fresh illumination from these pages. . . . the reader is left wishing it might have been universal in the South, and met with a corresponding spirit in the North.[50]

A reviewer in *Dial* wrote that there was no American who would not consider Robert Lee "among the most eminent of his fellow-countrymen," and that the book "will deepen this impression." *Current Literature* published an eight-page review, claiming that the book "has been awaited with much eagerness."[51] A reviewer for *The Nation* commented:

> . . . we feel quite at home in the family circle of the Lees, and can almost hear the voice of a man who was as conspicuously great in gentleness and goodness as he was in the art of war. Like that voice, the story is gentle and soothing.[52]

Perhaps there was no more representative commentary on what the nation was seeking, and what Lee's image could supply, than the remarks of a reviewer in *Outlook*. He noted that Lee's *Recollections* emphasized his father's character and postwar years.

> And well it is so, for the record of these years is the most precious legacy committed to the Southerner of the present generation. Lee's magnanimity in defeat, his ready acceptance of the new order of things, his moderation and restraint . . . his steadfast hope in the future of his section . . . constitute the most glorious chapter in a very noble life.[53]

The national response to Lee's book may have been partly motivated by the New England historian Charles Francis Adams, Jr. Adams's speeches and essays reflected the sharp change in the national mood. Like the Lee biography, the Adams critique displayed the retroactive process at work. Simultaneously, while Adams mirrored the changing opinions of Robert Lee, his writings helped to shape that opinion.

A descendant of President John Adams, he may well have typified historian Richard Hofstadter's description of the upper-middle-class New Englander of lost status who sought compensation in crusades. While some joined the Progressive reform movement, Adams turned to history. His presidency of the Union Pacific Railroad ended unhappily in 1890, and he suffered economic misfortune in the 1893 panic. Adams became disenchanted with the tawdry new industrial society of Boston, and buried himself in the American past. By 1895 he was the leader of the Massachusetts Historical Society, and in 1901 was elected president of the American Historical Association.

In his pursuit of history, Adams became intrigued with the career of Lee. Beginning with an address before the American Antiquarian Society in 1901, Adams initiated a decade of championing Lee as a national hero. He never wrote a biography of Lee, but he contributed a number of powerful essays. His 1901 address, *The Confederacy and the Transvaal: A People's Obligation to Robert E. Lee,* was later published in book form. So, too, were his 1902 Phi Beta Kappa address at the University of Chicago, *Shall Cromwell Have a Statue?*; his 1902 speech before the New England Historical Society, *The Constitutional Ethics of Secession;* and his 1907 address at the annual commemoration day at Washington and Lee University. These and other speeches and essays were incorporated into several books by Adams which defended the Confederacy, including *Lee at Appomattox and Other Essays* (1902).

Adams's devotion to Lee varied little from the theme of his address before the American Antiquarian Society. He said that Lee should be acclaimed on two counts—that he was a product of his environment and that he was a nationalist. Adams repeatedly defended Lee's decision of 1861 as a result of environment, and admitted that if he had been a Virginian in 1861, his decision would have been the same.

Adams also praised him as a great nationalist. Lee's decision in 1861 was viewed as one of special sacrifice because of the General's love for the Union. Adams took pains to stress Lee's postwar conduct. He saw great significance in Lee's refusing to continue guerrilla warfare and counseling moderation. In fact, Adams pioneered in arguing that Lee's postwar conduct helped to save the Union, and that the nation thus owed the Virginian a debt of gratitude. Had Lee behaved otherwise, the scars of war would not have healed; but by his example the South was restored to the Union.[54]

One reviewer of *Lee at Appomattox* noted that Adams gave Lee "great and deserved credit for a course which was perhaps the greatest factor in bringing the two warring factions . . . to the present conditions of harmony."[55] More significant was the national reaction to Adams's address at Washington and Lee. College officials had been impressed by Adams's championing of Lee's reputation and regarded him as an obvious choice for the centennial address. The centennial speech has been viewed as the climax of reconciliation between North and South. Actually it was more indicative of the existing national mood. The Chicago *Tribune* printed an editorial referring to the "national appreciation of the character and services of the great Virginian." *Leslie's Weekly* noted the significance of having the great-grandson of President John Adams uttering praise at Lee's tomb, while a perennially anti-Southern organ, the New York *Independent,* observed that "the country forgives Lee and Jackson."[56]

The reception given to the efforts of Robert Lee, Jr., and Charles

Francis Adams was not lost upon the South. One might speculate whether the Lee hero worship in the South was not in part a reaction to the nation's reaction. Some Southern writers now saw that adulation of the Virginian was not only acceptable but in vogue.

There is considerable evidence of this Southern awareness of changing trends. Both Robert Lee, Jr.'s biography and the *Life and Letters of Robert Edward Lee* (1906) by the venerable parson J. William Jones edited Lee's letters in such a manner that the General's national posture was improved.

What ensued was both a de-Southernizing and dehumanizing of Lee. Some phrases that expressed a severe attitude toward the North were lifted. Captain Lee omitted a sentence in a letter in which Lee referred to "rabid abolitionists." He also dropped from a letter a statement in which Lee warned that the Federal government would do as much injury to the Lee family as it could. "They look upon us as their most bitter enemies and will treat us as such to the extent of their powers. Witness their operations whenever they have got a foothold." Jones also omitted the comment, without inserting elision marks to indicate it had ever been there. In a letter in which Lee advised his wife to remove the family from Arlington, Captain Lee cut a section where his father voiced the opinion that war was inevitable because there was "such fury manifested against the South" in Washington that even if the government wanted peace "it may not be in the power of the authorities to restrain them." Reverend Jones omitted it as well, with his customary lack of elision marks.[57]

Another example of deliberate editing is shown in a prewar letter in which Lee gave his views on abolitionists. The General stated: "The views of the Pres: of the Systematic and progressive efforts of certain people of the North, to interfere with and change the domestic institutions of the South, are truthfully and faithfully expressed." When Lee advised his son Rooney as to the fate of the Arlington slaves, the letters were edited by Jones so that there was no segment where Lee suggested that the slaves' emancipation was not yet feasible, for "if the war continues I do not see how it can be accomplished but they can be hired out and the fund raised applied to their establishment hereafter."[58]

Neither book contained Lee's letter to his son Rooney in which Lee said:

> I fear I shall have to purchase a servant. I find it almost impossible to hire one, and nearly all the officers in the department have been obliged to resort to purchase.... At present I have a boy belonging to Major Marlin for whom I pay $20 per month. I have thought some one about Richmond might have a good family servant for

whom they are obliged to part, and for whom they would like to procure a master. Do you know of any?[59]

This "de-Southernizing" of Lee also made him appear less human. Both Captain Lee and Reverend Jones made Lee into a man of flaw-lessly polished language, devoid of personal problems, free of prejudice, and often without simple human emotions. Jones dropped a section from an 1858 letter which contained a strong statement against Mormons; Lee hoped the Mormons would not be permitted to continue where they were but would "be broken up and expelled [sic] the country." Sometimes the editors masked Lee's gloomy Calvinism. In a poignant letter after the death of his daughter in 1862, an anguished Lee cried: "When I reflect on all she will escape in life brief and painful at the best ... I cannot wish her back."[60] Captain Lee omitted this passage which told much of his father's attitude not merely toward death but toward life as well. He also deleted a paragraph from a letter from his father to Mary Custis Lee which observed:

> As to the reports which you say are afloat about our separation I know nothing. Any one that can reason must see its necessity under present circumstances. They can only exist in the imagination of a few so give them no heed.[61]

Another Lee biographer, Thomas Nelson Page, also sensed a change in the national view toward Lee. Page's biography, *Robert E. Lee, the Southerner* (1909), drew national criticism for its pro-Southern approach. For a later edition of the book he changed the title to *Robert E. Lee: Man and Soldier.* He also made revisions, which he saw were necessary on account of the current "attractiveness" of the subject. For example, the first biography contained only 39 pages on Lee's character and postwar career—favorite national themes. In the revision there were 120 pages on these subjects.[62]

There is no suggestion here of a literary conspiracy. Writings on Lee were nationally popular after 1900. The large amount of writing by the Lee cult, and the general Southern campaign to memorialize the Virginian, may have been a proud reaction to the nation's acceptance of Lee. Southern writers for decades had longed for a time when Confederate actions would be better understood by the nation. Perhaps the South now sensed that the time had arrived. Possession of Lee was cause for pride; declared one Virginian in 1906: "Whatever else we may have lost in that struggle, we gave the world Robert E. Lee."[63]

THE CONSTANT EMPHASIS on Lee's character went well with a nation concerned about the loss of values in an industrial society. It was no accident that shortly before the publication of Captain Robert Lee's biography of his father, *The Call of the Wild* and *The Virginian* achieved wide readership. The popularity of Jack London's novel was partly due to its protest against overcivilization and its glorification of a freer society not burdened with the pressures of the new industrialism. Owen Wister's *The Virginian,* which sold 300,000 copies in two years, was a social allegory. The novel was a protest against the loss of agrarian values in industrial anonymity and materialism. Wister chose the Virginian, representing the finest principles of the antebellum South, to teach the nation what character traits were being lost in the machine age.

Children's literature exhibited this admiration for noble ideals, even when struggling against difficult odds. Rudyard Kipling's *Captains Courageous,* Frances Burnett's *The Secret Garden,* Stewart Edward White's *The Magic Forest*—all stressed personal integrity, and the power of one's surroundings in shaping character.

This glorification of the traits molded by the non-industrial life-rugged individualism, duty, honor—was at the foundation of the Boy Scout movement, of Theodore Roosevelt's preachments about "the strenuous life," as well as of Daniel Carter Beard's Sons of Daniel Boone and Boy Pioneers, both absorbed into the Boy Scouts of America in 1910.

There was little doubt that the American of 1900, caught between urban squalor, industrial corruption, and the anonymity of city life, placed a high premium upon virtue and its relationship to the agrarian environment.[64]

Northern writing on Lee praised both his character and its steadfastness even when struggling against impossible odds. Gamaliel Bradford's *Lee the American* (1912) reflected the national response. (Bradford's importance as a psychological biographer will be discussed later.) Like Charles Francis Adams, Bradford, a descendant of William Bradford, fitted the stereotype of the displaced New Englander. His once promising New England career had been a disappointment. Ill health forced his early departure from Harvard. For almost twenty years thereafter, he gained little notice for his efforts as a poet and novelist.

Then Bradford discovered the medium of biography. Eventually he would write fourteen volumes which probed historic personalities, but none was more influential than *Lee the American* (1912). This book, which received great national acclaim, was more a character analysis than a narrative biography. What intrigued Bradford was the emergence in Lee of certain traits which guided his life. Bradford considered himself a psychological biographer, and dubbed his trade "psychography." After a process of selection, he magnified certain of Lee's personality traits which he considered to be the moving forces of the General's life, and then a life portrait was constructed around these traits.

What emerged was a popular but distorted image. Bradford's selection of Lee's traits was heavily influenced by his source material. He relied mainly upon works which preached the traditional Lee imagery, such as the writings of Fitzhugh Lee, J. William Jones, and Robert E. Lee, Jr. The result was the presentation of an almost superhuman figure.[65]

Exaggerated or not, Bradford's description of Lee fit well with the times. A reviewer in *Dial* considered the book indispensable because it gave "a superb and convincing portrayal of the actual soul of Lee." And the Boston *Evening Transcript* declared that it would help "to bind up the unity of the American nation."[66]

YET WHILE THE NATION found solace in Lee's example amidst the new industrial society, Americans also revered that society. Nationalism after 1900 was an American religion. The nation glowed over the feats of American imperialism, felt pride in the concept of Anglo-Saxon superiority, and accepted the racist novels of Thomas Dixon. America eulogized the same society it feared. Politicians, historians, popular writers —all paid homage at the shrine of nationalism.

They also paid tribute to Lee, whose image as a nationalist had been presented skillfully by the romantic Lee cult. Charles Francis Adams, Jr.'s insistence that the nation owed Robert Lee a debt of gratitude only reflected the sentiment of many Americans in the new twentieth century.

In 1909, while president of Princeton University, Woodrow Wilson praised Lee as one who had helped to mend the Union. In 1901, Robert E. Lee was among the first twenty-nine men chosen for the new Hall of Fame at New York University. A New York attorney said that Lee well deserved the honor because he was "a great reconciliator of the Union" and "belongs to the whole United States." Theodore Roosevelt also described Lee as having helped to save the Union. And in his popular biography, *On the Trail of Grant and Lee,* Frederick Hill saw the Virginian's true greatness emerge in the postwar years, when Lee toiled at "the rebuilding of the nation."[67]

So he had become a national hero in the years before World War I. Almost nothing that Lee had said or done escaped the pen of some writer anxious either to pay tribute to or to capitalize on a popular image. It was all far removed from that day in 1883 at Lexington when his devotees had paid homage only to the South's war hero.

Now Charles Graves, writing in *Harper's Weekly,* could describe Lee as "the pride of the whole country," and *Current Literature* could print a poem written in his honor by Julia Ward Howe, author of the

"Battle Hymn of the Republic."[68] The nation saw in the portrayals of Lee's character and the romanticized land from which he came elements worthy of imitation. Perhaps as well, the image of Lee after 1900 symbolized the meaning that Americans desired to attach to their experience in a Civil War. Caught in a gentle nostalgia in which a sense of reunion came more easily, the nation saw in Lee the best that could be produced from a bad war. The example of his good character striving to overcome the travail of Reconstruction, the portrayal of his love for the Union which led him to humble Lexington—this to Americans symbolized what was good in the Civil War.

CHAPTER V

LEE AND THE
SOUTHERN RENAISSANCE,
1920–1940

A T FIRST VIEW, Americans in the 1920s might appear to have shown little interest in the Civil War. The popular image of the era—sexual freedom, flappers, and bootleg whiskey—does not mesh well with Grant's long, monotonous siege of Richmond.

Yet during both the "roaring twenties" and the later Depression years, interest in the Civil War was a strong element of American popular culture. And although Robert E. Lee was well established as a national hero, his reputation reached its highest level during these years of the "Southern Renaissance" in American literature.

The image of the 1920s has suffered from the exaggerations of some popular authors who stressed the decade's social license. In 1931 Frederick Lewis Allen published *Only Yesterday,* a social history of the decade, which became an immediate best seller. *Only Yesterday,* a nostalgic look at the years before the Great Depression, discerned correctly that the mood of the twenties was restless and insecure. It was Allen's prognosis that was misleading. He collected numerous tales of back-seat petting parties and hip flasks to prove that a frenetic revolution in the nation's morals was in the making.

Washington journalist Mark Sullivan added strength to this image when he published *Our Times: The United States, 1900–1925.* Sullivan described the national psyche of the era as disillusioned by the Great War and twisted by despair.

Both studies were geared to reach a popular audience and no doubt overstated the case. Best-seller charts of the 1920s reveal little of the "lost generation" mentality. The decade's most popular writers avoided such topics. The most widely read novelist between 1900 and 1930 was Gene Stratton Porter, who wrote outdoor/moralistic works such as *Freckles* and *Laddie.* By 1932 four of Porter's efforts held the top positions as the best-selling novels of the century.

Most Americans were not involved in Allen's revolution of morals, but were concerned, rather, with the problem of how to retain old values in a new industrial society. Rumble-seat gymnastics were less popular than Bruce Barton's writings on practical Christianity, such as *The Man Nobody Knows.* Jazz and the new morality were the vogue in some circles. Still, Henry L. Mencken could grouse that one could toss an egg from any railroad car and splatter a fundamentalist. Most Americans of the 1920s wished anything but massive changes in social behavior. They sought the old rural code which seemed threatened by sprawling urban life and foreign immigration.

So the nation turned inward to grasp meaning from themes of history and patriotism. The mood was expressed by the Chicago mayor who offered to "punch King George in the snoot" and who campaigned against pro-British textbooks in Illinois schools. This "hundred percent" Americanism was evidenced in the remarkable growth of the second Ku Klux Klan. Between 1911 and 1925, the Klan's membership soared from five thousand to nearly five million. Despite its crusades against Jews, blacks, and other "undesirables," the Klan was able to project a patriotic image based upon what its Grand Wizard described as the "purpose and spirit" of pioneers.[1]

In this desire to return to old values, Americans were affected by the still visible image of the Civil War. It was not easy to escape the memory of the war. Only in 1914 did General Simon Bolivar Buckner die on his Kentucky farm, long after his surrender of Fort Donelson to U.S. Grant. Flora Cooke Stuart passed away in 1923, some seventy years after she had been wooed at a Kansas military post by the dashing Lieutenant J. E. B. Stuart. In 1927 General John McCausland died at his home in the Allegheny Mountains. In the year of the public adulation of Charles Lindbergh, McCausland's name could still provoke anger. He had burned Chambersburg, Pennsylvania, in 1864 after the abortive raid on Washington, D.C. In 1865, with a price on his head, McCausland had rejected surrender, slipped across the Rio Grande, and eventually wandered through Egypt. More than sixty years later, a Northern magazine, noting his obituary, described him as the "Hun of Chambersburg."[2]

Americans looked upon the war as part of a living past. A writer for the *Atlantic Monthly* walked on the Battery at Charleston, gazed at Fort Sumter, and recalled how "faint odors of acacia and orange blossoms are in the air."[3] The *American Mercury* reported on a 1928 Confederate reunion and pondered whether a better era had not passed, for "maybe, after all, they should have won the War. . . . It would have given us a technique of leisure, a calmer estimate of life's values."[4] Another journalist recalled her marches in Confederate Memorial Day parades on hot afternoons in Alabama, where "I had lived too close to those dead and dying things ever to break away."[5]

This desire to keep a connection to the past was obvious in widespread restoration movements of the twenties. Groups strove to preserve any seeming links with history, whether Fort McHenry in Baltimore harbor, James Monroe's law office in Virginia, or Henry Clay's palatial home in Kentucky. The Thomas Jefferson Foundation launched an elaborate fund-raising drive to restore Monticello. Governor Alfred E. Smith proclaimed Jefferson Week in New York, and schoolchildren throughout the nation held Jefferson's birthday celebrations.[6]

The interest in preserving George Washington lore became almost a fetish in the era. Fascination with Washington was enormous as the nation approached the 1932 bicentennial of his birth. The Washington image embodied national aspirations which gave comfort to a people who had experienced the Harding scandals and the Depression. The bicentennial celebration was a massive demonstration of a nation searching for its historic roots. Some 900,000 posters decorated classrooms, thirty million memorial trees were planted, and almost five million articles on Washington were published in newspapers.[7]

There was also wide attraction to the image of Robert E. Lee. While a national hero in his own right, Lee also gained notice because of the inescapable connection with George Washington. As in the past, Lee biographers emphasized their family ties and similar traits of character. In 1925 the New York *Times* endorsed a federal proposal to restore the Arlington mansion, calling the home as important a landmark as Mount Vernon because of the close Lee-Washington family relationship. The *Times* editorial compared Lee's character with that of Washington, and said that "had Washington met with Lee's failure," he would have exhibited "the same magnanimity and hopeful tolerance."

There was continuing publicity given to Lee-Washington minutiae, such as the discovery in the cellar of Washington's home of a sixteenth-century portrait once owned by Lee. The newly organized Society of the Lees of Virginia dedicated a memorial pew in the chapel at Valley Forge. Mrs. William Flournoy's book *Washington and Lee* (1928) compared their "distinguished ancestry, both of Norman stock, knights and gentlemen."[8]

The environs of the nation's capital in the 1920s offered a number of reminders of the family relationship. Just across the Potomac lay Arlington, built by Washington's adopted son and Lee's father-in-law. Up the concrete road to Alexandria lay Shuter's Hill; in 1922 workmen were completing the Masonic Memorial to Washington, on the site of the Ludwell Lee home. In Alexandria, Lee's boyhood home stood on Oronoco Street, where in 1829 Lafayette had paid respects to the widow of Washington's cavalry commander, Lee's father. Nearby was Washington's Christ Church, where Robert Lee was confirmed.

The restoration of the Arlington mansion was completed in the 1920s. Mary Custis Lee's struggle to regain the house had been continued by Custis Lee after her death. In 1882, the Supreme Court ruled him to be the rightful owner, and he agreed to sell the property to the government.

For decades the fate of the mansion was uncertain. Then in 1921 an Arlington association similar to that which had preserved Mount Vernon was organized. Four years later, Congress designated the mansion a national shrine, authorized its restoration, and ordered that Lee relics owned by the government be placed there.

It was an act that well suited the nation's desire to gain inspiration from hero symbols. A Michigan congressman who introduced the legislation spoke of Lee's "exalted character, noble life and eminent services." Lee's love for the Union had bound the American people "against common external enemies in the war with Spain and the World War."[9]

Even more publicity was given to the campaign to restore Lee's ancestral home at Stratford. In 1928 the Robert E. Lee Memorial Foundation was established to purchase and operate it to "perpetuate the ideals and character of the Lees." Within a year the home had been bought for half a million dollars, and the Foundation inaugurated a national drive to pay off the mortgage.

Organizations in two dozen states raised funds, and Lady Astor managed the campaign in Great Britain. Dinners were held in New York hotels, and a tour of colonial homes was conducted in Connecticut. There was even a bridge party on the roof garden of New York City's St. Regis Hotel. Stratford Days were sponsored in many states. The 1930 Stratford Week in New York City was endorsed by the New York *Times* as a means of "paying tribute to the greatness of one of Virginia's greatest sons." The *Times* published thirty-one articles on the Stratford movement. An annual Lee "death observance" was inaugurated at Stratford in 1930. Even a "May Celebration" was begun in honor of Lee's parents, complete with "plantation melodies" sung by local black residents.[10]

COMPETING FOR ATTENTION was the Lee Memorial at Stone Mountain, Georgia. Prior to World War I, Southerners had raised funds for a gigantic figure of Lee to be carved into the face of the mountain. With blasting powder and air drills, sculptor Gutzon Borglum had begun work on the figure of Lee astride Traveler. After the war, the project became a more sophisticated undertaking managed by the Stone Mountain Memorial Association, which planned a four-million-dollar carving of Lee, Stonewall Jackson, and Jefferson Davis. By the time of its partial completion in 1928, the work was as high as a ten-story building and a city block in width.[11]

The Association obtained public statements to help raise the necessary funds. President Warren Harding called the carving "one of history's most complete avowals" of national reunion.[12] Vice-President Calvin Coolidge also courted the Lee image—and the Southern electorate. He asserted that Lee was marked by "a purity of soul and high sense of personal honor" which none could question.[13]

Several gimmicks were devised by the Stone Mountain Association to publicize the effort, including the dedication of Lee's head in 1924. While assorted dignitaries looked on, tons of granite fell from a scaffold on the face of the mountain, American flags unfurled, and Lee's head appeared. Then the guests of honor ascended the mountain and were served lunch on Lee's face.

In 1924 the group's board of directors persuaded President Coolidge to approve the striking of the Stone Mountain half-dollar. The coin was designed to bear the image of Lee, Jackson, Davis, and Warren Harding, and was to be a memorial "to the valor of the Soldiers of the South."[14]

The coin was less a memorial to valor than an effort to raise money to complete the Lee carving. Coolidge authorized the coining of half a million fifty-cent pieces whose sale would be controlled by the Association. The government would sell the coins at par value to the group, who would then resell them at a profit. When coined, the half-dollar bore only the Lee and Jackson figures. Somewhere in the shuffle Jefferson Davis and Warren Harding were unhorsed.

By 1928 the carving of Lee's body was still incomplete and Traveler had scarcely been sketched, but a formal dedication was announced. A delegation of fifteen congressmen journeyed to Atlanta for the festivities, which included a fanfare of military parades, luncheons, and a ball. Mayor James J. Walker of New York City accepted the statue on behalf of the North, and the last surviving member of Lee's wartime staff gave the benediction. Master Robert E. Lee IV pushed a switch which unveiled the 130-foot-high carving. The New York *Times* praised the monument as "a wonder of the world."[15]

The most controversial of the Lee restorations was the proposed razing of the Washington and Lee chapel. The issue reflected not only Lee's status as a national hero symbol, but Washington and Lee University's continuing determination to use the General's image for fundraising purposes. In 1912 President Henry Louis Smith of Davidson College came to the Lexington campus to begin a long tenure as president, during which he freely invoked the Lee name.

Smith's most ambitious scheme was a proposal to demolish the old college chapel and construct a large, gaudy Lee Memorial Chapel. After the United Daughters of the Confederacy pledged $100,000 in 1921 to support the project, the university began a publicity campaign. A special "Lee Memorial Chapel edition" of its bulletin attempted to justify razing the old chapel. Describing Lee's tomb as "the South's most sacred shrine," the publication claimed that the existing chapel was unworthy to house one of such "matchless character and world-wide fame."

But the Lexington chapter of the United Daughters of the Confederacy protested Smith's proposed "desecration." A peace mission by some national Daughters to the local Lexington chapter ended in a donnybrook, with the Lexington group being labeled as "willful women" who "are making no end of trouble." Others soon criticized President Smith's project. The Virginia branch of the United Daughters announced its opposition. The hapless President Smith even motored to its state convention to lobby for his chapel proposal, although he insisted he would "rather be dragged through a mud hole or a sewer pipe" than attend the meeting.[16]

When the Virginia Daughters would not budge, Smith tried a new tack. A cluster of new university brochures, such as "The Final Solution of the Chapel Problem," announced that the old chapel would not be razed. Instead, this "sacred memento" would be attached to a new chapel. The joint building would be "a tribute of Southern womanhood to the South's ideal hero."[17]

Opposition to the new design, actually an architectural monstrosity, mounted quickly. "Lay not hand upon it ... for it is a holy thing," insisted one Virginia editor, while English playwright John Drinkwater issued a strong protest in the New York *Times*. Former President Woodrow Wilson and his wife announced that the proposed building would be "an outrageous desecration" of Lee's memory. On Lee's birthday in 1924, the university trustees surrendered and quietly dropped all plans to meddle with the chapel.[18]

The uproar over the chapel reflected more than American concern for preserving the living past. Lee's already strong image was also fortified by the cult of character. Popular culture in the 1920s was intrigued with the character hero, who personified those ideals needed in a time when a rising impersonality threatened the older creed of individualism.

The American obsession with hero worship has wrongly been attributed to public boredom. The public response to Charles Lindbergh's flight in 1927 produced a New York City parade with two thousand tons of ticker tape, three million fan letters, and hundreds of marriage proposals. Some writers have suggested that the adulation for

Lindbergh only reflected a national restlessness which sought any form of excitement. Yet one observer, Roderick Nash, viewed the popularity of such men as Lindbergh, Babe Ruth, and Jack Dempsey as expressions of an American "cult of the hero." In the images of military figures, pilots, and sports heroes, one could find the old ideals of stamina, courage, and fair play.[19]

This hero cult permeated popular literature in the twenties. Juvenile fiction preached self-reliance and moral rectitude. The Edward Stratemeyer syndicate, which had earlier devised the Rover Boys, published a dozen such series: Tom Swift, the Hardy Boys, the Ted Scott flying stories, and others. Pluck, courage, respect for elders—these were the ingredients of success.

Authors of popular reading for adults purveyed the same themes. Bruce Barton's best seller, *The Man Nobody Knows*, placed Jesus in the business world of the twenties and described how he became the Great Executive by practicing the ideals of public service and hard work. A Southern minister, Harold Bell Wright, sold over ten million copies of his moralistic novels, including *The Re-creation of Brian Kent*, whose characters represented such traits as greed and honesty.[20]

The best-selling nonfiction work of the early twentieth century, the Boy Scout manual, which sold almost three million copies during the twenties, stressed the importance of character. The growth of the Scout movement was phenomenal. Organized in the United States in 1910, by 1929 its membership had neared one million. The movement was designed to build character and to produce the clean-cut male. In a 1930 guide for Scout leaders, the organization asserted: "Our *Job* is to influence *Conduct* . . . to get the boy to build habits." Hence "we must get him to have the right attitudes."[21]

A MAN LIKE ROBERT E. LEE seemed a prime example of the good life. For a nation committed to the search for ideals, Lee represented the essence of the character hero.

In his greatness Lee was viewed as the supreme representative of a virtuous society submerged by the Industrial Revolution. Those who sung his praise dwelled upon his boyhood and devotion to his mother; his model West Point career; his sense of duty and sacrifice in 1861; his kind treatment of subordinates; his resignation and charity in defeat; and his refusal to accept lucrative business offers after Appomattox.

The tone of the praise was set by Franklin Riley's *General Robert E. Lee after Appomattox*. A professor at Washington and Lee, Riley used material that had been prepared for the "Lee Memorial Volume," the defunct 1870 project, and combined it with reminiscences of alumni who had known Lee. Riley's book extolled Lee's postwar conduct—his acceptance of defeat and his attempts to rebuild a shattered South. The publisher advertised the book as "a picture of a man of remarkable character." Though "Lee was dying of a broken heart," he still exemplified traits "strikingly different from those exhibited by many of the successful executives of today."[22]

Other writers stressed these same themes. The distinguished British military historian Sir Frederick Maurice eulogized Lee's personality in *Robert E. Lee the Soldier.* Historian J. G. de Roulhac Hamilton and his wife, Mary, wrote *The Life of Robert E. Lee for Boys and Girls.* A conventional portrayal of Lee's personality, this book, the authors felt, provided inspiration for youth, so that "the life and character of Lee may become more real to the generation of young Americans now growing up." William Johnstone's *Robert E. Lee: The Christian* discussed in tedious fashion Lee's temperament in such chapters as "General Lee and the Bible" and "A Man of Prayer." Meanwhile James Young's *Marse Robert: Knight of the Confederacy* asserted that "it may be doubted whether Lee ever committed an act that would reflect upon his moral self."[23]

A series of articles published in 1927 by *Collier's* well represented the nation's concept of Lee as the character hero. The magazine serialized the reminiscences of an aged black Virginian, Mack Lee, who claimed to have been Lee's wartime body servant. Although some critics labeled the accounts bogus, they captured the national imagination and were reprinted in Sunday tabloids across the country. The popularity of the articles reflected interest in "living history." Mack Lee said he was present at Chancellorsville and heard the General pray for victory. He recalled that fateful night at Arlington when Robert Lee elected to resign from the United States Army.[24]

INTEREST IN CIVIL WAR HISTORY continued to rise during the 1930s. No doubt much of the adulation for Lee was due to his national status, in company with Washington and Lincoln. Many Americans regarded him as the war's outstanding military figure, while all respected his character. Still, the memory of the Civil War held special meaning in the Depression years which ranged beyond mere admiration for Lee. Three images of the Civil War emerged, and Robert Lee was the dominant symbol of each.

During the Depression the national mood turned inward. In part this was an attempt to understand how a country reared on a history of inevitable success could undergo such a social catastrophe. A new self-doubt rejected the old thesis that Americans are always victorious. Millions who had been reared on the principle that hard work and moral uprightness produced success now found the sermon untrue. The doctrine of progress had failed badly, as many realized that it was possible to work hard, love your neighbor, and lose your job.

Southern writers were better able to understand this failure and to interpret its meaning to the nation. A literary and cultural renaissance swept the South. No other region could boast of such novelists and poets as William Faulkner, Allen Tate, and Robert Penn Warren. They were the last generation reared in the presence of the Confederate veteran, and had been nurtured on stories of Rebel defeat. They wrote of a society whose resources had been drained by a conquest which only the South shared with Europe—total defeat and occupation.

A nation disillusioned by its experience in the Great War and economic disaster became intrigued by the comparison with Southern failure. Stark Young's *So Red the Rose,* Hervey Allen's *Action at Aquila,* and Margaret Mitchell's *Gone With the Wind* were the most prominent of sixty Civil War novels published during the thirties. Douglas Southall Freeman's massive Pulitzer Prize biography of Lee dominated scores of nonfiction works on the war.[25]

Clearly the South won the book war during the 1930s. Only Abraham Lincoln served as a serious competitor to the number of writings on the Confederacy. *Saturday Review* editor Bernard De Voto groused that "the South lost the war but is in a fair way to win the renaissance." De Voto echoed the complaints of other observers who resented the stereotype portrayal which glamorized Confederate war heroes and often looked down on the industrial North.[26]

Ironically the same mood which doted upon the Confederate saga of defeat also relished a romantic image of Rebeldom. The economic doldrums of the Depression produced a widespread desire for escape. Some found solace in the new world of Hollywood sound films, whether the animated comedies of Walt Disney or the tinsel musicals of Fred Astaire and Ginger Rogers. Others retreated into the imaginary world of radio. By 1940, twenty-eight million families owned radio sets, from which programs like "Town Hall Tonight" and "Baby Snooks" temporarily shut out the realities of the Depression.[27]

Others sought deliverance in popular writings on American history and culture. The pocket-sized *Reader's Digest* expanded its circulation within the decade from a quarter million to nearly seven million. The best-seller lists of the decade were dominated by romantic, historical novels such as *Northwest Passage* and *Drums Along the Mohawk.*

The enormous response to Margaret Mitchell's *Gone With the Wind,* the best-selling novel of both 1937 and 1938, demonstrated what the public sought in the Confederacy. The cinema version in 1939, with its huge budget, for that day, of four million dollars, broke all attendance figures. Oddly, Mitchell's work, destined to influence strongly the average American's image of the Confederacy, was not a tale of Lee's

Virginia. It told, often with stark description, of General William Sherman's capture of Atlanta and of the war in central Georgia's red-clay country. Yet her romantic stereotype of the Confederacy is in the Virginia-dominated tradition of Southern novelists of the late nineteenth century. It told of the superior antebellum life overrun cruelly in wartime by a tawdry industrial society. The book depicted a land of yellow jasmine, cheerful servants, and good horses. Thus, when Scarlett O'Hara attended the fateful barbecue at Twelve Oaks, where she was to meet Rhett Butler, she sat on the lawn surrounded by "seven cavaliers . . . as handsome as blooded stallions and as dangerous." Around her were "grinning negroes, excited as always at a party."[28]

The cavalier imagery was not lost upon the reading public. Even a reviewer in the New York *Times* accepted the mythology, and reported that the Rebel South was a land of "loveable and happy" slaves, where "young men who come to call are furnished with mint juleps and bear such given names as Stuart and Ashley."[29]

Gone With the Wind was the apex of a Confederate view which provided escapism for Americans. By 1934 Stark Young had completed his saga of Heaven Tree Plantation. *So Red the Rose*, both a best seller and motion picture, told of a land where plantation houses were "lovely and secret," domestic slaves loyal and happy, and invading Federal troops ruthless and vulgar. Julia Peterkin's *Roll, Jordan, Roll* described a romantic society "never exceeded in America," while Francis Griswold's *Tides of Malvern* told of a mythical Southern family descended from ancient Normans.[30]

The romantic Rebel image was no mere escapist device. Many Americans strongly believed that men and events could alter destiny. Millions discarded their belief in the scheme of inevitable American progress and accepted the concept of the might-have-been. A few powerful men or some chance moments could better explain the past than the tired theme of irrepressible American advance.

For many, the Depression had undermined the Horatio Alger ideal of traditional Calvinistic progress. The failure of the Great War to bring lasting peace discouraged others. By 1936 the rise of Hitler's Brownshirts and the Italian rape of Ethiopia had further weakened the old notion that progress was inevitable. Even the Veterans of Foreign Wars campaigned for the Neutrality Act of 1937. Many Americans were disillusioned by the 1934 allegations by the Special Senate Munitions Committee. When Senator Gerald Nye contended that a handful of munitions magnates and international financiers had manipulated nations into World War I, the belief in the might-have-been was only given more credence.[31]

This distrust of traditional explanations of national destiny was applied freely to the Civil War. No era of American history received a more jaundiced reappraisal. An impressive array of historians, led by James Randall of Illinois, attacked the old shibboleths that had made the war a holy crusade. Randall coined the phrase "The Blundering Generation," and viewed the war as no righteous effort but a senseless turmoil of typhus, venereal disease, and agony. He belittled earlier historians who had seen the Civil War as an inevitable part of national progress, and termed it a huge blunder committed by irrational people. Charles Ramsdell of the University of Texas even charged that the outbreak of the war could be blamed upon the actions of Abraham Lincoln in the Fort Sumter crisis.[32]

Ramsdell's Lincoln article expressed a view of the Civil War held by many Americans of the 1930s. He stressed the power of the human being to alter history. A generation which suspected that individuals had manipulated the Great War could easily conclude that the outcome of the Civil War was also not inevitable.

All of this meshed well with the romantic-cavalier ideal. Bold men could change the direction of war. Hence escapist romanticism, mingled with disillusionment, produced what Bernard De Voto termed the "Everlasting If." De Voto observed that writers were intrigued with

> . . . the whisper of a great Perhaps . . . perhaps . . . Almost . . . four hours in Hampton Roads . . . a shot in the spring dust at Chancellorsville . . . spindrift blown back where the high tide broke on Cemetery Ridge. A passionate *if!* sleeps uneasily in the grandsons' blood . . .[33]

De Voto's "grandsons" were particularly adept at entertaining the "if" factor. Many Southerners who lived in the 1930s had never been reconciled to defeat because to do so was not in the psyche of the region's people. To admit that Confederate loss was inevitable implied an acceptance of the doctrine of progress. The Southern mind, steeped in a classical tradition of a never-changing existence, could not do this. The war was still an eternal moment, not an obscure link in a chain of national destiny.

Southern writers expressed this sense of the power of chance and human strength to change destiny. William Faulkner explained it in *Intruder in the Dust,* when lawyer Gavin Stevens described to a young nephew why the South always looked backward. Stevens mused that for every Southern boy, it was always—and would always be—that afternoon on July 3 when General George Pickett stood ready to attack. Pickett's charge had already occurred, but to Southern boys, it had not yet happened, and perhaps "this time" would succeed.

Other writers—North and South—used freely this concept of the "Everlasting If." To a character in Clifford Dowdey's *Bugles Blow No*

More, George McClellan's Federals would have been swept from the fields surrounding Antietam Creek "if we had one more division." To Joseph Hergesheimer in *Swords and Roses,* the fatal day was at Shiloh, where Confederate leader Albert Sidney Johnston bled to death from a freakish wound. Had Johnston lived "perhaps even the Confederacy might have survived for a period . . . of its own choosing."[34]

In 1942 historian Henry Steele Commager spoke for a decade of such thought when he mused that Southern defeat had not been inevitable, for "the South had, from the beginning, an excellent chance to achieve independence, and that chance was not finally lost until the end of 1864."[35]

To Commager and others, Robert E. Lee was the epitome of the might-have-been concept. No other war figure so exemplified the varied images of the Civil War. Lee was the great character struggling amid the non-American tradition of defeat. He was the romantic leader of that band of cavaliers, the Army of Northern Virginia. And, too, Lee was that strong character who possessed the power to control history.

IN A DECADE of American failure, Lee emerged as the man of good character who experienced defeat. He was the image of anti-success, magnificent even when failing. The emphasis was upon the lesson of his life which gave solace to the Horatio Alger generation—that good men can lose. He was the moral non-achiever, who could now provide inspiration. A speaker at Washington and Lee University in 1931 urged his audience to heed Lee "over the radio of history." They would learn that Lee's "material failure was a moral success," and that "human virtue can be equal to human calamity." Another speaker issued a "Call for Lee Leadership," urging the nation to observe Lee's posture in defeat. Francis P. Gaines, president of Washington and Lee, emphasized the relevance of the Lee example. In 1933 Gaines described Lee as the non-achieving hero, yet "one of the world's noblest losers," because of his ability to bear calamity.[36]

Some pedestrian studies praised Lee as the noble loser. William Johnstone's *Robert E. Lee: The Christian* (1933) compared Appomattox and Gethsemane, with a resurrection in both incidents. Charles Rhodes's *R. E. Lee: The West Pointer,* Stanley Horn's *A Boy's Life of Robert E. Lee,* and S. A. Steel's *Lee: The Passing of the Old South* used the same theme. Steel's long epic poem, a tribute to great character caught astride failure, was designed to "get inspiration to go forward by looking backward."[37]

Popular drama echoed the theme. A 1934 radio broadcast from Arlington, produced on the anniversary of Lee's birth, centered upon the non-successful hero. While musicians played "Carry Me Back to Ole

Virginny," and servants barked, "Yassuh!" a rider galloped from Mount Vernon to Arlington. He informed Lee of the foolish decision of the cotton states to secede, and then remarked to Mary Custis Lee: "Cousin Mollie, Virginia deeply loves the Union, which she so largely helped to create. She has always opposed secession, in North or South! But . . . she will NOT make war upon her sister states."

As he spoke, a messenger arrived from Washington informing Lee of Abraham Lincoln's call for volunteers to suppress the rebellion. Amidst the strains of "Old Black Joe," Lee made his decision.

Thus emerged the traditional doomsday figure, cognizant of the hopelessness of the South. Though Mrs. Lee protested the South's weakness, Lee "must share the miseries of my people."[38]

Two network radio programs at the close of the decade used this imagery. In 1940 Du Pont's Cavalcade of America featured "Robert E. Lee," a live broadcast from Richmond. Based on Freeman's biography, it depicted his magnificent posture in defeat. Lee was introduced as "a courageous, gentle and loveable character—a man who, in his life and deeds, stands as a bright symbol of the indomitable spirit of the South."

The scenario opened with the offer to command the Federal army, which Lee refused because he was willing "to sacrifice everything for the Union. Everything but honor." As Lee wrote his resignation, he agreed with his wife that "this means the end of everything you've worked for . . ." Through the war the narrative took Lee, sturdy in adversity, toward eventual failure. So Lee went to Lexington, and the final pages of the script reiterated his advice to young men on how to rise from misfortune. Lee advised: "Remember—the truth is this: The march of providence is so slow and our desires so impatient; the work of progress is so immense and our means of aiding it so feeble . . . that we often see only the ebb of the advancing wave and are thus discouraged. But we mustn't be discouraged. . . . Remember—it is history that teaches us to hope."

Nine months later, the Ford Sunday Evening Hour on the Columbia Broadcasting System featured a lecture about Lee on the anniversary of his birth. The program asked why Lee's birthday, above that of other Southerners, was so remembered. The lecturer, T. J. Cameron, felt that in Lee "we are confronted with a fame supported *By The Power Of Character Alone.*" He stressed that Lee's career was no success story —no tale of renown "for political service, for literary achievements, for scientific discoveries." It was Lee's character, not any success, that made his life great.[39]

More serious biographies also lauded Lee as a symbol of defeat. In *Lee of Virginia,* William Brooks saw him as "one of the noblest tragic figures the world has ever produced." Although a good man, Lee became entrapped in defeat, and "there are times that one thinks of Hamlet."

Robert Winston's 1934 study, *Robert E. Lee: A Biography*, developed a similar approach. Winston wrote of a tragic figure engulfed in matters beyond his control. "Lee's situation was distressing and the pity of it was its hopelessness. . . . the situation was tragic—others and not himself had created it."[40]

The theme was repeated in 1936 when the city of Dallas, Texas, dedicated a massive statue of Lee. President Franklin Roosevelt unveiled the monument, and Lee was eulogized by Jesse Jones, head of the Reconstruction Finance Corporation. Though Jones believed Lee possessed "the noblest traits of man," it was the pressure of adversity that made his example brightest.[41]

Somehow it all came together on a cold winter day in 1940 when aged Henry Wickham addressed the Virginia General Assembly. Wickham not only possessed that peculiar Southern sense of enduring time but could also call for Lee's example in the present. Once he had been a lad of Hickory Hill who prowled between Arlington's columns while Colonel Lee was absent on the Texas plains. He could still remember a breakfast with Lee at Arlington, and how he saw the elderly ex-general while a postwar student at Washington and Lee.

The Depression was not over, and a new conflict was shaking the world. In those critical times, Wickham reached back to Lee for lessons applicable to the present. The oratory was grandiose, but the message was clear. In Lee's example of behavior in defeat, "the guidon is still there, and it points the way."[42]

LEE WAS ALSO the prime symbol of the romantic-cavalier imagery of the war. Romance could be found in almost any Southern region. Stark Young's *So Red the Rose* was set on a Natchez plantation, with "the garden with the box walks, the tiny pavilions in blue lattice, the camellias, roses, azaleas, jasmines, gardenias." For Francis Griswold in *A Sea Island Lady*, the cavalier lived in the low country of the Carolinas, where "the streamers of moss that fell from the old live oaks waved gently in the sea-scented wind that stirred up the river."[43]

For Joseph Hergesheimer in *Swords and Roses*, the entire Rebeldom was one huge romance. Hergesheimer admitted that he desired to escape to happier times, and he roamed the South, seeking the ghosts of the Confederacy. He discovered what he wanted in an Alabama manse, with "dark mahogany beds with solemn canopies and feather mattresses, linen fragrant with lavender."[44] It was there in Albert Sidney Johnston, who carried hair-trigger pistols, played chess, and read Shakespeare.

Still, it was Robert Lee and his Virginia army who were the show-pieces. For those seeking romance in the Civil War, Lee possessed obvious appeal. His image was strengthened in the 1930s by a surge of regional pride in the South. Some Southerners even resented the nation's use of Lee as a hero figure. Poet Donald Davidson argued that Lee rightfully belonged to the South as a sectional hero, and feared that the region was surrendering Lee to the nation by diluting his image into the "milder, more yielding Lee, the college president and quietist."[45]

For most Americans, however, the cavalier Lee image was a mosaic of his English ancestry, his colonial family ties, and the supposedly idyllic life of antebellum Virginia. Writers often mixed the elements. S. A. Steel lamented the demise of the older Virginia, which had lost

> *The elegance of social speech . . .*
> *the charming female modesty,*
> *And all the courtly gallantry*
> *That did our manners grace.*[46]

L. W. Allen's *An Epic Trilogy* praised Lee as the beau ideal of the cavalier:

> *And was he not the Old Dominion's child*
> *And son of Light-Horse "Harry"? Was he not*
> *Being son of Henry Lee, the noble son*
> *Of noble sire with nature deeply hued*
> *By the best blood of Southern lineage,*
> *Patrician of patricians?*[47]

Flournoy's *Washington and Lee* waxed at length on the colonial cavalier and the old South, but also talked of "Lancelot Lee, fighting by the side of William the Conqueror at the battle of Hastings." A speaker at a meeting of the Illinois State Colonial Dames spoke of Lee as "the White Knight of the Confederacy—the Sir Galahad of the South," while a lecturer at a Lee birthday celebration in Alabama noted that the Virginian boasted "the best blood of the Cavalier in his arteries." And a speaker at an Ohio celebration of Lee's birthday traced his ancestry to quite a medley:

Thomas Randolph Earl of Moray, Walter the High Stewart . . . Duncan, the murdered Scotch patriot; of Malcolm, who defeated Macbeth . . . of David, the Earl of Huntington; and of Robert Bruce, the Lord of Annandale, as well as of Robert Bruce, the King.

Even a more critical observer such as biographer William Brooks described Lee as a member of "the nearest approach to a hereditary aristocracy in America."[48]

Virginians relished such symbolism. Despite economic hard times, tournaments were held throughout the commonwealth. Clad in medieval costumes, knights tilted for rings, hopeful of crowning their favorite as "Queen of Love and Beauty."

This desire for escape and the pride of an impoverished Southern state culminated in the annual "Robert E. Lee Week" at White Sulphur Springs. As though on a trip to Mecca, Virginians crossed the Shenandoah Valley to the Allegheny spa for a yearly flurry of cavalier balls and polo matches played in Lee's honor. In 1932 the week began with the opening of "Old White," the summer cottage occupied by Lee, while a lawn party served frozen watermelon, which Lee had offered to children in 1867. Mrs. Woodrow Wilson led the grand march to the Lee ball. While a New York *Times* reporter rhapsodized about the costumed ball, colored "mammies" hustled Virginia's young elite out of carriages into re-creations of antebellum lawn parties and the children's fancy-dress ball.

The best commentary on this early journey back to cavalier land was supplied by two events during the final week. Douglas Southall Freeman lectured on "Stratford: A Landmark in American Genetics," while players assembled for a "Traveler's round-robin tennis tournament."[49]

LEE AND THE ARMY of Northern Virginia also embodied the "Everlasting If" of a generation that distrusted the historical inevitable. The desire to question the doctrine of progress—that the South *had* to lose —naturally centered upon the Rebels' best hope for success, Lee's army.

It was no surprise that the "if" factor concentrated upon Lee at Gettysburg. Stephen Vincent Benét in *John Brown's Body* had looked long at Gettysburg, where

> *Pickett came*
> *And the South came*
> *And the end came.*

Then *Scribner's* in 1930 featured a series of historical "ifs," regarding Lincoln, Lee, and Napoleon. The first, "If Booth Had Missed Lincoln," was prefaced by the editor: "Chance often plays a leading role in the drama of man's career and of history. These articles are brilliant conjectures on what DID NOT happen but what might have happened." *Scribner's* published another "if" article, by Winston Churchill, "If Lee Had

Not Won the Battle of Gettysburg," about which the editor wrote that Churchill "views the new world which would have been created merely if the South had won a single battle."[50]

Some writers saw the whole issue hanging in the balance that July 3 afternoon of 1863. To Robert Winston, Gettysburg was where "the backbone of the Confederacy was broken," while William Brooks described Pickett's charge as "the high-water mark of the Southern flood."[51]

Although Douglas Freeman's distinguished *R. E. Lee* will be discussed in a subsequent chapter, it is important to note here that this biography was the bible of Confederate revisionism. Freeman saw the war's outcome as hinging upon a few powerful men and events. He wrote an entire chapter, "What Can Detain Longstreet?", on that officer's alleged slowness at Gettysburg on July 2. And in dealing with Lee's retreat, Freeman considered the comparative might-have-been of Stonewall Jackson and Longstreet. What if Stonewall had not been struck by the bullets at Chancellorsville and had lived to march to the assault on July 2, an attack Freeman saw as perhaps opening the road to Baltimore or Philadelphia? It was a tragedy which Freeman viewed as "the turning point" in the fortunes of Lee's army.[52]

The Lee commemorative address at Washington and Lee University each January gave speakers the same opportunity to flay Longstreet as had been done in the 1870s. Typical was a 1931 lecture, in which a speaker contended that without doubt Lee would have won at Gettysburg, "the high tide of the Confederacy," if "Longstreet had cooperated as Jackson would have done."[53]

Even Bernard De Voto, perennial critic of the "if" philosophy, would admit that all hinged on a few hours at Gettysburg, where "the Civil War was decided." To De Voto, the chance actions of men and events there determined even more—"the pattern of Western civilization." So here "the egg was fertilized of which the future was born, where all might have gone otherwise."

Only the human element could reverse great events. It was men such as Longstreet and J. E. B. Stuart who failed Lee in critical circumstances at Gettysburg. De Voto suggested that one could sense the alteration of American destiny merely by visiting the Gettysburg field. In each step across the battleground, the visitor could feel "the forces of human effort," where "things happen when men act together."[54]

No writing better summarized the mood of the era than did Donald Davidson's poem *Lee in the Mountains*. There stood Lee in the Lexington sunset, on the rocky path to his modest office, pondering what might have been achieved. It could have been different, he mused, had Jefferson Davis in 1865 taken his advice to abandon Richmond while time remained:

The mountains, once I said in the little room at Richmond, by the huddled fire, but still the President shook his head. The mountains wait, I said, in the long beat and rattle of siege guns at cratered Petersburg. Too late we sought the mountains and those people came.

It is all summed up in Lee's brooding commentary—his image as a symbol of defeat, romance, and the epitome of what might have been. As he walked the path he murmured, "I am alone, trapped, consenting, taken at last in the mountains."[55]

CHAPTER VI

THE MIDDLE-CLASS HERO:
FROM FREEMAN
TO THE CENTENNIAL

H E TOURED THE MANASSAS BATTLEFIELD with Hindenburg's military attaché, General Friedrich von Boetticher. When he completed the first two volumes of his six on George Washington, *Time* published a seven-page article on his curious working schedule and rated him America's foremost military historian. In the days before the Normandy invasion, General Omar Bradley's major reading was the three-volume *Lee's Lieutenants.*

He was the man of whom David Lloyd George remarked, "He is one of the most intelligent people I ever met in my life." In 1938, when the country commemorated the seventy-fifth anniversary of Gettysburg, scores of newspapers, from the Elmira *Star-Gazette* to the Tulsa *Tribune,* featured in headlines his seven "live" reports from the field.

He was the Pulitzer Prize winner of 1934 for his four-volume *R.E. Lee.* His publisher had hoped for a sale of 4000 sets; by 1948 the figure had topped 35,000. When the volumes on Lee were published, the New York *Times* observed that Lee is "complete for all time," while the *New Republic* titled its review "The Definitive Lee." When Winston Churchill visited Richmond to tour the Peninsula fields, he made it clear that one person he desired to meet was Douglas Southall Freeman.[1]

And so it was that Freeman, editor of the Richmond *News Leader,* became the leader of modern Lee biographers.

Already, of course, Lee had been ennobled as perhaps the greatest military figure of the Civil War. His superb generalship and character had since 1900 placed him among the nation's most respected hero symbols. But with the advent of the Freeman era, Lee's stature would grow to even greater heights. He would be elevated to such a position that one observer would call him the "untouchable Galahad of the Confederacy." The Civil War would more than ever be regarded as a contest for Virginia. Lee's new biographers would advance him as the epitome of the middle-class hero, an image which during the years of the Civil War Centennial would add strength to the General's lofty reputation.

Even before Freeman began to solidify the General's image, the groundwork was laid by the continuing use of Lee's name by Washington and Lee University. Though defeated in his efforts to raze the chapel, President Henry Smith found a myriad of other uses for the Lee name. A Lee Memorial Fund in 1921 sought donations in memory of Lee's "lofty purpose and exalted character." A 1922 Lee Memorial Movement requested money for a variety of projects, from the "sacred task" of renovating his mausoleum to the establishing of the Lee Memorial School of Engineering.[2] Smith skillfully played down Lee's war service and stressed his value to the business community. His promotional material struck a more pleasing chord—that "when the long roll is finally called," Lee's postwar career in attempting practical educational reforms "will outshine and outweigh" his more "transient glories" as a soldier. Nationally distributed pamphlets, such as *Lee the Educator,* strove to restructure his image into that of a practical man. Hence when "heaven's unerring calculus" measured the General's life, military fame would be outshone by "Lee the Educator . . . the creative Engineer of a new Industrial South."[3]

Smith's successor, Dr. Francis P. Gaines, also campaigned to reshape the Lee mystique into that of a practical businessman who sought common-sense training for youth. It was Gaines who described the "New South" Lee in his famous address, "Lee: the Final Achievement," before a New York audience in 1933. The Lee of the Civil War had become remote by legend, superseded by the practical Lee of Lexington, where one would "learn something of the real man."

For thirty years President Gaines publicized this concept. Lee's postwar contributions were his greatest, because he sacrificed fame and wealth to train young people. Lee opposed the traditional Southern classical education, and tried instead to give students practical courses in commerce, journalism, and engineering. Gaines even asserted that Lee could be credited with the South's rise from the ashes of defeat in the war. "It should not be forgotten" that much of the industrial South "unrolled itself first in the brain of Lee."[4]

The highlight of the Gaines era was the university's bicentennial celebration in 1949, which was both an observance and a fund-raising venture. The institution mounted a three-million-dollar drive emphasizing the Lee image. One publication, *Two Great Investments in Faith,* invoked the familiar comparison between Lee and George Washington. Both generals were men of a practical bent who "looked down the vista of the future and made two great investments" in Washington and Lee University.[5]

In 1948 Congress authorized a Washington and Lee Bicentennial Commission which included President Harry Truman and several congressmen. They sought to commemorate, not Lee the general, but the practical man who "gave the last five years of his life to the service of education in this college."[6]

In later years university officials established the "Robert E. Lee Associates" for donors of $1000 and "The General's Council" for donors of at least $10,000. In 1965 the university celebrated the centennial of Lee's acceptance of its presidency with more printed tributes to his educational foresight. Five years later, Washington and Lee commemorated the hundredth anniversary of Lee's death with more promotional literature which stressed the twin concepts of sacrifice and sagacity. One publication asserted that "Lee turned out to be one of the farsighted educational statesmen of the nineteenth century."

Perhaps the best commentary upon the university's penchant for using the Lee name came in another circular, *Robert E. Lee: Innovative Educator*. The brochure was designed both to commemorate the centennial of his death and to solicit funds. In a special section entitled "Will Your Gift Match Maggie's?" the pamphlet recalled a vignette of 1870. After Lee's death, a nine-year-old child sent to Mrs. Lee money that she had earned doing chores, to help pay for the Lee mausoleum. Noting the incident—and the school's need for $800,000 that year—the pamphlet concluded: "We appeal to you, in the spirit of Maggie and Lee, to give Washington and Lee all that you can."[7]

By the 1930s Douglas Freeman was regarded as the leading Confederate scholar. He had served almost twenty years of apprenticeship in Civil War writing before achieving eminence. In 1915 he had edited *Lee's Dispatches,* a massive compilation of previously unpublished communications from Lee to Jefferson Davis. That same year, the twenty-nine-year-old editor of the Richmond *News Leader* signed a contract with Charles Scribner's Sons for a one-volume study of Lee. Gradually the project grew into a four-volume undertaking which required nineteen years of work. After the publication of *R. E. Lee* in 1934, there was little question that Freeman had established his predominance as the ranking Lee scholar. His reputation was solidified by three additional brilliant volumes on the General's subordinates, *Lee's Lieutenants.* These seven volumes on Lee and his commanders were to have considerable influence upon the modern perception of Lee.

Freeman viewed Lee as the central figure of the Southern experience, for "it took five generations of clean living and wise mating to produce such a man."[8] In turn, Freeman saw the Southern heritage as a great teacher for the United States in the crisis years of the Depression and World War II.

Freeman's desire to explain to the nation the peculiar Southern tradition came in part from his own background. While a student at Richmond College, he had attended his first Confederate reunion. Then, and later, he not only saw the rank and file of Lee's veterans— which included his own father—but glimpsed such notables as Longstreet and Fitzhugh Lee.

Frequently he attempted to recapture this sense of standing astride two civilizations. In a 1936 speech before the Columbia Graduate School of Journalism, Freeman mused on his own background:

> I have seen a man who attended the funeral of John Marshall. I knew two men who had seen Edgar Allan Poe. I knew quite a number of people who had heard Henry Clay and Daniel Webster debate . . . I mention these things because they show in a sense how close we are to the great past of America.[9]

That same year, in an address before the Virginia General Assembly, he caught the moment of time and place:

> Did the decaying blinds rattle in the winter's storm and beat against the unpainted clapboards of our gaunt abode? Grandfather would lift his head and listen: "Ah," he would say, "it sounds like the rattle of our volleys just such a day as this, that time in December '62, when we threw 'em back at Fredericksburg."[10]

In a 1935 address at Columbia, Freeman attempted to explain the psychology of a Confederate reunion parade. He admitted that an onlooking Northerner "would be puzzled or bewildered or outraged by what he saw." But Freeman reached in his own memory:

> After a while there was a murmur and a stirring and the distant pulsing of a bass-drum. "They are coming, they are coming," the spectators would say with one voice—and would begin to choke with tears before the first red banner appeared down the street . . . a clatter of hoofs, a burst of cheers, the quaver of the rebel yell from throats as youthful as those in which that same yell had been frozen in death on Cemetery Ridge, an answering quaver from the street, and General John B. Gordon, as erect as when he dashed into the Bloody Angle, is acknowledging the greeting.[11]

Freeman saw this sense of history as a stabilizing factor in a time of rapid change. Lee's career provided special comfort. In a radio address, "How a Great Leader Met Adversity," he found an analogy in Lee's postwar difficulties and the economic miseries of the 1930s. Since Lee's great character prevailed, "might not that message from the invincible spirit of a man whom the world called defeated" be of use in the present? In a later speech Freeman said that the example of Lee could be a guide through "this dark crossing of the Valley of the Depression." "Rallying now on Lee," the nation could rebuild.[12]

After war erupted in Europe, the Lee image could again provide "strength of soul" in a time when one saw "a mighty wave of attacking Messerschmitts and defending Spitfires all too few." Before a convention of bankers in 1940, Freeman spoke of how Pickett, facing Cemetery Hill, had urged his men not to forget they were Virginians. Forecasting America's entry into the war, Freeman warned that the nation "may have to fall in across the field from some Cemetery Ridge," and should remember "in that hour that you come from America."[13]

It was no mere ritual that when en route to his office in Richmond Freeman always saluted the Lee statue and promised: "I shall not fail to do that as long as I live." Lee's birthday was "a personal holy day," and he has described a young mother bringing her daughter to Lee "to be blessed." In fact, Lee "is one of the few, the very few of her sons, whom America offers at the altar of the ages as worthy by reason of his character to be exempted from the else-universal sentence of death."[14]

In Freeman's mind Virginia society held a special place. Once, speaking of the Army of Northern Virginia, he boasted: "Our Southern fathers made up an 'Army of Gentlemen.' They lived the tradition of gentlemen. . . . Richmond is different. Virginia is different."[15] Frequently he sprinkled his narratives and speeches with such sentiments. In Colonel John Washington, a member of Lee's staff, Freeman saw "a gentleman of the highest type and a true aristocrat," and Robert Lee "justified" the aristocratic concept of society. In an address at Stratford, Freeman described Lee's home country in the Westmoreland district as "the Western Attica, the birthplace of a larger number of notable men of the past than ever saw the light in an area so small."[16]

In 1919 Freeman addressed the Virginia General Assembly on the three hundredth anniversary of the organization of the House of Burgesses. He argued that it was Virginia that "carried the standard of advanced free government on the continent," and it was the commonwealth

> who wrote the bill of rights, she who gave an empire to unity, she who called the Annapolis convention, she who enacted the model law for religious liberty, she who, with the patience of patriotism, breathed the oxygen of an invigorating ideal into the lungs of a slow-pulsed, dying Confederation.[17]

At the dedication of the Stratford shrine in 1935, Freeman indicated why he believed Virginia culture was superior and why Lee was its finest example. He asserted that the greatness of Virginia aristocracy lay in its mixture of breeding and the public-service concept of *noblesse oblige*.

Much of the Lee family's greatness was attributed to blood ties. Freeman recalled "not more than two or three instances" when a Lee "married persons who were not equal in blood and station with themselves." The result was "the steady maintenance of the physical stamina and intellectual vigor of the stock for generations" that continued "until its perfect flowering in one of the greatest human beings of modern times, Robert E. Lee."[18]

One felicitous kinship was with the Carters, on Lee's mother's side. Freeman wrote that the Carter stock "bred greatness on the female side." Even when Robert Lee fought at Fredericksburg, his genealogy was influential. As Lee observed Burnside's advance across the Rappahannock River, "the blood of Light-Horse Harry fought in his veins with the calmer strain of the peace-loving Carters."[19]

Yet the Virginia society which produced Lee involved more than breeding. Freeman described the desire for public service which prompted Virginians to make "citizenship their avocation." Freeman imitated earlier Lee biographers by waxing long on the family's sense of public duty. In numerous passages he praised the record of the Lees and their kinsmen. Indeed, "in eastern Virginia there were few families of the highest standing whose members Robert Lee did not call cousin." To Freeman, this was proof that "names and blood still count in Virginia."[20]

Freeman's brilliant portrait of Lee and his society in *R. E. Lee* is remarkably consistent with the picture put forward by Virginia writers during Reconstruction. To Freeman as well, the South centered all its hopes upon both Virginia and the General. In a lecture, Freeman had declared that "Richmond became the prize for which both armies contended ... she was set as the goal for the Federal advance." Later he called Richmond the South's Verdun, the ultimate hope of the Confederacy.[21]

Thus, even in his first months of command, Lee is described as bearing the burden of the war. Of Lee's train ride from Arlington to Richmond in April 1861, Freeman mused, "If the Southern cause ever depended upon him and him alone, was there in him the stuff of which military dictators are made?"[22] In two sentences Freeman covered the disasters at Shiloh and Island Number Ten in the spring of 1862. His concern was: "How could the South be saved if Virginia were lost?" For Lee's Army in the Seven Days was "the first line of the South."[23]

Like writers of the 1870s, Freeman assumed that the South looked to Lee's army on the Peninsula for its salvation. Lee's victory in the Seven Days made him the "first captain of the Confederacy," and he had achieved success "at a time when the Confederates on other fronts had been able to do nothing to relieve the pressure on Virginia."[24]

But there was no speculation here about Lee's responsibility to relieve pressure on western commanders. At this time, western armies under Generals Braxton Bragg and Kirby Smith were beginning an invasion of Kentucky that would carry them to the Ohio River.

Also familiar was Freeman's description of Lee as virtually flawless in physical appearance. Lee was still the model that had graced the pages of J. William Jones's biography in the 1870s. When he was a cadet his hair had "a wave that a woman might have envied," while his arms were "beautiful and symmetrical." In 1861 Lee was without "a blemish on his body," and possessed superb vision, teeth, and hearing, a "rich and resonant voice," and great powers of endurance. Lee had a strong nervous system, which resided in a "fine large head" that matched his "massive torso."[25]

In company with the earliest Lee biographers, Freeman saw no equal to his subject in character. As a West Point cadet, Lee was dignified and considerate, and was possessed of candor, tact, and good humor. He was courteous, unpretentious, frank, unselfish, non-egotistical, slow to anger, gallant to women, and tactful. In addition, he had a good sense of humor, practiced a simple religious faith, lacked jealousy, and abjured flattery. The superhuman image was furthered by examples of Lee's practice of self-control, self-denial, and self-discipline.[26]

Freeman also presented the traditional portrait of Lee as both a mind reader of his opponent and a prophet who foresaw events beyond the comprehension of others. His decision to attack McClellan's army in 1862 outside Richmond was "based in part on Lee's knowledge of McClellan." After the Seven Days, Lee ignored Stonewall Jackson's fear of General John Pope's army mobilizing in central Virginia because "he had known Pope casually in the old army and had no very high estimate of his abilities."

Thus when Lee detached part of his army to attack Pope, leaving McClellan behind on the Peninsula, the psychic factor was again present. For "he was beginning to read with more assurance the minds of the men who opposed him. Pope he never took very seriously; McClellan he respected but understood." And when Pope came to grief at Second Manassas, it was partly because he "had not been so fortunate ... in reading the mind of his opponent."[27]

At every turn Lee seemed to possess psychic powers. He divided his force in the Maryland campaign in part because "by every test of known temperament and previous behavior, McClellan would organize thoroughly before advancing at all." When McClellan was removed after Antietam, Lee stated that "I fear they may continue to make these changes till they find some one whom I don't understand."[28]

His new adversary, Ambrose Burnside, was no match for Lee's ability to read an opponent. Lee anticipated his moves "with a precision that was almost pre-science." When Burnside was replaced by Joseph Hooker, Lee jested mildly over "the apparent inability of Hooker to determine on a course of action."[29]

Lee also possessed prophetic talents. He viewed matters in a broader perspective—was less enthusiastic about secession, less sure of the South's hopes for victory, and less sanguine about the shortness of the war. Hence he took no part in the "wild" rejoicing in Alexandria after Virginia seceded, for "his knowledge that war would be long and terrible kept him from any statement or action." Instead he boarded a train for Richmond and mused about the oncoming war as he observed joyous crowds gathered at stations en route. These throngs "may have been talking of easy victories and easy independence," but Lee knew better. He foresaw "a bloody test, a long war, a doubtful issue." Lee continued to be anxious when he stood in the capitol rotunda awaiting presentation to the Virginia convention. With prophetic bearing, "Lee's mind was running ahead" to the South's future problems.[30]

As he waited in the rotunda Lee gazed at the statue of "his great hero Washington." Like the early writers, Freeman frequently used the Lee-Washington imagery. Washington was Lee's model, and "the strong Washington tradition and influence" helped shape the General's life. When Lee wed Mary Custis, "in the eyes of the world" he became the representative of the Washington family.

Lee's belief in honor and public service had its root in the fact that "he had made Washington his model." Lee's decision in 1861 was influenced by his hero worship, because "Washington, his great model, had embraced a revolutionary cause." Only Lee's modesty prevented him from drawing "the very obvious analogy between his situation and that of Washington in 1775."[31]

Nevertheless, Lee's decision was accompanied with deep anguish. Again Freeman repeated many of the themes, and went further to provide the fullest account yet of the traditional "Virginia argument." Virginia (and Lee) loved the Union more than other Southerners, disliked secession, and hated slavery. Virginians had little use for the cotton South, and Lee "had no regard at the time for the South as a section. . . . His mind was for the Union."[32] But Lee's sense of duty had determined from the outset that he would adopt the course of his beloved Virginia. And like other Virginians, "he could not bring himself to fight against the states that regarded secession as a right."[33]

Thus the temptation to remain in the United States army and his feeling for the Union made Lee's decision a special case of anguish. Yet "duty was plain. . . . All the Lees had been Americans, but they had been Virginians first. . . . Dearly as Lee loved the Union . . . he would not bear arms against the South."[34]

So Robert Lee joined the Confederacy, and again Freeman's use of the insights of Reconstruction writers was familiar. He repeated the "bridled strategist" theory, according to which Lee was prevented from using his skills to best advantage. In 1862 Jefferson Davis rejected the idea of an actual commanding general because it invaded his constitutional rights, and instead assigned Lee "with the conduct of military operations in the armies of the Confederacy."

This assignment involved only "the minor vexatious matters of detail and the counseling of commanders in charge of the smaller armies." Freeman admits that Davis consulted Lee on larger strategic matters, but never was the General "given a free hand to initiate and direct any plan of magnitude."[35]

This frustration continued throughout the war. Until Braxton Bragg became general-in-chief in February 1864, Freeman noted, Davis considered Lee "still his principal adviser." Yet Freeman implied that while Lee sometimes knew better, the boundaries of his authority and his own concept of the constitutional prerogative limited what he would accomplish.[36]

The limited nature of Lee's power also explained his handling of his subordinates. Like earlier writers, Freeman saw Lee as not only the bridled general, but the bridled commander. Lee's concept of field direction had stemmed from his years of association with Winfield Scott. Lee would devise the strategy, deliver the troops to the field, and leave tactical operations to lieutenants such as Jackson and Longstreet.

Thus Freeman often blamed Lee's failures on his subordinates. He admitted that Lee had blundered tactically in the Seven Days but chiefly criticized officers like Jackson and Benjamin Huger for the failure to crush McClellan. At Second Manassas, "Longstreet was guilty of behavior that would have justified Lee in having him court-martialed." Freeman joined past writers in blaming Stuart and Longstreet for Gettysburg.[37]

If Lee's subordinates repeatedly failed him, why did he not dismiss them? Freeman explained that although Longstreet deserved court-martial and Jackson "had been a like disappointment" at Seven Days, Lee simply had a shortage of good officers. Hence "he could not chop off a head, as Grant or Pershing could, with reasonable assurance that the man he promoted was as good as the man he relieved." After Longstreet "failed Lee again, more disastrously," at Gettysburg, "whom could he have put in his place?"[38]

Later Freeman changed his explanation. Lee's dependence upon his officers in the Seven Days was attributed both to his training with

Winfield Scott and to his gentle character.[39] By the time of Second Manassas, Freeman had injected a theological concept. He quoted Lee's own statement to the Prussian observer Scheibert:

> I plan and work, with all my might to bring the troops to the right place at the right time; with that I have done my duty. As soon as I order the troops forward into battle, I lay the fate of my army in the hands of God.[40]

Freeman stressed Lee's gentle temper and inability to deal harshly with subordinates. Lee was thus constrained by his own great character and could not discipline those officers who behaved like erring children. Thus Freeman's position was that if Lee succeeded, it was due to his skillful use of his generals; if he failed, it was because his lieutenants failed him, often because of his own human kindness.[41]

One Lee subordinate who continually drew Freeman's attention was Stonewall Jackson. Sometimes Freeman appeared almost as desirous of lowering Jackson's reputation as were postwar authors like Fitzhugh Lee. By combining his skillful pen, honest scholarship, and a hint of suggestion, Freeman colors Jackson as an officer in whom Lee only grudgingly showed confidence. Freeman views him in 1862 as a "strange young soldier" who a junior officer confided to friends "was insane beyond all doubt." Jackson, "regarded by some of his comrades as eccentric to the point of madness," was "darkly Calvinistic in his manner."[42]

Once the stereotype of Jackson was established, Freeman probed his ambition. He recalled that Jackson after First Manassas wrote to his wife that God "makes me content to await His own good time and pleasure for commendation." This statement was not unlike many which Lee uttered before and during the war. Nevertheless, Freeman continued:

> He was "content to await," but not to be denied "commendation." Did he mean "fame"? Was ambition burning under that faded blue coat he had brought to Manassas, from V.M.I.? . . . his large blue eyes had blazed with a strange light during the battle: what did that portend?[43]

Again, by innuendo, Freeman toyed with Jackson's ambition as a reason for his sluggish conduct during the Seven Days battles. He spoke of how "ugly tales of Jackson were in circulation. He was reported to have said that he did not intend his men should do all the fighting." And while

Lee never doubted Jackson's ability, "he may have feared that Jackson was ambitious and ill-disposed to fight under another."[44]

Jackson thus emerged from the Peninsula as an erring child yet to earn Lee's final approval. Freeman took pains to note that in the army's reorganization after the Seven Days, Longstreet was allotted twenty-eight brigades and Jackson only seven. Such disproportion "must reflect, to some extent, Lee's belief at the time regarding the comparative willingness of the two men to cooperate." For now if Jackson "was to prove recalcitrant, his power to thwart the general strategy of the army would be limited"—"a safe inference from the facts." Only after Antietam, when Lee recommended to Jefferson Davis that Jackson be promoted to lieutenant general, does Lee show "the final dissipation of all his doubts as to Stonewall's willingness to cooperate."[45]

Freeman questioned not only Jackson's ambition but also his real contributions to Lee's success. Jackson's bold move around General John Pope's flank to Manassas Junction was played down as merely an operation "conducted on Jackson's part without a serious mistake of any sort." Jackson's infantry tactics in the Shenandoah Valley campaign were described as "commonplace," and "lifted above the level of mediocrity by nothing save an intelligent effort to co-ordinate the three arms of service."[46]

Freeman did admire Jackson greatly. But it was an admiration tempered by that same rivalry displayed by early Lee writers. One almost senses a mild resentment when Freeman spoke of Jackson's hero status in the spring of 1862, at a time when Lee lacked popular approval. He wrote:

> Stonewall's victories had come, moreover, when they inspirited a discouraged Confederacy. Press and people did not know, and would not have responded differently had they known, that the larger strategic plan was Lee's, not Jackson's.[47]

Freeman's sense of rivalry came through clearly in his treatment of Chancellorsville. As did the earliest Lee biographers, Freeman emphasized that the credit for the flanking march around Hooker belonged to Lee. When Lee asked how they could attack Hooker, "Jackson answered, in substance, that it was for Lee to say. He would endeavor to do whatever Lee directed." When Lee, after studying the map, suggested a march around the Union right flank, "Jackson at once acquiesced." Again Freeman repeated that "Jackson was thus entrusted with the execution of the plan that Lee had determined upon." And after Jackson's attack demolished Hooker's flank, Lee was cheered by the troops, "sensing that he had fashioned their victory."[48]

Freeman may have presented the familiar Lee image, but never before had it been done with such research, writing skill, and scholarly respectability. The extent of the praise accorded Freeman became an important contribution to the Lee reputation. Both *R. E. Lee* and *Lee's Lieutenants* were greeted with such acclaim that one historian observed: "To him was accorded the rare honor of being accepted, while still alive, as a great historian, as the authority in his field . . ."[49] From the *North American Review* to the *Catholic World,* and from the *Review of Reviews* to *Time,* critics agreed that there was little left to say about Lee.[50]

The old image of Lee was now sealed by Freeman's magnificent writing. The popular view that nothing was left to be said of Lee was well expressed by one critic who said that any other books will be those of "after-gleaners."[51]

In some respects Freeman's monumental study proved harmful. His scholarship wrapped Lee in an almost impregnable mantle and deterred further examination of his career. Freeman deliberately discouraged probing into Lee's personality, and scorned those who would do so. Lee was a simple man, governed by an uncomplicated combination of self-denial and self-control, "the supreme rule of his life."

Freeman was impatient with those who sought to investigate more deeply beyond the marble exterior of Lee's character. He derided those biographers who had "in vain" suggested that Lee's outward reserve masked "some deep spiritual conflict." Freeman simply closed the book. "It is not so," for "his was a simple soul . . ."[52]

Given Freeman's intensive research, he could have said much more of Lee's personality. Were there dark currents in Lee's mind? Why did he for years badger his children with dour letters on self-conduct? Why did he possess a seeming obsession with death and a tendency toward self-deprecation?

Some have suggested that Freeman shunned such questions because he disliked attempts to describe what a subject was thinking. Certainly he had little use for the psychological biography of Lytton Strachey. He railed against the psychological approach to history as the worst of "all the frauds that ever have been perpetrated on our generation."

Though Freeman admitted that he had "lived" with Lee and George Washington for years, "I am prepared humbly to submit to you that I do not know what either of them ever was thinking at a given moment . . ." In fact, "how dare a man say what another man is thinking when he may not know what he himself is thinking.' "[53]

Actually, in *R. E. Lee,* Freeman often attempted to judge what Lee was thinking. When Lee prayed in Christ Church shortly after his resignation in 1861, "as he prayed, it must have been for his divided country." Freeman spent pages supposing what was on Lee's mind when, a few days later, Lee's train rode down to the Chickahominy Valley. A year later, in his capacity as military adviser to Jefferson Davis, Lee returned from a visit with General Joseph Johnston:

> ... he trotted homeward—with what thoughts, one wonders. ... Was he doomed to remain always a headquarters general? Had his long preparation brought him only to this?[54]

However, Freeman never tried to penetrate the inner Lee personality. One observer has suggested that here Freeman was influenced by his own upbringing—that he "was a Virginia gentleman writing about a Virginia gentleman." Hence, "because he was like Lee," Freeman saw nothing unusual in a pattern of behavior that he assumed was normal.[55]

There is much to be said for this notion. Freeman himself believed in the great eternals which moved men to action, such as self-control, self-denial, and honor. Once he explained to students at Columbia the code under which he was raised:

> Pain is inevitable; man was born to suffer "as the sparks fly upward." That was part of the philosophy of the old world. Suffering is inevitable, bear it as strongly as you can.[56]

For Freeman's Lee, the eternals were his traits of character. "Character is invincible—that, it seems to me, is the life of Robert E. Lee in three words."[57] When Freeman summarized Lee's behavior in his eloquent chapter "The Pattern of a Life," he did not examine personality but depicted the simple character of a Virginia gentleman. "His language, his acts, and his personal life were simple for the unescapable reason that he was a simple gentleman." Freeman believed that this "gentleman of simple soul" grounded his life in simple verities.[58]

To the very last sentence of his biography, Freeman refused to look beyond this code. He concluded:

> That is all. There is no mystery in the coffin there in front of the windows that look to the sunrise.[59]

To some authors, that was *not* all, but their questions were greeted with criticism. By totally enshrining the Lee image, Freeman had unknowingly generated a new era of paranoia among Civil War writers.

A few biographers and historians did try to approach the Lee image critically. In 1933 Major General J. F. C. Fuller issued his *Grant and Lee: A Study in Personality and Generalship.* Fuller represented a new school of British observers of the American Civil War. Earlier English writers such as Garnet Wolseley and G. F. R. Henderson had stressed the glory of the offensive. But World War I, with its defensive trench warfare, introduction of armor, and adoption of the concept of "total war," spawned a new breed of theorists. In *Grant and Lee,* Fuller argued that Grant was Lee's superior because he possessed a broad strategic grasp of the war in contrast to Lee's parochial outlook.[60]

Fuller's views were supported by perhaps the most respected British military theorist of his generation, Basil Liddell Hart. A lieutenant in the Yorkshire Light Infantry, Liddell Hart was wounded on the Western Front in 1915. He was deeply impressed by the battle of the Somme and became convinced that conventional infantry assaults only brought slaughter. While recuperating from his wound, Liddell Hart wrote an impressive account of the Somme that launched a distinguished career as a military analyst.

Gradually Liddell Hart's interest in mobility, armor, and changing strategic concepts led him to study the western theater of the Civil War. In part he saw the 1864 campaign in Georgia as demonstrating the use of two of his own notions of changing warfare. He believed that the "indirect approach," threatening two or more points simultaneously, would force the enemy either to overextend his resources or to abandon territory. Liddell Hart also admired the "baited gambit," a combination of offensive strategy and defensive tactics.

In 1929 he called for more study of the western theater and took to task Henderson's *Stonewall Jackson* for unduly influencing young British officers to study only Lee's campaigns. That same year, his highly acclaimed biography of Sherman praised that officer as being years ahead of his time in such matters as mobility and the use of economic and social warfare.[61]

Criticism of Freeman's *R. E. Lee* was predictable. Liddell Hart wrote two review essays in the *Saturday Review of Literature.* In "Lee: A Psychological Problem," he showed little sympathy for Freeman's praise of Lee's immaculate character and spotless West Point record. To him such steadiness promised only "every prospect of admirable mediocrity." In addition, Lee's loyalty to Virginia augured only a "limitation of outlook" not compatible with a good strategist. Bound too closely to both Virginia and antiquated offensive tactics, Lee bled the South to death, and his casualty lists "spelt bankruptcy to his country."

In a second review, "Why Lee Lost Gettysburg," Liddell Hart claimed that Lee was no "true grand strategist" because he was unable to grasp the conditions on which such planning hinged. For example, Lee's continual costly frontal assaults indicated that he had little understanding of the South's resources.[62]

Fuller and Liddell Hart's criticisms received little support until the 1950s. Then, in 1955, historian T. Harry Williams wrote an article reevaluating Freeman as a historian. Actually Williams was examining

both Freeman and Lee. Freeman's tendency to be "a little too worship-
ful of Lee" and to make "excuses for his hero" was understandable.
Both author and subject were products of a limited society. Neither
Freeman nor Lee recognized that the Civil War was a modern struggle,
and both clung instead to the "old tournament notion of war."[63]

Four years later Allan Nevins revived the matter of Lee's parochialism. In his *War for the Union*, Nevins saw Lee's decision to join the
Confederacy as colored by "a parochial type of patriotism" which
lacked "a certain largeness of view." Such limitations affected Lee's
generalship. Nevins pointed to Lee's invasion of Pennsylvania at a time
when Vicksburg was in peril, and observed that "it is difficult to believe
that Lee either knew or cared much about the Mississippi front."[64]

This handful of critics encountered rebuttal which bordered on
paranoia. Nevins was answered in 1961 by Avery Craven in the annual
Lee Birthday Address before the Virginia Historical Society. Craven
began with a furious attack on Nevins's view of Lee's generalship. With
regard to Nevins's charges of provincialism, Craven saw Lee's action as
"the natural one for a Virginia gentleman." In a sentence that revealed
the power of the Freeman legacy, Craven added: "If Douglas Freeman,
speaking to the future, saw no reason for explaining Lee's action, I most
certainly can find no excuse for doing so on this occasion."[65]

Williams's re-evaluation of Freeman also provoked criticism. A
Richmond native and acquaintance of Freeman, Joseph Harrison, Jr.,
criticized Williams in the *Virginia Magazine of History and Biography*.
Harrison's article was a hodgepodge of hastily delivered salvos. Williams
could not understand Freeman because he did not understand "the
Virginia gentleman's type." Williams exaggerated Lee's concern for
Virginia. Harrison ridiculed the assertion that Lee held the "old tournament notion of war," and observed that "this sort of talk is still heard
from time to time."[66]

J. F. C. Fuller was a favorite whipping boy for a generation. As late
as 1964 a defender of Lee berated Fuller for being one of those who
"speak with uncertain voices" on the subject.[67]

A more modern critic who met resistance during the Civil War
Centennial was Marshall Fishwick, a professor at Washington and Lee.
Fishwick's penetrating analyses of Virginia culture, such as *Virginians
on Olympus*, irritated professional defenders of the commonwealth.
He spoke of Virginia's penchant for hero worship and conceit, and
described a mosaic of "Anglophilism, biracialism, hero and ancestor
worship, and the force of a gloriously remembered past."[68]

Fishwick was intrigued with Virginia's veneration of Lee as the
"southern Saint George," the closest thing to a saint possessed by white
Protestant Virginia. He thought Lexington had become a shrine where
relics such as "locks of Lee's hair ... and the skeleton of his horse

Traveler are reverently displayed."[69] Such veneration clouded Lee's true character and worth. In his *Lee after the War* (1963), Fishwick returned to the theory of Charles Francis Adams—that Lee's greatness came after the war, and not on the plains of Manassas. It was "the old man moving among Lexington's children" that should provide the simple lesson that "human virtue was equal to, if not superior to, human calamity."[70]

Although Fishwick's writing was a thoughtful tribute to Lee, his efforts to humanize a tradition was criticized by the Virginia establishment. Clifford Dowdey, a pretender to Freeman's mantle as Virginia's historian of the war, missed Fishwick's interpretation completely. He labeled Fishwick an iconoclast, his writing as pedestrian, and his attitude as beset with an "airy irreverence." Fishwick was only "taking pot shots at the establishment," and lacked the background—or Virginia credentials—to do so.[71]

At first glance these often angry rebuttals to criticism of Lee appear puzzling. In an era when Civil War writing had become more sophisticated, and when the Centennial invoked sentiments of harmony, why did unfavorable comments on Lee provoke ire?

It was not a case of Southerners defending the reputation of one of their own. One could scarcely envision any fiery defense of Beauregard or even Stonewall Jackson. In fact, some of Lee's staunchest defenders in modern times have been non-Virginians or non-Southerners.

But one does not tinker lightly with a national image. By the 1930s Lee was well established as a major American hero symbol, ranking in esteem with Washington and Lincoln. He was beloved by a nation which respected both his great character and his military prowess.

Americans have always demanded perfection in their heroes, and resent attempts by writers to detract from their image. Dixon Wecter, in *The Hero in America*, noted that "hero-worship is a secular religion" in the United States. Americans like to foster a self-portrait of common sense and practicality, but they approach their national heroes with an air of folk worship. Individuals such as Washington and Lee have become almost Christ-like symbols viewed as lacking flaws. And Americans dislike hearing that they may very well have had a few flaws.[72]

The determination to maintain the stainless quality of such men was demonstrated by the reaction to criticisms of George Washington. Two biographies of Washington published in 1926, by William E. Woodward and Rupert Hughes, attempted to penetrate the Virginian's protective mantle. They wrote of such controversial matters as Washington's snobbery, drinking, and alleged love affairs. Both books met with wrath from Americans unwilling to accept flaws in a national symbol.[73]

There is another American prerequisite for hero status which bolstered the modern Lee image. Lee became the South's war hero during the Reconstruction partly because he represented the noble loser who fell to overwhelming odds. In part this sentiment reflected the Lost Cause mentality of Southerners who sought to rationalize defeat.

Yet it was also in the tradition of what Americans require of their great hero symbols. Dixon Wecter noted that we have always been affected by "our sympathy for the underdog, our respect for minorities, our sentimental weakness for lost causes, even our admiration for failure." So "handicap, struggle and failure has much to do with the popularity of heroes."[74] Napoleon is remembered far more vividly than Wellington, and Hannibal more than Scipio Africanus. Americans admire the traditional success story, but also venerate those who struggle against great odds. The hero of the Revolution, George Washington, scarcely won a battle.

The defeat syndrome also provided the Civil War's strongest hero images. Abraham Lincoln's long climb from poverty to the White House ended in tragic death. Ulysses Grant's journey from pauperism in Galena to national adulation and the presidency also ended in painful death. And Robert E. Lee, the noble figure who endured, was brought down by irresistible odds. All three well suited Walt Whitman's verse, "Vivas to those who have failed. . . . And to all the generals who lost engagements, and all overcome heroes."[75]

In the years from Freeman's writings to the Centennial, another traditional American requirement for heroes resurfaced to further protect Lee from criticism. As the modern image began to crystallize, he became the symbol of the middle-class Protestant ethic, a man possessed of the virtues of the American Everyman. He exemplified the well-proportioned life sought by the nation in its heroes—a military hero but no warlord; intelligent but no intellectual; religious but not wrapped in piety.

Certainly the publicity campaigns at Washington and Lee, stressing the General's common sense and business acumen, fortified the ideal. Lee's prestige also derived strength from Freeman's portrayal of a gentleman possessed of simple virtues such as decency and devotion to principle.

The Civil War Centennial also fortified the modern image. In fact, so many books about the war were published that one editor complained that "the last surviving scraps" from "every sutler, cook and camp follower who could write" had been printed. An Alabama group spent $100,000 to re-enact the inauguration of Jefferson Davis, while the battle of Bull Run was refought at a cost double that amount. Journalist Harry Golden recalled a friend who was "killed" at Bull Run, only to die for his country in three later re-enactments.

Business realized that the Civil War was still the proverbial rich man's war and poor man's fight. The Chrysler Corporation advertised a specially made Valiant, the "Dixie Special," to be sold only in Southern states; it boasted a paint finish of "Confederate gray." A New York firm offered a canine "turncoat" for poodles, one side blue, the other gray. The National Civil War Centennial Commission set up a subcommittee to help businessmen to capitalize on the fad. It supplied such advice as: "Tobacco advertisers can point to the clandestine barter in smoking and chewing tobacco that brought enemy soldiers together."[76]

Mass-media accounts of the war made it appear as a struggle for Virginia. The New York *Herald Tribune* syndicate's cartoon strip introduced a young Confederate hero who announced: "My name is Johnny Reb and I'm a Virginian. When I heard about how the Yankees was going to invade us, I joined up to fight for my state and for the South." On television, a cavalier fantasia, called "The Gray Ghost," which described the exploits of Lee's cavalry, achieved impressive ratings from Boston to Los Angeles. Another network carried "The American," a blue-gray epoch of war in Lee country. In the first week of its availability Parker Brothers sold 25,000 copies of its "1863" board game, and other games, such as "Gettysburg" and "Chancellorsville," were also successful.[77]

As usual, Virginia was the center of the war. Shortly before the Centennial, *Time* featured a poignant Memorial Day pictorial on the war. Eleven battlefield photographs—nine of them of Lee's army—were selected for such comment as: ". . . across the graves of Appomattox, perhaps, the memories and meanings of the Civil War echo most truly and most nobly."[78] *The Saturday Evening Post* published an article, "The Lost Rag Doll of Appomattox," which traced the fate of a doll that was in the room when Lee surrendered. The writer noted that the doll was part of history on that day "when Lee surrendered to Grant, ending the bloodiest war this hemisphere ever knew."[79]

Such articles reflected intense interest in Lee and Virginia. A naval ballistic-missile submarine christened the *Robert E. Lee* was launched at Newport News. Du Pont's Cavalcade of America filmed "Sunset at Appomattox" for television, while Walter Cronkite interviewed Lee twice in his "You Are There" series. The British Travel Association issued *Explore the Lee Country in Britain.* The booklet suggested that it seemed appropriate during the Centennial for Americans to visit "the home of the ancestors of Robert E. Lee." One tour north from London was a journey into a land where "the imprint of the Lees is everywhere."[80]

THERE WAS no more popular military writer in the 1960s than the longtime journalist and editor of *American Heritage*, Bruce Catton.

Ironically, a century before, it had been William Swinton, historian of the Federal Army of the Potomac, who had first called the nation's attention to Lee's exploits. Now Catton, the latter-day historian of the Army of the Potomac, focused on Virginia.

Swinton and Catton advanced a similar theme. The greatness of the Federal army lay not in its string of inept commanders, but in the endurance of the common soldier. The army was afflicted with generals who were no match for Lee. Only the tenacity and courage of the private soldiers saved the hour. Catton, like Swinton, emphasized Lee's greatness to prove the point. His combination of praising Lee and damning the Potomac force's generals was evident in *This Hallowed Ground:*

> Robert E. Lee played cruel games with its generals, deceiving them and leading them on so that they would get many of their men killed to no good purpose. . . . Its men were fatalists, doing the best they could do . . . and coming back for more.[81]

Catton had become intrigued with Lee's army while working as a Washington journalist. "Virginia lay across the river, and Virginia was magic soil." Catton's trilogy on the Army of the Potomac, which included the Pulitzer Prize-winning *A Stillness at Appomattox,* established him as the war historian of the popular reading public. Much of his success was due to his superb writing style. It was evident in his famous passage in *Glory Road,* recounting how Federal troops awaited Pickett's charge:

> They were old soldiers and had been in many battles, but what they saw then took their breath away, and whether they had ten minutes or seventy-five years to live, they remembered it until they died. There it was, for the last time in this war, perhaps for the last time anywhere, the grand pageantry and color of war in the old style . . . fighting men linked up for a mile and a half from flank to flank.[82]

Catton's later books, such as his multivolume *Centennial History of the Civil War,* continued to describe the war as a struggle for Virginia. Richmond was the "heart and core" and "keystone" of the Confederacy. Gettysburg was a land where Longstreet "argued, grumbled and sulked." And Federal soldiers were "ready enough to admit that the greatest general of all" was Robert E. Lee.[83]

If there was a Southern counterpart to Catton, he was the Richmond journalist and novelist Clifford Dowdey, whose experience before the Centennial years included three decades of eulogizing the

Army of Northern Virginia. Dowdey wrote a trilogy on that army, a massive 700-page biography of Lee, and the volume on the Confederacy in the "Mainstream of America" series.

Dowdey's streak of professional Virginianism came through plainly. The dust jacket of his *The Land They Fought For* asserted that because Dowdey had an ancestor at Jamestown, he possessed the right to speak for "our side." When Dowdey compared Lee with Jefferson Davis, the Virginia elitism was obvious. Davis was a crude example of the "self made Bourbons of the new cotton kingdom." Lee was "the real thing, the perfect product of the ruling class."[84]

Dowdey's writings seemed a carbon of the Lee cult of the 1870s. Virginia was "the battleground" and the "backbone of Southern defense." Davis was an incompetent who succeeded in curtailing Lee's genius. When Lee was appointed as Davis's military adviser in early 1862, he came to Richmond "to save the war for the Deep South secessionists."

But Lee remained the bridled general. He was given "an ignominious office job" by a jealous President. Had Lee possessed authority to exercise his brilliance, "clearly the war would have taken a quite different course." Then came the wounding of General Joseph Johnston and Lee's assumption of command of the Army of Northern Virginia when the Confederacy was "on the verge of total collapse."[85]

Another prominent writer was Virginius Dabney, the editor of the Richmond *Times-Dispatch*. Dabney stated that "we Virginians modestly admit our superiority to citizens of all other American states." To Dabney, the war was also a fight for Virginia soil, and "the last war fought between gentlemen" ended at Appomattox Court House.[86]

Such observations were often accepted at face value during the Centennial era, when Americans desired an easy synthesis of four years of carnage. It was simpler to view the war as a titanic struggle between Grant and Lee than to cope with the careers of men such as Rosecrans, Bragg, Thomas, and Albert Sidney Johnston. Appomattox was a more cogent symbol of defeat than surrenders at far-flung places such as Durham, North Carolina, and Citronelle, Alabama.

Gettysburg was a crucial element in the nation's search for neat verities in a confusing war. It was easier to understand the great crisis of 1863 as a contest between Pickett's men and the Federals for the rock wall on Cemetery Ridge, rather than deal with Grant's arrival at Grand Gulf or Rosecrans's operations against Chattanooga.

Gettysburg was a stereotype into which all the fortunes of the war could be compressed. In *The Atlantic Monthly*, historian Oscar Handlin provided a concise explanation for Rebel defeat which represented the national view. In 1863 the Union was in peril, as England and France stood ready to intervene in behalf of the Confederacy, and

Robert Lee rode north into Pennsylvania seeking the *coup de grâce*. Then came Lee's defeat, and General George Meade's army would "bury there the delusion that secession might succeed."[87]

Gettysburg provided other symbolism. Bruce Catton echoed the sentiments of many when he described the entire nation as the "real victor." To Catton, here was the tragedy of Lee, whom he considered the battle's "central figure." The rise of middle-class America was on the horizon, but when Lee invaded Pennsylvania, for him "the stars in their courses were going in the other direction."

Lee could not understand that the Union victory was the great divide of American history, a cathartic which allowed the rise of the middle class and a modern industrial state. Thus, far more than other battlefields, Gettysburg held powerful symbolism. It was a place where men could catch a glimpse of "a vista extending far into the undiscovered future."[88]

Catton was reflecting a nation's self-image of the war, that somehow modern America had risen out of the narrow valley between Seminary and Cemetery ridges. He brought the symbolism together in the last paragraphs of *Glory Road*, when he pictured Lincoln's visit to consecrate the battlefield cemetery. It was "the valley of dry bones," the framework of a new America, which awaited Lincoln's speech.[89]

Other historians agreed that the war had transformed an earlier age into a modern America. Ulysses Grant was often hailed as representing the rise of the pragmatic business order. Grant became the impatient hammerer of Fort Donelson, Vicksburg, and Richmond, the man anxious to crush the archaic Southern order and get on with the task of building the industrial state. Grant was the ever-practical man who believed that "what lay back of a person mattered nothing in comparison to what lay ahead of him."[90]

Yet it was not Grant, but the man whom he defeated, who dominated the military side of the Civil War Centennial. For half a century Robert Lee had been a national symbol, revered for both his character and his military prowess. In addition, his flexible image had continually provided meaning for those who sought to understand the war. To the generation of 1900, Lee was the nationalist who had striven to restore the Union; thirty years later, in the Depression, he represented the cavalier ideal. Certainly his reputation would have endured without these specific appeals, but they did reinforce his prestige. The same became true in the Centennial era. To a nation that considered the war a victory for middle-class America, Lee became the central war figure. His image emerged from the Freeman years as that of the middle-class hero. The loser of Gettysburg, whose defeat supposedly released the forces which Americans esteemed, now epitomized those ideals.

Two decades before the Centennial, Dixon Wecter analyzed what

Americans require of their heroes. He surmised that the essential ingre-
dient was steadiness, the concept of the well-proportioned life. Common sense is valued more than high intellect, and character more than
shrewdness. Hard work, honesty, enterprise, the proper use of power
—all such traditional middle-class virtues were demanded of the nation's strongest folk images.[91]

Character and balance had been at the core of the Lee image since
Appomattox. Lee's life was great in its own right. But that concept of
steadiness, the heart of Freeman's character analysis of Lee, gave special meaning to the Centennial generation. As one historian observed,
"What is ultimately pleasing is the well-proportioned life."[92]

Two examples serve to illustrate this. In 1961 Interlaken Mills of
Rhode Island issued a booklet entitled *The Noble Lee*. The masthead
bore Woodrow Wilson's famous commentary on Lee:

> . . . a leader of men in war and peace, a champion of principles, a
> humanitarian, a man who devoted his entire life to the benefit of
> others without regard to himself. Time after time, he was offered
> opportunities to gain fame and wealth, but neither factor in-
> fluenced his decision to take a course of action he conscientiously
> believed to be right.

He was lauded for his consistency, for a devotion to duty "never abandoned to personal emotion." He was the man who did not capitalize on
his power: as a general he "could have enjoyed the luxurious treatment" accorded to high officers, but chose "to share the privations of
his soldiers."[93]

An article on Lee's character in *American Heritage* was announced
as the first in a new series on "The American Hero." The editor asked
what qualities Americans demand "in the men they elevate . . . to the
exalted rank of hero." The response was given by a long-time Lee
student, Stanley Horn.

Horn asked why a soldier such as Lee had become a national symbol, since "the fame of but few soldiers has survived such failure as he
experienced." The answer was not in his soldiery but in his character,
"primarily in his greatness as a man." It was the greatness of steadiness,
of "such high ideals and principles that his whole conduct was governed
by them."[94]

Thus the Lee image emerged from the Centennial, more than ever
adored by a nation. He represented everything that was good which
emerged from a war so terrible that Allan Nevins could find little compensation for it save "all the heroism, all the high example we find in
Lee's character and Lincoln's wisdom."[95]

THE MARBLE MAN:
A REAPPRAISAL

So THERE HE LIES in the crypt at Lexington, beneath the marble figure carved by Edward Valentine.

What was he truly like, this man whose personality has been obscured by a century of near sainthood? The real nature of Robert Lee has remained an enigma.

Some biographers have been frustrated by the difficulty in probing beneath the protective covering of the Lee image. Stephen Vincent Benét described him as the "marble man," a curious personality who remains safe from the "picklocks" of biographers. T. Harry Williams considered Lee "a strange, almost baffling creature," while Bruce Catton observed that Lee was "one of the most profound enigmas of American life." Perhaps the Confederate diarist Mary Chesnut expressed it most clearly when she pondered, "Can anyone say that they know Robert E. Lee?"

But what more is there to learn about him? His personal habits have been described exhaustively in a score of biographies. We know that he loved horses, read little, and delighted in kissing young ladies. We know that his favorite dish was smothered chicken and that he enjoyed romping with his children as they tickled his feet.

Still, one is haunted by Mrs. Chesnut's query. None of his biographies tells much of the inner Lee, of the drives that shaped his life. Many writers have been content to describe Lee only in terms of his character traits, and have closed the book on his inner soul.

The *Oxford English Dictionary* contains several definitions of the word "character." Usually, when biographers wrote of Lee's character, they referred to what the Oxford authorities regard as "moral qualities strongly displayed." If Lee was courteous, humble, or considerate to an erring lieutenant, such was his character.

Yet the Oxford compendium also suggests that character may be defined as "the sum of the moral and mental qualities which distinguish an individual—viewed as a homogeneous whole." Given this broader definition, one must admit that far less is known of Lee's inner spirit.

For if one's character is regarded as the sum of those qualities viewed as a whole, much remains to be said of the man. What provoked his savage outbursts of temper, or produced those deep moods of depression so dreaded by members of his wartime staff? What prompted his long-time fixation with death, so prominent an element in his correspondence for almost a decade before the Civil War? What was the source of his tendency to look upon life as an unhappy, transient existence? Why did a man known in earlier years for his vibrant personality become morose in the years before the war?

It is not surprising that the answers to such questions have been obscured for over a century. Much of the power of the Lee mystique exists because knowledge of the inner man has been scarcely pursued beyond the invocation of stereotyped phrases. The non-knowledge of Lee has fortified the superhuman structure of his image.

Attempts to penetrate more thoroughly into Lee's inner nature have met with resistance from several quarters. Certainly the image, fashioned by a century of admirers, discourages further exploration. The real Lee has become so intermingled with the hero symbol that his human traits have been overlooked. Too, the American penchant for shielding its national heroes and the protectiveness of some Lee devotees have perhaps intimidated biographers who would probe more deeply. Then Douglas Southall Freeman sealed the issue with his insistence that Lee was a totally uncomplicated man.

Certainly none would quarrel with Freeman's general description of Lee's conduct. He was a good man, whose qualities often far transcended the pettiness of many who surrounded him in the Civil War years. No one would question that he was a man of grace, dignity, humility, and deep religious convictions. Yet this says little about Lee's humanity. The constant depiction of such traits has made Robert Lee into a rigid individual who often seems more marble than flesh. Lee was not the simple character portrayed by many authors. Much of his greatness may have been due to his ability to control the elements of frustration, self-doubt, and unhappiness which troubled his life.

Too often Lee has been evaluated as the middle-aged, reserved general of the Civil War years. This Lee was the product of over a half century of personality development, a matter that has often been overlooked. One can discern three stages in the shaping of Lee's character. Prior to the 1850s, he was a vibrant, outgoing person who at the same time was beset with inner frustrations. During the decade before the Civil War, he had become a reserved, morose individual who appeared to have made some conscious decisions about his life. The Lee of the Civil War would be strongly affected by these resolves.

. . .

LEE'S FRUSTRATIONS and strains included his unsatisfactory marriage, complicated by his need for emotional release. In some ways, his marriage was more duty than happiness.

Mary Anna Randolph Custis was the spoiled child of Arlington, never quite able to sever the umbilical cord. She was the daughter of George Washington Parke Custis. Custis, the grandson of Martha Washington and the adopted son of George Washington, had inherited the Arlington property from his father. In 1802 he began construction of the mansion. Two years later he married Mary Lee Fitzhugh, the sixteen-year-old daughter of William Fitzhugh of Chatham, and brought his bride to Arlington.

George Washington Parke Custis had three passions in life—his mansion, George Washington, and his daughter Mary. He was a splendid ne'er-do-well, raconteur, genial host, and visionary. Washington had hoped to provide him with an education, but young Custis was removed from school when Washington found it "impractical to keep him in college with any prospect of advantage, so great was his aversion to study."[1] Custis then attempted an army career, but found it incompatible with his artistic temper. So he retired to Arlington, where he made a hobby of puttering on the estate farms, extolling the virtues of Washington, and idolizing his daughter.

Custis, proud of his nickname, "the Child of Mount Vernon," loved to give orations on Washington's brilliance. A frustrated thespian, he composed numerous historical dramas and wrote gaudy epic poems about Washington's greatness. He also turned Arlington into a museum of Washington lore, which he delighted in displaying to visitors. The house contained the china presented to Washington by the Society of the Cincinnati, the lantern from the hall at Mount Vernon, Washington's books and bookcase, the bed upon which he died, clothing, and many other items. The household even harbored Mrs. Washington's maid, Caroline Branham, who had been present at Washington's death.

Custis gave lavish parties, at which he regaled guests with stories of Washington. He enjoyed the good life, and was determined that his daughter Mary should experience the same. The Custises had four children, but all save Mary died in infancy. She became the idolized daughter, the "Child of Arlington" on whom Custis and his wife lavished all of their affection.

Mary Custis never seemed to break away from the father to whom she was devoted—or from Arlington. She loved the spacious gardens of hyacinths and bluebells-of-Scotland. The magnificent boxwoods, the snowball bushes, the eleven varieties of roses—all were dear to Mary Custis. Later her daughter Mildred recalled that "her thoughts were ever in the past at Arlington—always Arlington."[2] As a young woman she enjoyed the society of northern Virginia and Washington. A stream of suitors crossed the Potomac to pay her court, including Congressman Sam Houston. Later, when she married Robert Lee, her bridesmaids were from the blue book of northern Virginia aristocracy.

After her marriage, held in the Arlington drawing room in June 1831, somehow Mary Lee never left the mansion. Following a long wedding party, the couple prepared for the journey to Lee's post assignment at Fort Monroe, Virginia. Mary Lee was unhappy, for the small, cramped quarters of a second lieutenant were a far cry from the hospitality of her father's estate, and her personality did not encourage contentment. She did not make friends easily, and unlike her gregarious husband, she detested parties. Prior to the marriage, Lee had been very active in the fort's social life, sometimes escorting the wives of absent officers. But now he refused many invitations. In fact, Lee sometimes expressed pleasure at Mary's absence from the fort, which gave him the opportunity to socialize. Of one such absence he confided to a friend, "I am as happy as a clam at high water."[3]

Mary's absences became more frequent, for her family ties were a powerful force. Only a few days after the first departure for Fort Monroe, her mother wrote:

> I will not attempt to tell you how I felt at your departure. I hastened to turn from my own loss to a contemplation of your happiness. United to the man of your choice, you could I am sure find enjoyment in far less favorable circumstances than those in which you are now placed.[4]

Meanwhile, her daughter would respond: "What ... would I give for one stroll on the hills at Arlington this bright day."[5]

Her visits back to Arlington lengthened. In December of that first year, the young couple returned on leave to Arlington for Christmas. An active social season revived the old memories. Shortly after the holiday, Mary Lee confided to a friend that "I am now a wanderer on the face of the earth and know not where we are going next and hope it will be East." Of her visit with her mother, Mary Lee exclaimed, "What happiness! I am with mine now—the past and the future disregarded."[6]

So when Lee prepared to return to Fort Monroe, both daughter and parents begged that she be allowed to remain for a while. But the stay lengthened into months of separation. Impatiently, Lee wrote her early in May that "I can't consent to your remaining longer than the first of June." By June 2, he wrote:

> Yet you say everything is for the best, though I must acknowledge it sometimes passes my poor comprehension to understand it. But

Molly we have been writing mighty short letters to each other lately. I think your last was even worse than mine. And what fatigued you so much? . . . I will tell you Mrs. Lee before you come down that I will keep a remarkably tight rein over you this summer and you will not be allowed to do as heretofore.[7]

Mary Lee returned to Fort Monroe in the summer, but so unable to bear separation from her family that Mrs. Custis came also. Through 1832 she continually returned to Arlington. Then, eager to improve her quarters, Mary and her mother brought servants to the fort. A frustrated Robert Lee then wrote:

I know your dear mother will be for giving you *everything* and she has; but you must recollect *one* thing, and that is, that they have been accustomed to comforts all their lives . . .[8]

Not all of her absence from Lee was due to devotion to parents and Arlington. Beginning in 1835, Mary Lee, never of a strong constitution, entered over thirty years of constant illness which would eventually reduce her to a total invalid. After the birth of their second child in the fall of 1835, she became ill with what doctors termed "rheumatic disthesis." Weak and emaciated, she suffered from painful abscesses in her groin and was unable to stand. She was bedridden for months, and it was the spring of 1836 before she was able to walk.

Her sickness was a constant topic in her husband's letters. That first October he reported that his wife "is still as weak and helpless as ever and confined to bed." Later, "she is dreadfully reduced and so weak that she cannot stand." In November 1835, Lee admitted that "I have been now more than a month under most miserable apprehensions."[9]

But recovery did not come. In early 1836, Lee reported her "very liable to cold and its effects." In June 1837, Lee left his family at Arlington for duties at St. Louis. He was absent until Christmas, and planned to return in warmer weather with Mary, though he feared "the discomfort she will be put to."[10]

Mary Lee stayed in St. Louis for a year, spoke of little but returning to Arlington, and despite her husband's pleas, insisted in May 1839 on a return to Virginia. Sadly Lee took her to Arlington and went back to St. Louis, "turned out upon the world again as a *lone man.*" Not until Christmas, after another eight months of separation, did Lee get back to Arlington.[11]

During these absences, Lee vented his frustration and loneliness. In 1840 he begged his wife to

write regularly and often. While both of us are changing our positions so frequently, we ought not to allow many days to intervene between our letters or to wait for replies, or the consequence will be that we shall hear rarely and unsatisfactorily of each other.[12]

In 1853, from Jefferson Barracks, Missouri, Lee wrote:

I am conscious however, of having lost a great deal that is desirable and what I value more than anything else, the society of you and my children. Still . . . I could not have done otherwise. . . . I did not consult my ease or personal pleasure, but what I conceded to be my duty.[13]

Later, Lee expressed irritation at his absence: "I feel it the more in consequence of my separation from you and my inability personally to administer to your comfort . . ." Lee hoped to be with her, but "I unfortunately belong to a profession that debars all hope of domestic enjoyment." Such a profession "cannot be performed, without a sacrifice of personal and private relations . . ." Lee grew morose when he thought of his children, and thought sadly that "probably they and I will never meet again."[14]

As the secession crisis gathered, Lee in 1860 deplored these absences:

We must hope that in time they will end and that they are now permitted by our merciful God for our good. We must therefore lay nothing too much to heart: desire nothing too eagerly, rejoice not excessively . . .[15]

But the opportunities did not come in time. Mary Lee could scarcely walk, and eventually was confined to a wheelchair. Lee's wartime letters are filled with sadness. From Savannah in 1861 he wrote his daughters, "I wish indeed I could see you, be with you, and never again part from you." In the spring of 1862 he wrote his daughter Agnes:

I think of you all, separately and collectively, in the busy hours of the day and the silent hours of the night and the recollection of each and every one while away the long night . . .[16]

In the summer, on the Peninsula line, he expressed his frustration to Mary:

I want to see you all very much but have not time. . . . I hope our merciful father in heaven will in his own time relieve us from our present troubles and enable us once more to enjoy the society of each other and our dear children.[17]

The years of strain were prompted by more than Mary Lee's Arlington ties and her ill health. One must ask why Lee married her.

Several possible reasons emerge besides love. Four decades after his mother's death, Robert Lee, himself with scarcely a year of life remaining, could recall his sorrow at her bedside as if it were "but yesterday." It had been a summer in 1813 when poverty-stricken General Light-Horse Harry Lee, possessed of wretched health and tarnished reputation, had shambled aboard a ship bound for Barbados. Anxious to recover his health and to escape the disgrace of his financial escapades, Harry Lee in effect abandoned his family and never returned. Already a stranger to his children because of disinterest and long absences from home, he would be only a memory. His wife, Ann Carter, would speak of herself as a "widow."[18]

Lee's biographers have stressed the care Robert devoted to his mother after the family moved to Alexandria in 1813. It was a poignant saga of the devoted son ministering to a mother who was ill. With sons Carter at Harvard and Sidney Smith at sea in the navy, Ann Carter Lee became dependent upon Robert, so much so that when he left for West Point she observed, "How can I live without Robert? He is both son and daughter to me." Young Robert Lee was the housekeeper, managed the grounds, and attended to the marketing. Often when his schoolmates were at play, Lee would be taking his invalid mother for a carriage drive, amusing her with conversation, or mixing her medicines.[19]

To her death, Robert Lee was his mother's son. He missed the companionship of a father, and Light-Horse Harry's pathetic letters from his various places of exile could only represent to Robert a lesson of the misspent life. Lee also missed the benefits of a normal, carefree youth. He did not abandon all the usual boyhood pursuits—he was an excellent swimmer, horseman, and skater. But his constant attention to his mother made for an austere youth. When Ann Carter Lee died in 1829, shortly after Lee's graduation from West Point, he was at her bedside, mixing her medicines and ministering to her.

The sobriety of the household and the precepts that Ann Carter Lee passed on to her son affected his personality in many ways. His concept of duty, his self-denial and self-discipline, his fear of personal failure—all were rooted in his abnormal boyhood experience. Rooted there as well were drives that perhaps affected his marriage. Lee hungered for the happiness of a normal family situation. More important, he longed for affection.

He was probably deeply influenced by his first assignment as a young lieutenant of engineers in 1829 when he was ordered to Cockspur Island, in the Savannah River. Before reporting for duty, Lee stopped in Savannah to visit the family of an old West Point chum, Jack Mackay.

Lee became enamored of the entire Mackay family. The Robert Mackay home on Broughton Street radiated both happiness and hospitality. Urbane, Edinburgh-educated Robert Mackay was dead, but his widow Elizabeth maintained a lively social life with her six children. Two of the daughters enchanted Lee—twenty-year-old Margaret and her beautiful younger sister Eliza.

Lee never forgot his happy times in the Broughton Street home. To him, the Mackay home was "that spot of spots, that place of places." A letter from the Mackay family was deemed "worth a dozen from any other spot." Lee would tell his friend Jack that "I am famishing for the sight" of the Mackays, for "the idea alone thrills through the heart, like the neigh of my blooded stallion . . ."[20]

His interest in the Mackay women was important. Despite his austere boyhood, Lee was a passionate soul, flirtatious and easily led into love. Lee men had always been notorious admirers of women. Robert Lee fell in love with both Mackay sisters. The eldest, Margaret, whom he claimed to "love dearly," rejected him and married a Georgia doctor-planter.[21]

Even after his engagement to Mary Custis, Lee was still enamored of dark-eyed Eliza Mackay. In the spring of 1831, months after becoming engaged to Mary Custis, Lee told Eliza that "I have not had the heart to go to Savannah since you left it." He reflected on how the two of them had once exchanged sketches, and asked her to "recollect you have been *owing* me a drawing (and some other things too) for a long time." In 1832, six months after his own marriage, Lee heard of the impending wedding of Eliza and wrote his apology for not attending the ceremony:

> . . . this cannot be Miss Eliza (my sweetheart) because it only arrived here last night, by this token that I have been in tears ever since the thought of *losing* you.[22]

Two years later he chided Jack Mackay for "not one word about them all on Broughton Street, the place I most wished to hear from," and especially "not a syllable concerning Miss Eliza." Lee's fascination with Eliza Mackay would be enduring. From the Texas frontier in 1856 he wrote her, speaking of a recent letter received from her:

> I have carried it with me in all my wanderings—Have read and re-read it and each perusal has brought me fresh and pleasant thought.[23]

Also, Lee may have sought a mother image in Mrs. Custis. Like his mother, she was deeply religious, quiet, and deferred to her husband's wishes. Lee may have seen in her the embodiment of his own mother. He deeply loved Mary Lee Fitzhugh, and often referred to her as his mother. Once, musing over a possible return to Arlington, Lee wrote Mrs. Custis: "Then mother we could all live together and enjoy the daily expansion of our little children."[24] When she died in 1853, a grief-stricken Lee remarked that "as a son I have always loved her, and as a son I deeply mourn her," for "she was to me all that a mother could be . . ."[25]

Arlington offered other advantages. Lee was poor and had no prospect of inheritance. Lee men usually married well, and Robert Lee had been trained in the family tradition: "Never marry unless you can do so into a family which will enable your children to feel proud of both sides of the house." A serious student of his family genealogy, Lee must have realized that in the previous five generations, his male ancestors had bettered or maintained their status by fortuitous marriages. Often these unions involved younger sons, of little property, who wed wealthy heiresses.[26]

The marriage to Mary Custis would make Lee the heir to the tradition of Mount Vernon. Perhaps he was as much enamored of Arlington as he was of Mary. Douglas Freeman observed that Lee "had come to view duty as Washington did, to act as he thought Washington would, and even, perhaps to emulate the grave, self-contained courtesy of the great American rebel."[27] Nor was it exaggeration when a Lee relative, Edward Childe, observed that the Lee-Custis marriage, "in the eyes of the world, made Robert Lee the representative of the family of the founder of American history."[28]

Washington was the central hero of Lee's life. His practice of duty, tact, and self-discipline often seemed a conscious effort to emulate Washington. Governor Henry Wise once twitted him, "General Lee, you certainly play Washington to perfection."[29]

He not only identified with Washington, but basked in the glory of the Washington heritage. Washington had been a close companion of his cavalry commander, Light-Horse Harry Lee. After Harry Lee's disgrace, the family moved to Alexandria, a Washington shrine. Christ Church maintained Washington's pew Number Five, and had a Bible once owned by the first President which George Washington Parke Custis had given the church. Washington had drilled his militia in the old marketplace, and had repeated the response in the Masonic Hall. As Freeman observed, in the Lee home "God came first and then Washington."[30]

As children, Robert Lee and Mary Custis romped through the Arlington gardens and visited the slave quarters to talk with servants who had lived at Mount Vernon. The Washington carriage—still the Custis family vehicle—stood in the carriage house.[31] Long before he paid court to Mary Custis, Lee doubtless was intrigued with this treasury of relics of his hero. Douglas Freeman noted that "to come into the atmosphere of Arlington was to Robert Lee almost like living in the presence of his foremost hero."[32]

Whatever prompted Lee's marriage to Mary Custis, it did not provide him with the emotional satisfaction he desired. His love for Mary appeared almost devoid of romance, a duty both strained and strengthened by her invalidism. The marriage may have brought him more frustration than anything else. Long absences at far-flung military posts, concern for Mary's health, homesickness, brooding over the fate of his children, the near formality of a marriage between Mary Custis and the man she called "Mr. Lee"—all affected his personality.

It produced in Lee a craving for affection and emotional satisfaction. Though his boyhood may have been severe, Lee by the end of his West Point career was handsome, robust, attractive to women, and exceptionally gregarious. Thus he found escape in a type of relationship with women, frequently engaging in harmless flirtation and sometimes falling in love.

Lee's personal letters to friends are filled with humorous, almost spicy remarks concerning women whom he escorted—or flirted with— at military social functions. In 1832, while Mary Lee hovered with her parents at Arlington, Lee joked to her about these activities:

> Let me tell you Mrs. Lee, no later than today did I escort Miss T. to see Miss Kate! Think of that Mrs. Lee. And hasten now, if you do not want to see me turned out beaux again.[33]

From Fort Monroe, Lee, always fond of a "frolick," wrote Jack Mackay:

> As for the Daughters of Eve in this country, they are formed in the very poetry of nature, and would make your lips water and fingers tingle. They are beginning to assemble to put their beautiful limbs in this salt water, and among the rest we expect some friends of ours![34]

In February 1835, Lee's brother Sidney Smith married Anna Maria Mason. Robert Lee wrote exultantly to Mackay of the "grand frolick" which had lasted for a week. Of the extravagant party at Arlington, Lee reported to another comrade, Andrew Talcott:

> My spirits were so buoyant when relieved from the eyes of my

Dame, that my Sister Nanie was trying to pass me off as her spouse but I was not going to have my sport spoiled in that way and deceived the young ladies and told them I was her younger brother. Sweet innocent young things, they concluded I was single and I have not had such soft looks and tender pressures of the hand for many years.[35]

Particularly up to the 1840s, Lee spiced his letters to close friends with accounts of "frolicks" or general comments about women. In 1835 he instructed Mackay to "kiss *all* of your family for me and any of the pretty girls that will let you."[36] In 1836, after the birth of a daughter, he confided to Andrew Talcott that "I have given all the young ladies a holy day and hurry home to her every day."[37] He apologized for not writing Jack Mackay from Arlington, blaming his military duties and "the no less important ones to the pretty girls—God bless them." In 1837, from St. Louis, he wrote a friend that most things there displeased him save "the pretty girls, if there are any here, and I know there are, for I have met them in no place, in no garb, in no situation that I did not feel my heart open to them like a flower to the sun."[38]

Aside from such general teasing, there was a deeper longing for affection. From his youthful days at Fort Monroe through the Civil War, he showed the need for some emotional relationship, often half fatherly, with women.

The first was Harriet Randolph Hackley of Norfolk. A kinswoman of Mary Custis, she came to Fort Monroe as the bride of Lee's close friend and superior, Captain Andrew Talcott. Harriet Talcott's portrait by Thomas Sully reveals a stunning woman. For ten years Robert Lee was her devoted courtier. He never addressed her by first name, but by several pet nicknames, including "my beautiful Talcott" and "Talcott my beautiful." They teased often, in many letters. Harriet Talcott seemed always to be in his thoughts. In November 1834, he implored Andrew to "give my love to *my beautiful Talcott* and tell her I am sparing her that she may recruit herself for a separate epistle which I will inflict upon her as soon as I get time." In notes to her husband, he always sent "my love to *my beautiful Talcott.* In one letter to Andrew, Lee wistfully wrote:

Please give our best love and thanks to Mrs. T. and say that in all things she displays a pure and elegant taste except—Oh me! in choosing you instead of myself.

Shortly thereafter, he expressed disappointment in not receiving a note from her, as "I had anticipated that by this time *our beautiful* Talcott had *something* to tell me." In another letter, Lee told her husband:

Tell Mrs. T. that I am afraid to send her any more messages: that I delight to pay compliments to those so well deserving them, though I am not ambitious to pass encomiums on her good nature however just in the manner she insinuates. I hope for those already presented she will give me her pardon, and attribute my errors to a slight use of spirits occasioned by a coincidence of several events.[39]

Lee would see less of Harriet Talcott after 1835, for the following summer her husband resigned from the army. Deeply disappointed, Lee "was thereby left in ignorance too of your future plans . . . as well as the opinions and feelings of my *beautiful Talcott* upon this *unnatural* separation." His infatuation with her had been a source of emotional nourishment, however vicarious the relationship had been. Perhaps nothing is more revealing than a note Lee sent her in 1836:

I had much to say to you which I must now keep for the next time, and in the language of a young nimrod from the West, declining an appt. of this year to the M. Acad. "I hope my country will not be endangered by my so doing." But *Talcott my Beauty*, how could you have served your uncle so![40]

The successor to Eliza and Margaret Mackay and Harriet Talcott as the source of Lee's pleasure was Martha Custis Williams. By 1840 "Markie" Williams, great-granddaughter of Martha Washington and a cousin of Lee's wife, was a beautiful teenager who often stayed at Arlington.

Markie Williams and Robert Lee maintained a voluminous correspondence that lasted over twenty-five years. However harmless, it seems evident that Markie Williams was the object of Lee's love.

The closeness of the relationship was first evidenced in 1844, when Lee was stationed at Fort Hamilton, New York. Lee's letters are filled with gentle affection: "Oh Markie, Markie, when will you ripen?" "I cannot refrain from thanking you for your charming long letter, which I have been enjoying ever since its arrival." "My dearest Markie . . . if we had have required to be reminded of you, you would have constantly been brought before us through the power of *association*." "Your good long letter my dearest Markie gave me infinite pleasure. I have thought upon it, dwelt upon it . . . and have not done with it yet. I only wish you had brought it yourself . . ."[41] By 1851 Lee, after not writing to her for three months, would say:

On paper Markie, I mean, on paper. But oh, what lengthy epistles have I indited to you in my mind! Had I any means to send them, you would see how constantly I think of you. I have followed you in your pleasures and your duties, in the house and in the streets, and accompanied you in your walks to Arlington, and in your search after flowers. Did you not feel your cheeks *pale* when I was so near you? You may feel pale; but I am happy to say you never write as if you were pale; and to my mind you always appear bright and rosy.[42]

Lee reflected upon his engineering work at Baltimore, and how steam pile drivers were poor topics for correspondence.

If it was not for my heart Markie, I might as well be a pile or stone myself, laid quietly at the bottom of the river. But that has no hardness for you, and always returns warmth and softness when touched with a thought of you.[43]

For years the gentle relationship continued. While superintendent of West Point in 1854, Lee received a letter and immediately attached it to his pocket watch,

where it now feels the beatings of a grateful heart for your consideration and remembrance. So long as that heart beats it will be full of affection and gratitude for you.[44]

Lee was true to his word. In late August 1870, the correspondence still continued. Lee wrote from the Virginia Hot Springs, hoping for a visit from Markie, that "it is late for you to come here Markie for I am just going away." Within three months he was dead.[45]

Lee found affection in correspondence with a number of other women through the years. Two of these were his cousins Margaret and Caroline Stuart, beautiful daughters of Cedar Grove in King George County. Once he wrote their mother:

I cannot express the pleasure I have experienced in the society of your sweet daughters. They have furnished the only sunshine, save the occasional glimpse I have had of my own family, that has shone on my path during the war.[46]

It was a warm, half-fatherly, half-courtly correspondence which lasted from Fredericksburg into the Wilderness. From Orange Courthouse in the winter of 1863, Lee explained to Margaret its importance to him:

I take advantage of a few quiet moments this Holy morning to write to you for the thought of you always brings me pleasure, and

adds to my cause of gratitude to our Merciful God for all the bless-
ings bestowed upon me.[47]

He also corresponded with the cousin and wife of his son Rooney,
Charlotte Wickham of Shirley. After the marriage in 1859, Lee often
wrote "Chass" until her early death in December 1862. Beneath his
reserve, the inner warmth of Lee was revealed in this correspondence,
as from Richmond in 1862:

> . . . dearest Chass, and write to say that I have taken time to read
> it and enjoy it too, and shall always do so long as I love, so do not
> hesitate to write. I want to see you very much, and am always
> thinking of you. It is very hard, I think, for you to say that you did
> not want to come to me. I hope, at least, F. will be able to go to
> you, and if he does you must tell him to kiss you for me double and
> triple . . .[48]

It was the outlet described once by Lee to his friend Andrew
Talcott in 1837, when noting the social life in Washington, where
"among them were some very pretty girls, in whom you know I take
great pleasure."[49] The inner loneliness of Lee, the repression of a vibrant spirit, was basic to his nature.

EQUALLY VITAL was his sense of failure as a father of his children, as a
man, and as a career army officer. In 1860, when Lee congratulated
Rooney on the birth of a son, his warm note displayed fears that he had
failed as a father. He offered thanks "for this promising action of my
scattered house, who will I hope resuscitate its name and fame."[50] Lee
inwardly believed that the family name had been besmirched, and that
his long absences from home did not give proper direction to his children.

As early as 1838, while stationed at St. Louis, Lee initiated an
exhaustive research of the Lee family, which he attributed to "a little
curiosity relative to my forefathers."[51] But he knew that the golden age
of the Stratford Lees had been rocked by scandal. Robert Lee had been
three years old when the sheriff's officers had evicted his family from
Stratford Hall. It had not been the first visit. He had seen the chains his
father had secured about the Stratford doors to keep out his creditors.
Now all of the furniture was attached, adjoining estate lands were sold
for debts, the horses were gone, and the Lees were evicted.

This was the beginning of the end of Light-Horse Harry Lee's
career. He had resigned from the army in 1782, in the middle of a love

affair, and after a stint in Virginia politics, had plunged into visionary financial schemes, investing money in land speculations in the Mississippi country and other ventures. Desperately unhappy and disatisfied, he cast his net in various directions—borrowing large sums from friends and even attempting to obtain a general's commission in the revolutionary armies of France.

For a time Lee's self-control—and luck—stabilized. He succeeded temporarily in recouping his fortunes by marrying Anne Hill Carter of Shirley, seventeen years his junior and the daughter of Charles Carter, probably the richest man in Virginia. While Anne Carter Lee bore him several children, Henry Lee served another term as governor of Virginia and one in Congress, led the army that crushed the Whiskey Rebellion, and was even mentioned as a possible successor to George Washington as President.

Then Lee again lost his self-control, and attempted to accumulate a fortune. Speculation followed speculation. Heavily in debt, he neglected his family, spending time away from home in various enterprises, including a plan to join Aaron Burr in the West.

By the time Robert Lee was two years old, his father's reputation had collapsed. The family credit was gone, and Lee was twice imprisoned for debts. Repeatedly the sheriff's officers came to Stratford, until Light-Horse Harry and his family were forced to remove to Alexandria. In 1812, he was wounded by a mob in a Baltimore riot, and the next year he left for Barbados.

It was a shabby affair, but not the end of the Lee scandals. Henry Lee, Robert's half brother and heir to Stratford, inherited his father's love for dalliance. In 1817 he had married Anne McCarthy, the richest heiress in Westmoreland County. Relishing the life of the country gentleman, Henry Lee neglected the Stratford lands and soon accumulated heavy debts.

Henry, later dubbed "Black-Horse Henry," had an affair with his wife's sister, whom he had succeeded in making his ward. A child was born, and later the courts discovered large deficits in her estate under Henry's care. By 1828 the Lee empire had collapsed. Stratford was sold for $11,000 and passed forever from control of the Lees.[52]

To a man long absent from his family and desirous that his sons "resuscitate" the "name and fame" of the Lees, such events could only be object lessons. Robert Lee was troubled by the memory of the family disgrace, and by the fear that his constant absence from the children might have the same results.[53]

He wrote long exhortations to Mary Lee on the subject of child care, and preachments to his children regarding their behavior. As early as 1837, referring to the conduct of one of the children, Lee wrote:

. . . it is our duty if possible to counteract them and assist him to bring them under his control. . . . I have also tried to show him that I was firm in my demands, constant in their enforcement, and that he must comply with them. . . . I *must* believe now that I have been unfortunate in my efforts since the result has been so unsuccessful . . .[54]

Two years later Lee urged his wife "to be very prudent and careful of these dear children," to "exercise firm authority over all of them," and not let them "run wild in my absence." Particularly after 1850, Lee voiced frustration that he was unable to guide the children. Once he told his son Rooney:

When I think of your youth, impulsiveness, and many temptations, your distance from me, and the case (and even innocence) with which you might commence an erroneous course, my heart quails within me, and my whole frame and being trembles at the possible result.

Lee hounded his children with long letters on conduct. To a child in 1845 he implored, "You must endeavor to learn, in order to compensate me for the pain I suffer in being separated." To his son, the object lesson was his brother Rooney, who had recently lost the tips of some fingers in an accident at Fort Hamilton. Lee only briefly mentioned the accident, and spent paragraphs moralizing upon its implications. It was, he hoped, "a warning to you to meddle or interfere with nothing with which you have no concern . . ." Of Rooney and his damaged fingers, Lee wrote little save to hammer at his sins:

Although he is at times obstinate and disobedient, which are grave faults, he has some very good qualities. . . . I hope this will be a lesson to him and that in time he will correct his evil ways.[55]

Lee's concern for the "evil ways" of his children increased as years of separation convinced him that he was failing in his duties as a parent. In 1846 he instructed a son to take care of his mother and sisters:

To do that you must learn to be good. Be true, kind, and generous, and pray earnestly to God to enable you to keep his commandments, and walk in the same all the days of your life.[56]

The separation during the Mexican War intensified Lee's fear for his children. En route by ship to Mexico, he wrote his two eldest sons:

I shall not feel my long separation from you if I find my absence has been of no injury to you, and that you have both grown in goodness, and knowledge, as well as stature. But oh, how much I will suffer on my return, if the reverse has occurred![57]

Lee told his children they should strive to be achievers, and should do so for the sake of the family. One letter sermonized: "At times the temptation to relax will be hard upon you, but will grow feebler and more feeble by constant resistance . . . I know it will confirm you in your present resolve to try and do your best," for "the happiness which it brings to father and mother. . . . Hold yourself above every mean action. Be strictly honorable in every act, and be not ashamed to *do right.*"[58]

To his daughter Annie, while he was superintendent at West Point in 1853, Lee also emphasized upholding the family name. He hoped that "you will endeavor to improve and so conduct yourself as to make you happy and me joyful all our lives." Lee explained that "I do not know what the cadets will say if the Superintendent's children do not practice what he demands of them."[59]

Lee's preachments increased as he served on the Texas frontier, and as his sons took up their own army careers. In 1858 he apologized to Rooney: "You see I am following my old habit of giving advice," a habit "which proceeds from my great love and burning anxiety for your welfare and happiness."[60]

Lee's obsessive concern for training his children shows up in his diary, which contains long notations on child rearing. He stressed the need "not only to make the child obey externally but internally to make the obedience sincere and hearty." He mused over numerous theories as to how this could be done:

Cultivate in the child's mind, a love of candor, straightforwardness, integrity, along with a corresponding hatred of falsehood. . . . The cultivation must be by the training of motives and principles into confirmed habits.[61]

When he was home, Lee was unrelenting. Robert, Jr., remembered the intensity of his father's supervision. Upon receiving his first pair of skates, Lee asked him to make regular progress reports. After he began swimming, his father "made me describe exactly my methods and strokes, explaining to me what he considered the best way to swim, and the reasons therefor." When young Lee was allowed to have his own bedroom, his father "went through the form of inspecting it to see if I had performed my duty properly" in cleaning it.[62]

One can only conjecture about the effects of nearly two decades of such badgering, but a warping seemed evident in the personality of the

Lee children. The influence of Robert Lee upon his eldest son, Custis, has already been observed. Agnes Lee also reflected her father's consciousness of sin. There is no more poignant item in the voluminous Lee papers than the journal Agnes kept in her adolescence. She described the struggle for her soul:

> I do wish I was a Christian! but it is so hard to be one. I am afraid I don't feel that I need a Saviour as deeply as I ought. . . . Oh, that I could believe there was a place in Heaven for me . . .[63]

Later she confided, "Why I am so miserable I can't find out . . . I have such longings, sometimes, such yearnings for something I know not what." She confessed that there were occasions "when my poor, weak, miserable nature makes me despise myself." Unhappily, she prayed, "O may a time come for me, weak and wicked as I am, when I may be perfectly happy."[64]

Her sister Annie exhibited similar tendencies. In 1857, Annie wrote her friend Helen Bratt regarding long absences, and used language that smacked of her father,

> Still, Helen dear, it is best. He knows what is best for us, it will teach us not to be too happy or think too much of earth, but to lay up our treasure in Heaven, that glorious, happy home. If we could only realize that only a few short years must pass and then all must leave, how different would be our lives.

She spoke of her own moral unworthiness, and implored her friend to "take the peace and joy of casting every care and sorrow on One who had done so much for you, even shed his own precious blood that you might live."[65]

They were old before their time, trained by a father who believed that his own inadequacies made him a failure as a parent.

THE KEY TO LEE'S ATTITUDE toward his children was a belief in his failure as a man. The image of the ever-confident Lee, dominant in the Civil War over quavering opponents, is untrue. Nothing is more important to an understanding of Lee than his concept of self-failure. By the 1850s, he believed his army career had failed. Promotion had come slowly. Although he had been advanced to first lieutenant in 1836, it would be nineteen years—long after his achievements in the Mexican War—before he was promoted to lieutenant colonel.

Lee's letters, particularly after 1850, were often tinged with discouragement. From San Antonio he wrote Mary:

... unfortunately I belong to a profession that debars all hope of domestic enjoyment and the duties of which cannot be performed without the sacrifice of personal and private relations, one or the other must be abandoned.[66]

He saw little hope for the future, and told Mary that "our sons are fairly launched forth on the everchanging and tempestuous life. . . . Probably they and I will never meet again."[67]

Eventually he considered resigning from the army. In 1857 he confided to his friend Albert Sidney Johnston:

I can see that I have at least to decide the question, which I have staved off for 20 years, whether I am to continue in the Army all my life, or to leave it now. My preferences which have clung to me from boyhood impel me to adopt the former course, but yet I feel that a man's family has its claims too.[68]

Lee's growing dissatisfaction with his army life was often masked by an appeal to Divine Providence. He philosophized to his wife that "God helps those who help themselves in his own good time," and that they should "desire nothing too eagerly, nor think that all things can be perfectly accomplished, according to our notion." And when his wife hopefully mentioned that his name had been advanced for a promotion, Lee replied, "We are all in the hands of a kind God, who will do for us what is best, and more than we deserve." Hence he urged her, "Do not give yourself any anxiety about the appointment. . . . You will be sure to be disappointed . . ."

Despite such game attempts, Lee's attitude toward his future after 1850 was one of dejection. He wrote a son that as long as his children "strive to respond to my wishes . . . I can meet with calmness and unconcern all else the world may have in store for me." Later he spoke movingly of Christmas at Arlington:

Though absent, my heart will be in the midst of you, and I shall enjoy in imagination and memory all that is going on . . . I can do nothing but hope and pray for you all.[69]

In 1859, after a visit to Arlington, he prepared to return to Texas, noting that "I have no enjoyment in life now but what I derive from my children." And from San Antonio, he told Mary that "my departures grow harder to bear with years."[70] By late 1860, Lee was totally pessimistic about his future. His frustrations boiled over when he wrote his daughter:

God knows how often I think of you and long to see you. If you wish to see me you will have to come out here, for I do not know when I will be able to go in there. It is better too I hope for all that I am here. You know I was much in the way of everybody and my tastes and pursuits did not coincide with the rest of the household. Now I hope everybody is happier.[71]

Lee's sense of failure reflected a deeper conviction of inadequacy as an individual. It was a self-distrust, not unlike the depression which Light-Horse Harry Lee had undergone prior to his resignation from the army. In Robert Lee this attitude became very obvious in the 1850s. The jaunty correspondence of his earlier years was replaced by letters of a religious bent, imbued with self-criticism.

He wrote Markie Williams from West Point confessing that "I am conscious of my faults . . . and make many resolutions and attempts to do better, but fail. . . . You who know my weakness will I fear have little confidence in my success."[72] When he was ordered to Jefferson Barracks, Missouri, in 1855, Lee viewed this new separation as "a just punishment for my sins," and prayed that "I may truly repent of the many errors of my life, that my sins may be forgiven . . ." And when his grandson was born in 1860, Lee told Rooney that "I wish I could offer him a more worthy name and a better example," hoping that the new grandchild could "avoid the errors I have committed."[73]

Lee sensed a moral estrangement from God. When his wife was forced to leave Arlington in 1861, it was because "we have not been grateful enough for the happiness there within our reach." From South Carolina in 1861, he wrote to his daughter that "you see what a poor sinner I am, and how unworthy to possess what was given me; for that reason it has been taken away."[74]

Even on the march to Gettysburg, Lee's mind was turned to his sense of failure. When he learned he had been made a director of the Confederate Bible Society, he wished he "could feel worthy of these attentions, or do anything for the glory of God." Until the end, Lee evinced this spirit. From Petersburg he lamented, "How thankless and sinful I have been."[75]

LEE'S SENSE OF UNWORTHINESS was an element in his fierce devotion to Arlington and Virginia. His love for Arlington was shared by his entire family. In 1853, when his daughter Agnes prepared to move with the family to West Point, she wrote in her diary, "How can I say farewell to Arlington! How can I quit this dear place?" Later she wrote, "I long for Arlington my precious Arlington. . . . O if I could only see that peaceful spot in the woods dearer than anywhere else." Decades later, in 1890, the only surviving daughter, Mildred would hear a familiar hymn in a Lexington church and "instantly my thoughts flew to the old garden at Arlington—to a wooden bench, almost hidden by a droopy branch of seriga, my favorite hiding place in those days of long ago . . ."[76]

Arlington also haunted Robert Lee. In 1857, after the death of George Washington Parke Custis, Lee became the executor of the several family mansions. In November he obtained a two-month leave from his post at San Antonio and journeyed eastward to settle affairs. But the leave of absence developed into two years beset with frustration. The Arlington house and lands were in poor condition. White House and its four thousand acres, bequeathed to Rooney Lee, were burdened with ramshackle buildings and debt. At Romancoke, the legacy of Robert, Jr., the buildings were run-down and the fields were worn out.

For years Lee was forced to stretch the already thin Custis funds, eroded by some ten thousand dollars in debts. He also faced the problem of the eventual freeing of nearly two hundred slaves. By the terms of Custis's will, they were to be emancipated within five years. In 1860 Northern newspapers were accusing Lee of maltreatment of the slaves. So violent were the assaults that Mary Lee deemed them "villainous attacks upon my husband by name and upon my father's memory in language I would not pollute my lips by repeating."[77]

It was ironic that during the years of lonely outpost life, Lee had longed to return to Arlington. Now, when he was in the process of restoring the properties, war removed the lands from his wife's family.

Losing Arlington was a severe blow to Lee. Foremost was the sense of guilt at the loss of his wife's estate, incurred by his siding with the Confederate cause. In early May, Mary Custis Lee and the children fled Arlington and sought refuge with relatives and friends in the vicinity.

Lee deplored the necessity which forced his invalid wife to abandon the mansion. On May 25 he wrote:

I sympathize deeply in your feelings at leaving your dear home. I have experienced them myself, and they are constantly revived.[78]

By late 1861, Lee's remorse was growing. To Mary he wrote:

In my absence from you I have thought of you very often, and regretted I could do nothing for your comfort. Your old home, if not destroyed by our enemies, has been so desecrated that I cannot bear to think of it.[79]

Lee said he would rather have had the mansion "wiped from the earth" than for it "to have been degraded by the presence of those who revel in the ill they do." Lee viewed the loss of the mansion as atonement for his shortcomings:

> You see what a poor sinner I am, and how unworthy to possess what was given men; for that reason it has been taken away.[80]

The forfeit of his wife's property continued to trouble Lee during the war and until his death. At Christmas in 1861, he told his wife of his guilt, and noted:

> As to our old home, if not destroyed it will be difficult ever to be recognized. . . . It is better to make up our minds to a general loss. They cannot take away the remembrances of the spot, and the memories of those that to us rendered it sacred.[81]

In 1863, when Arlington was threatened with seizure for unpaid taxes, Lee endeavored to save his wife's lands. He told Custis Lee that "I have been much exercised as to how I can pay my taxes," and urged him to find information as to what was owed. The Lees were unable to make arrangements to pay the delinquent amount, and Arlington was sold by an auctioneer, never to return to the Custis heirs.

After the war, remorse at having caused the dispossession of his wife's estate must have borne heavily upon Lee's mind. Until his death, Arlington was a bitter memory. For several years he contacted attorneys in hopes of regaining the property, but his attempts were of no avail. A family friend, Captain James May, urged the Lees to apply to the government to return at least the Washington relics. President Andrew Johnson consented, and ordered the Secretary of the Interior to return the relics to Mrs. Lee. But an ensuing turmoil in Congress killed the project.[82]

LEE'S ATTACHMENT to Virginia was equally powerful in shaping his prewar personality. Some biographers have suggested that in wartime Lee was a parochial figure whose concern for Virginia damaged the broader Confederate effort, and have attributed his attitude to his closeness to the Virginia land. Yet it may have been his absence—not his closeness —which influenced his behavior. Few elements of frustration in Lee's prewar personality emerged more strongly than his constant homesickness for Virginia while on military duty.

Lee's intense wartime commitment to Virginia had two possible roots. One was his love for the Virginia landscape. He had been reared in the Westmoreland country, in the twilight of the eighteenth-century Virginia dynasty. He had been surrounded by the mementos of his idol, Washington, and by men who had known him.

The resultant localism was evident even when Lee was a young lieutenant. Perhaps he failed to take advantage of the opportunities which military travel presented to him. Instead of broadening the horizons of one who had never traveled or read widely, the absence from Virginia only made him perpetually homesick. From St. Louis in 1838, Lee complained, "I wish all were done and I was back in Virginia." From a steamer on the Missouri River, Lee mused, "Surely Rob't Lee you have fallen upon evil times or evil times upon you and that is because you have left Virginia."[83]

It was when he spoke of Virginia that the usually unpoetic Lee could produce admirable description. In 1861 he wrote about the western Virginia Alleghenies:

> . . . the mountains are beautiful, fertile to the tops, covered with the richest sward and blue grass and white clover. The enclosed fields wave with a natural growth of timothy.[84]

Always there was that boyish, wistful sensation. Even during the war, he eagerly wrote to a daughter who had described to him her visit to his birthplace at Stratford. Lee said that Stratford "is endeared to me by many recollections, and it has always been the desire of my life to be able to purchase it." Lee especially recalled that "the horse-chestnut you mentioned in the garden was planted by my mother," and noted that "you do not mention the spring, one of the objects of my earliest recollections." Movingly, he exclaimed, "How my heart goes back to those happy days!"[85]

Particularly by the 1850s, Lee seemed to consider himself a wanderer prevented by army service from living in Virginia. In 1853 from St. Louis, he wrote to his wife that "I am conscious however of having lost a great deal that is desirable, and what I value more than anything else, the society of you and my children." Yet he seemed resigned:

> . . . in my view of the matter I could not have done otherwise nor has my opinion changed. I did not consult my ease or personal pleasure, but what I conceived to be my duty. . . . It [separation] was a just punishment for my sins. It might also be intended to prepare you and my children for any longer absence.[86]

By the end of the decade, his misery had intensified. In 1860 he wrote Mary from San Antonio:

... my departures grow harder to bear with years. Still as there is a necessity for it they must be borne and ought not to be made worse by useless repining. We must hope that in time they will end . . .[87]

Ironically, even when he was defending Virginia during the war years, Lee felt homeless. There was almost a touch of the Cincinnatus in his letters, perhaps a conscious imitation of Washington, in his longing to avoid public life. After Antietam, Lee wrote Mary:

If God spares me to the end of the war, I trust to be with you all, at least, for the few remnant years of life; but until the war is ended . . . do I consider that anybody else has anything else to do, and during that period must make up his mind to forsake home and family.[88]

It was an expression he often used, once to a daughter in 1861. Then he had said, "I wish I could see you, be with you, and never again part with you."[89]

Lee's love for Virginia was perhaps his greatest frustration. He, of course, had never been a landholder. In late 1857, when he returned to take charge of the Arlington farm, his spirits had lifted. His son Robert, Jr., has written:

He often said that he longed for the time when he could have a farm of his own, where he could end his days in quiet and peace, interested in the care and improvement of his own land.[90]

But when Arlington was lost in 1861, Lee wrote his wife sadly:

I wish I could purchase Stratford. It is the only other place I could go to now acceptable to us, that would inspire me with pleasure and local love. . . . It is a poor place, but we could make enough cornbread and bacon for our support, and the girls could weave us clothes.[91]

It was the pipe dream that never materialized. Even in his last years, Lee lived in the college-owned house at Lexington. He once confided to a son:

I should have selected a more quiet life and a more retired abode than Lexington. I should have preferred a small farm, where I could have earned my daily bread.[92]

.   .   .

THUS, BENEATH THE SERENE LEE IMAGE, so often mentioned by his biographers, lay an unfulfilled person. How did his frustrations affect his personality? What meaning did they have for the postwar years?

Since his earliest biographers, Lee has been described accurately as a humble man. It is no contradiction to suggest that he possessed an extreme consciousness of self. The "self-conscious" Lee was a product of his self-image, which was a curious mosaic. Lee regarded himself as the savior of the family name which had been harmed by the reckless conduct of his father and his half brother.[93]

Lee was also conscious of his status as a gentleman. He was a product of the Lee-Carter marriage, had been educated in a boys' school on the Carter land, was a frequent visitor to Shirley, Stratford, and other eastern Virginia estates, and married into the aristocracy of Arlington. His military education and almost four decades of Federal service had been spent in the rigid caste system produced by West Point.

He was no social leveler; he was a man who owned slaves and who could speak of the Plains Indians as people who "give a world of trouble . . . a poor creature, they are not worth it."[94]

It was this consciousness of being a Virginia gentleman that may have motivated his kindness toward subordinates during the Civil War. Lee's courtesy to junior officers and private soldiers reflected his great human spirit. Perhaps also it was moved by a conviction that he was a gentleman and saw no need to prove it. During the war he set down his code of what such a man should be:

> The forbearing use of power does not only form a touchstone, but the manner in which an individual enjoys certain advantages over others is the test of a true gentleman. The power which the strong have over the weak . . . will show needlessly and unnecessarily remind an offender of a wrong he may have committed against him.[95]

Lee was also conscious of his popularity. Strikingly handsome, he was a welcome guest at levees, parlor conversations, and officers' parties. A son later recalled that in Baltimore, Lee "was a great favorite . . . as he was everywhere, especially with ladies and young children." As superintendent of West Point, "he was always a great favorite with the ladies, especially the young ones."[96]

More important, he was deeply aware of his position, during the war and Reconstruction, as a Southern hero symbol. Amidst the acclaim given him as commander of the new Virginia state army in 1861, his friend Bishop William Meade told him:

> ... it has been a relief to me that in the Providence of God so important a station has been assigned to you ... you are better qualified for the same than any other of our citizens of Virginia.

And W. C. Rives, another family friend, said that "the confidence and heart of the whole state are with you ..." Lee was aware of this, and in the early autumn of 1861 he warned Governor John Letcher that "you overrate me very much, and I feel humbled when I weigh myself by your standard."[97]

By 1862, after his successes against McClellan and Pope brought him more reknown, Lee confided to his wife that "I tremble for my country when I hear of the confidence expressed in me."[98]

After the war, Lee's self-awareness only intensified. Six days after Appomattox, he reluctantly consented to sit in Richmond for a Mathew Brady photograph. He reportedly asked Brady, "How can I sit for a photograph with the eyes of the world upon me as they are today."[99]

Lee was also constantly reminded of his hero status among all Southerners. Given his inner frustrations, this would have been pressure enough. The other root of Lee's self-conscious nature only complicated matters. He had a deep distrust in himself, a fear that he would err and mar the image that had been cast upon him. Particularly from the 1850s, his letters are often critical of his own behavior. Words such as "transgressions," "unworthiness," and "weakness" are seen frequently in his writing.

The origins of Lee's low opinion of himself were varied and are difficult to place exactly. Perhaps he worried that the excesses of his father's later career would be repeated by the son. His deeply entrenched Calvinistic sense of guilt may have produced his self-doubts.

Whatever the origins, this attitude, when merged with Lee's awareness that he bore a public image, produced an intriguing self-conscious individual. Aware of what others expected of him and of what he desired to be, Lee seemed to fear that his conduct would fall short of the mark.

Lee became one who had made a decision to guide his life by strict conformity to certain principles. No doubt his ideals and his concern for duty had roots much deeper than his state of mind during the 1850s. Yet the rigid personality which surfaced after the Mexican War appeared almost a deliberate effort to adopt a code of conduct. Duty became obsessive. The notes in Lee's diary on "Education" are replete with demands for blind obedience to duty, as were his letters to his children.[100]

Lee learned duty from his mother or, as Douglas Freeman suggested, absorbed it as a tenet of the aristocratic society in which he was reared. Still, the stress of the ideal may have been a compensative element, used by Lee to make up for his chronic homesickness. More than once he explained that despite deep yearnings for family and Virginia, duty demanded that he remain absent and unhappy.

Lee's self-denial also became almost Biblical. Douglas Freeman recalled the young mother who brought her baby to Lee "to be blessed," only to hear him admonish, "Teach him he must deny himself." Self-denial was also a lesson rooted in Lee's boyhood.

He had transformed a long-held attitude into a rigid principle. It produced a rationale to deal with loneliness in drab military posts. It provided compensation for an officer whose army promotion was slow while others used political channels to curry favor. Lee's diary notes on "Self-dependence" and "Moral Training" stressed the beauty of the ideal:

> The main thing to be acquired consists in habits of industry and self-denial. . . . The first business of education is to draw forth and put into habitual exercise the former dispositions, such as kindness, justice, self-denial.[101]

This same pattern may have fitted Lee's concept of self-control. Despite his violent temper, observers never failed to comment upon his serenity and self-presence. Lee once observed that humans possess various desires, some requiring encouragement, "others which for their own comfort and that of their fellow creatures must be kept in subjection." A young student at Washington College recalled the advice Lee gave him on how to achieve self-discipline:

> You will find it difficult, at first, to control the operation of your mind under all circumstances . . . but the power can be gained by determination and practice. . . . If it had not been for this power, I do not see how I could have stood what I had to go through with.[102]

Lee also reacted to his inner problems with a steady immersion in religion. His religious character has been traced since the early biographies. Lee held a simple faith in God which guided his conduct. His deeper humanity was reflected in such traits as his kindness to Federal prisoners, a willingness to share privation with his soldiers, and a concern for the army's religious welfare.

But some intriguing niches of Lee's spirituality could be overlooked. One senses that he went through the motions of formal religious practice. He had been reared in the staunch Episcopalian faith of the Lee and Carter families, and was taught the catechism at Christ Church, Alexandria. When possible, Lee attended Episcopal churches while on military duty, and in 1843 was elected a vestryman while serving at Fort Hamilton, New York.

Yet it was not until 1853, at the age of forty-six, that he was formally confirmed in the Episcopal Church. Although he never explained the reasons for the delay, they may have been tied to his view of religion. Lee was basically a Christian humanist whose religion was more of the inner self than of formal practice. He shunned debate and disliked sectarianism. Lee cared far less for a person's faith than for his spiritual life. He was moved less by loyalty to the Church than by his interest in any activity that replenished the soul.

Lee's concept of the Christian life was essential to his behavior. In the 1850s, he began a steady retreat into certain concepts of a private religion that would guide him thereafter. The same frustrations that produced his self-consciousness led him toward religious codes that would have great impact on his personality.

One was a total commitment to Divine Providence, an admission that his own unhappiness was the will of God and thus should not be questioned. This belief was evident in many of his writings. Two family members died in that decade. When Mary Lee's mother, Mary Custis, passed away in 1853, Lee said, "As a son I have always loved her, as a son I deeply mourn her." To Mary he wrote, "May God give you strength to bear it and enable us to say 'his will be done.' "[103] The same code applied in 1856 when he learned of the death in Paris of his sister, Mildred Childe. Alone with his grief on the Texas plains, Lee trusted "that our merciful God only so suddenly and early snatched her away because he saw that it was the fittest moment to take her to himself."[104] The same code applied to other frustrations. He explained to his daughter Mildred that her mother's growing invalidism was God-sent:

> Perhaps God has thus afflicted her to try her children and give them an opportunity of showing their appreciation of all she has done for them. Do not invite his anger by your neglect.[105]

He often sent similar explanations to Mary Lee. From Texas he wrote that "we must bow with humble resignation to all the chastisements of our heavenly Father."[106]

Lee also used Divine Providence as a rationale for his unhappiness with military service. By 1857, separation from his family and concern for his wife's illness had become almost unbearable, and Lee contemplated resignation from the army. He preferred to stay, "yet I feel that a man's family has its claims too." Whatever the outcome, "we must not repine, but be resigned, knowing that [God] will not afflict us but for our own good."[107]

Other facets of Lee's prewar army life were seen as controlled by God. During the time of slow promotion, when his wife hoped that he might be elevated in command, Lee wrote that "we are all in the hands of a kind God, who will do for us what is best . . ." Later in 1860, after his return to Texas, which only promised more loneliness, Lee wrote to Custis, "But God's will be done! It will only prepare us for a longer separation soon to come."[108]

Lee's belief in God's intervention was an important part of his wartime personality as well. Much has been written of the Puritan nature of Stonewall Jackson. Yet Lee was no less a Puritan. He saw the Southern army as controlled by a divine hand, and believed that battles were determined by God. After the victory at First Manassas: "I hope God will again smile on us . . ." When an attack plan failed in the 1861 West Virginia campaign: "I had taken every precaution to insure success . . . but the Ruler of the Universe willed otherwise, and sent a storm to disconcert the well-laid plan." In 1862, when McClellan menaced Richmond, Lee hoped that "a kind Providence will protect us and drive them back." When Burnside's army threatened Fredericksburg, Lee wrote that "I pray God that he will confuse their counsels and return them to their own country."

In the critical spring and summer of 1863, his philosophy never wavered. After defeating Hooker at Chancellorsville, Lee issued a General Order offering thanks "to the only Giver of Victory." When he rode northward to failure at Gettysburg, Lee hoped that God "will deliver us by his Almighty-hand." To his cousin Margaret Stuart, Lee interpreted the defeat as a situation where "God willed otherwise."[109]

Lee was totally convinced of the justness of the Southern cause. How could such a noble effort fail? He often interpreted defeat as punishment by God for his own shortcomings or those of the Confederate people. Arlington was lost because "we have not been grateful enough for the happiness there within our reach." The disasters of Roanoke Island, Fort Donelson, and Fort Henry in 1862 came because "it is necessary we should be humbled and taught to be less boastful, less selfish, and more devoted to right . . ."

But Lee watched the Southern war effort steadily crumble. He finally explained the collapse as the work of the inscrutable will of God. A remark uttered after his own loss at Malvern Hill summarized his credo: "God knows what is best for us."[110]

By the 1850s, Lee had not only committed himself fully to God's designs, but had adopted a death fixation and a sense of otherworldliness.

He seemed to believe that death would be a welcome release from this world. When his mother-in-law, Mary Custis, died in 1853, Lee observed that he did not grieve for her; rather, as he told his wife:

> ... it is for you, your poor father, for myself, the children, relatives, friends and servants, I grieve. Not for her. She has gone from all the trouble, care and sorrow to a happy immortality.

When her husband, George Washington Parke Custis, expired in 1857, Lee said that "we must hope the one taken is best prepared to go, the time selected is the best for that one." And on the death of his sister Mildred, Lee noted that she "has preceded me in that long journey, on which we are all hurrying."[111]

When his daughter Annie passed away in 1862, Lee comforted her sister Mildred by saying that "we should rejoice at her translation from this world of sorrow." And to his wife Lee wrote, "When I reflect on all she will escape in life, brief and painful at the best ... I can not wish her back."[112]

Sometimes Lee's comments on the pleasant release of death revealed an almost suicidal tendency. After Gettysburg, when he brooded over the Confederate casualties, he remarked that "my only consolation is that they are the happier and we that are left are to be pitied." After First Manassas, the emphasis again was on the pleasure of death. To Mary Lee he wrote:

> Do not grieve for the brave dead. Sorrow for those they left behind —friends, relatives, and families. The former are at rest. The latter must suffer.[113]

In 1857 Lee wrote to Mary from a dusty Texas outpost just after he had read the funeral service for a dead child. He believed that it was better for the child to die "in purity and innocence," because he "has been saved from sin and misery here." Or perhaps it was better said by Lee when he observed the encircling Federal lines shortly before the surrender at Appomattox. Realizing now that he was defeated, he remarked, "How easily I could be rid of this, and be at rest. I have only to ride along the line and all will be over!"[114]

Lee's frequent mention of the release that death would provide revealed another element of his personality. Early biographers always lauded his serenity and self-possession. Actually Lee's mood of depression became a central part of his behavior. He seemed to pity himself, and was convinced that his star had been ill-destined.

Lee's wartime correspondence often showed unhappiness and self-pity. When he spoke of the loss of Arlington he said that "my own

sorrows sink into insignificance." In 1862, when he lamented his continuing separation from his family, Lee wrote, "I hope our merciful father
in heaven will in his own time relieve us from our present troubles."
Yet he soon reflected, "I can not see a single ray of pleasure during this
war." Of his daughter Annie's death, Lee mused, "It is a bright angel
in Heaven, free from the pains and sorrows of this world." And later
came other comments, such as: "Old age and sorrow is wearing me
away" and "I know affliction has been sent me by a merciful God for
my good."[115]

So ROBERT LEE came to the years of secession and war. What did his
personality portend for his generalship? His wartime career has often
been described in a vacuum, with scant treatment of the effects of the
previous fifty-four years upon his leadership.

We know much—and little—about Robert Lee as a secessionist and
war leader. We do know that in 1861 Lee was held in high esteem by
professional military men, for both ability and character. Certainly at
the time of the Fort Sumter crisis, Lee was scarcely known by the
average Southerner.

But his popularity among peers dated back to the Mexican War.
Lee was in that cadre of favored officers who fought with Winfield Scott
from Veracruz to Mexico City in 1847. After the capture of the Mexican
capitol, men like Lee, McClellan, and Beauregard formed a long-lasting
fraternity, the Aztec Club. They would see much of each other within
the next thirteen years, and were the framework of most important
military commands. For example, in 1855, the officers of the Second
Cavalry made up a roster of future Civil War luminaries—Lee, Albert
Sidney Johnston, George Thomas, Earl Van Dorn, and others.

None of these men spoke of Lee save in terms of affection and
respect. One of his captains, later the Confederate General John Bell
Hood, said that early service on the Brazos River instilled in him an
undying "affection and veneration" for Lee.[116] Another who knew Lee
well during the Texas days was the staunch Unionist—and later Ohio
governor—Charles Anderson. He recalled that when Lee came in 1860
to command the Department of Texas, the Virginian was "the nearest
in likeness to that classical ideal, Chevalier Bayard—*Sans peur et sans
reproche.*"[117]

More important, Lee by 1861 was clearly the favorite lieutenant of
the nation's ranking military officer, Winfield Scott. He had won his
fellow Virginian's respect by his remarkable service as a scout on the
long march from Veracruz to Mexico City. His bold reconnaissances did
much to ensure victory in the battles of Cerro Gordo, Contreras, and
Churubusco. Lee was commended in Scott's battle reports more than

any other officer, and was characterized as "constantly distinguished," "conspicuous," and "daring." Shortly after the occupation of Mexico City, Scott's officers feted him at a grand banquet. At the close, Scott rose, rapped on the table, and offered a toast to "the health of Captain Robert E. Lee, without whose aid we should not now be here."

Scott's admiration for Captain Lee never diminished. After the Mexican War, he remarked to Colonel Erasmus Keyes that "if hostilities should break out between our country and England, it would be cheap for the United States to insure Lee's life for $5,000,000 a year!" In 1854 he told an Ohio politician that Lee was "the best soldier in Christendom."[118]

It was no surprise that in 1861 Winfield Scott tried to make Lee the principal Union field commander. The exact nature of the offer remains vague. Twice Lee rode across the Potomac to discuss his future in the United States army. The first occasion, shortly after his return from Texas in March, involved a three-hour conversation in which, Douglas Freeman surmises, Scott offered Lee the second-in-command of the army. Lee himself later recalled that the subject of his being given the command of Union forces was never discussed with Scott. Yet Scott later told Charles Anderson that in one of the two conversations he informed Lee that "if you remain by the old flag . . . you will be placed in supreme command of the armies of the United States, subject only to a normal command in myself."[119]

Certainly the offer appears to have been made. On April 18 Lee again crossed the Potomac to meet at Blair House with Lincoln's trusted adviser, Francis Blair. Blair had talked with Lincoln of Lee's future, and now made the outright offer. A large field army, perhaps 100,000 men, would soon be mobilized to suppress the rebellion. Not only Winfield Scott but Abraham Lincoln too wanted Lee to have the command.

After Lee's historic refusal, he went immediately to Scott's office. He told Scott of the offer and of his unwillingness to take up arms against Virginia. Then followed Scott's oft-quoted reply, "You have made the greatest mistake of your life, but I feared it would be so."[120]

Lee well knew that a thirty-year career in the military—the only profession he had ever known—was being abandoned. He also realized that his reputation as a career officer was at its peak. He was spurning the outright offer of advancement from colonel to commanding general of the Union's main field force.

There were other matters which Lee probably reflected on as he rode back to Arlington after the last meeting with Scott. Lee disliked secession, and had observed earlier in the year that "secession is nothing but revolution." He felt that the framers of the Constitution did not intend for the government "to be broken by every member of the Confederacy at will," and resented the "selfish, dictatorial bearing" of the cotton South. He reminded a son a few months before his resignation that in the early days of the Republic secession was considered treason. Hence, "What can it be now?"[121]

FOR A CENTURY serious military observers have considered Lee the South's greatest military leader. To William Swinton, Lee was easily "the Confederacy's foremost military leader." Historian T. Harry Williams, who sometimes viewed Lee's abilities with reserve, described him as "the Confederacy's best general."[122]

The qualities of military genius that have attracted such praise are also well known. These attributes were a mark of the still important power of the individual in military leadership. Certainly Lee's formal military education entailed those same rudiments of West Point theory taught to men whom he defeated. General John Pope, of the class of 1842, had been tutored by Professor Dennis Mahan in the same Napoleonic-Jominian principles used by Lee when he boldly divided his army and routed Pope at the battle of Second Manassas. General Joseph Hooker, class of 1837, was equally well exposed to Colonel Guy De Vernon's textbook on the science of war. Yet Hooker's division of force at Chancellorsville, a truly Napoleonic movement, collapsed in humiliation.

Hooker's mental disintegration at Chancellorsville underscored a well-known quality of Lee's generalship. Whatever the alchemy, much of Lee's success was due to his character. The Civil War, though altered drastically by the Minié bullet and the railroad, was still fought in an era when the moral force of a general could prove decisive.

Napoleon mused that "the personality of the general is indispensable, he is the head, he is the all of an army." The Prussian theorist Clausewitz spoke of times when an army, weary or demoralized, resisted its own commander, and could be overcome only by "great force of will." T. Harry Williams dissected this element and described it as a "mental strength and moral power" which enabled a strong man to deal with crisis.[123]

Lee certainly possessed this element of strength. At its heart was that balance in his outward nature. It involved the ability to dominate —but not one's subordinates. It entailed being able to raise an army's élan by one's very presence, yet not to become intoxicated by knowledge of such power. It was a refusal to be intimidated by exaggerated accounts of an enemy's numbers, while maintaining a cautious respect.

Lee's character was well summarized in a vignette related by Bruce Catton. It was the spring of 1864, and General James Longstreet's corps had just returned to Virginia after seven hard months on the western front. Shabby and weary, Longstreet's veterans had little but bitter memories . . . the fruitless victory at Chickamauga . . . the slaughter at the battle of Knoxville . . . the miserable eastern Tennessee winter.

Now Lee rode out to welcome them back, and a bugle signaled his arrival. He gazed upon them, and then slowly removed his hat. The men cheered wildly. Forty years later, an observer recalled that "the effect was as of a military sacrament."

In his command relationships, Lee lived his credo—that a gentleman possessed authority, knew it, and applied it judiciously. Such a man "does not needlessly and unnecessarily remind an offender of a wrong," and not only forgives "but can forget."[124]

Lee's practice of this belief explains much of his military success. A long-time colleague on the western front, Braxton Bragg, could not cope with his officers. His command was one long tale of blaming his generals for defeats, of arrests, and of public humiliation of subordinates.

Lee avoided such conduct, even when he believed that his officers had failed him. In fact, his remark to General J. E. B. Stuart at Gettysburg—"General Stuart, *where have you been?*"—was one of his strongest rebukes. His response to failure usually involved a quiet reallocation of responsibilities, to make the best use of good men who had demonstrated flaws.

This trust was reciprocated by Lee's officers. Once Lee explained to the Prussian observer, Captain Justus Scheibert, why he gave wide latitude to subordinates. Until the fall of Richmond, Lee steadfastly believed that his duty was to bring his troops to the right place and time for battle, and allow his lieutenants considerable responsibility. There were obvious defects in this philosophy. One wonders what might have occurred on the evening of July 1 at Gettysburg if Lee had not given his corps and division leaders, Richard Ewell and Jubal Early, so much discretion in planning.

But Lee's command technique succeeded more than it failed, because his officers were not afraid to use their own discretion. Bragg's treatment of his lieutenants produced a timid group who feigned responsibility, and threw away opportunities for success for fear that failure would earn them recrimination.

Typical of the way Lee handled his officers was the army reorganization after the battle of Seven Days. The conduct in battle of Generals Benjamin Huger, John Magruder, and Theophilus Holmes indicated that all three had little capacity for command. There were no arrests or rebukes. Magruder and Holmes were transferred to duties west of the Mississippi River, and Huger was made an artillery inspector.

More indicative was Lee's treatment of Stonewall Jackson, whose performance in the Seven Days had been mediocre at best. He had failed to attack promptly at Mechanicsville and Gaines' Mill. He then suffered an unexplainable day's delay in crossing White Oak Swamp on June 30, and had not supported the attack at Savage Station. Jackson's principal biographer, Frank Vandiver, noted that "Jackson had fallen far short of the reputation earned in the valley," and surmised that Lee had doubts about whether army commander Jackson could serve as a corps officer:

> . . . undoubtedly he asked himself if Jackson's nature would permit him to function under someone else's direction. Was he the type who chafed under subordination?[125]

Lesser men than Lee would have taken advantage of Jackson's vulnerable position. He came to join Lee on the Peninsula as the Confederacy's idol, and some editors had compared his boldness with a lethargy they charged to Jefferson Davis and his military adviser, Lee. Before the Seven Days Lee had absolutely no reputation as a field commander. The chance bullet that felled General Joseph Johnston on June 30 enabled Lee to demonstrate his own brilliance, and gave him the power, if he so desired, to harm the reputation of Jackson.

Lee shunned this chance to downgrade a rival and to explain away some ill-spent opportunities of the Seven Days. While Jackson was not praised in his battle report, there was not a single line of censure, nor was there rebuke in private. The only action that reflected any doubt about Jackson's talents was a reshuffling of the army command. Jackson's force was reduced from fourteen brigades to seven, while Longstreet's new corps was augumented from six brigades to twenty-eight.

No analysis of Lee's greatness has failed to praise his audacity in combat. His combative spirit may have portended serious problems for the overall Confederate war effort, but in field command Lee was not intimidated by the enemy. His division of force in the face of McClellan at the Seven Days; his detachment of Jackson's corps to strike Pope's communications at Second Manassas; and his detail of Jackson to strike Hooker's flank at Chancellorsville—all were marked by singular boldness.

Lee personified Napoleon's "first quality" of a leader. He possessed that nature "which receives exact impressions of things . . . which never allows itself to be dazzled, or intoxicated, by good or bad news." How well the French general described a score of other Civil War leaders when he portrayed men who lacked the commitment to give battle at the critical moment, who painted "mental pictures," faltered, and passed the initiative to the enemy.[126]

Still, a comment upon his daring by his artilleryman, E. Porter Alexander, indicates there is much to Lee's generalship that remains obscure. Alexander recalled a conversation in 1862 with a member of the President's staff, Colonel Joseph Ives. Ives had said that Lee "will take more desperate chances and take them quicker than any other general in this country, North or South." Alexander agreed, but admitted years after the war that "it seems, even yet, a mystery." Lee's boldness was a puzzle because it seemed to contradict his "dignity of character" and "calm self-reliance," and one might be aware of these external qualities "without deducing from them, also, the existence of such phenomenal audacity."[127]

Countless descriptions of Lee's greatness as a commander, the listing of traits of genius—these leave some important matters unresolved. As a secessionist, war strategist, and army commander, Lee is still an enigma. Why did a man, so sensitive to the concept of duty, throw aside his military oath in 1861 and seemingly violate his own code?

There are intriguing questions regarding Lee's conduct in 1861. His dislike of secession, his love for the Union, and his conviction that Virginia's alignment with the Confederacy would eventually bring disaster to the state, all are familiar. In view of these attitudes, one wonders why Lee did not endeavor to use his influence within Virginia to squelch the secession movement. He certainly might have been able to do it. Even before he resigned his commission in the United States army, the Virginia convention on April 19 had voted for the appointment of a major general to command state troops, and the advisory council had recommended Lee. On April 21, the day after Lee resigned, Governor John Letcher formally tendered the offer. Two days later, after Lee's acceptance, he was treated to praise and an ovation when he addressed the convention in Richmond.

How can Lee's rapid change of attitude toward secession be explained? If his loyalty to the Union and his pain of resignation were as intense as his biographers indicate, the switch was abrupt. Within a week after resigning his commission, Lee was a major general commanding the Virginia state troops. During that same week he began working tirelessly to get the army in shape for war with the United States.

Lee's conduct as a Confederate general also raises pertinent questions. Given his pre-eminence in the war effort, why did he neglect to submit advice on vital matters of civil-military policy, such as the possible removal of the capital from Richmond to a less exposed area? And when he offered military advice to Jefferson Davis—which was frequent—why did his views reflect an almost obsessive concern with the Virginia theater?

Perhaps such questions remain unanswered because the crucial element of personality has been absent in many biographies of Lee. It is not enough to list his qualities of military genius or character, for unless one examines the personality which Lee brought to the Civil War, the concept of the marble man remains undisturbed.

Essentially, Robert Lee by his middle age, in 1861, was a child of the seventeenth-century New England mind, and not of the later Enlightenment. In fact, his idea of death as caused by sin, his belief that men's actions are directly controlled by God, smacked more of the pen of Cotton Mather than that of Thomas Jefferson. In 1857 he wrote to Mary Lee:

> I know in whose powerful hands I am, and on Him I rely and feel that in all our life we are upheld and sustained by Divine Providence.[128]

In this, Lee's was an exaggeration of the antebellum Southern mind, which, like Puritanism, stressed an ever-present link between man and his creator. To the Southerner, as to the seventeenth-century New Englander, such a belief implied an unquestioning spirit which submitted to unseen forces. In Lee, it also produced an inward isolation, and a denial of the reasoning process.

After his decision in 1861, he saw himself and others as controlled by forces beyond the power of men. A few days after Virginia's secession, he wrote:

> I fear it is now out of the power of man, and in God alone must be our trust . . . but trust that a merciful Providence will not dash us from the height to which his smiles had raised us.[129]

Even when Lee spoke of his techniques of command, the emphasis was more on destiny than reason. To one he explained:

> I think and work with all my power to bring the troops to the right place at the right time; then I have done my duty. As soon as I order them into battle, I leave my army in the hands of God.[130]

Lee also exaggerated another element of the prewar Southern mentality—the concept of the tragic hero figure. One wonders whether Lee, perhaps subconsciously, viewed himself as a Southern Hamlet, destined by fate to live unhappily in a troublesome world.

Lee's writings often hinted at such a complex, and this would only fortify his self-containment. He spoke of one dead as having been saved "from sin and misery here," while the living "are left to be pitied." He talked of "the pains and sorrows of this world" and how one should rejoice at the departure of someone "from this world of sorrow." And when Stonewall Jackson was killed, Lee admitted that he did grieve for Jackson, but "for our sakes not for his. He is happy at peace."[131]

By the war years Lee believed that life had dealt him a cruel hand which he must bear unquestioningly. For example, he hoped "God should spare me a few years of peace," but by 1862 "year after year my hopes go out, and I must be resigned."[132]

Another element in Lee's personality reinforced this detachment. His code of duty, self-control, and self-denial had about it an austerity which may have had some important effects on his behavior.

Lee saw duty as an abstract force, tied closely to Divine Providence. Together they steered one's life along paths that were not to be questioned. Lee's code was to decide upon what he considered his duty, obey it, and trust the remainder to Divine Providence. After the war he explained that "we are conscious that we have humbly tried to do our duty. We may . . . with calm satisfaction, trust in God and leave results to him."[133]

For Lee, duty as a principle had nothing to do with reason. He later explained that in wartime "I did only what my duty demanded." During the war he wrote that "there is a true glory and a true honor; the glory of duty done."[134]

But Lee's rigid devotion to duty seemed to affect his thinking processes. He sometimes reacted from the narrow base of his concept of duty and nothing more. One almost senses a decision to do what he felt he was obligated to do and to go no further. Before the war Lee advised his wife:

> Do not worry yourself about things you cannot help, but be content to do what you can for the well-being of what properly belongs to you. Commit the rest to those who are responsible. . . . It is the part of wisdom to attend to our own affairs.[135]

There was often the self-imposed limitation beyond which Lee would not carry himself. He had difficulty in grasping the relationship between war and statecraft and saw his responsibility as a commander of an army and little more. When a Confederate senator sought his advice on whether the capital should be moved from Richmond, Lee refused to comment. Although he led the South's most successful army, he regarded such a matter as beyond his definition of duty. He replied:

> Whatever talents I may possess (and they are not unlimited) are military talents . . . I think the military and civil talents are distinct, if not different, and full duty in either sphere is about as much as one man can qualify himself to perform.[136]

One might conjecture whether Lee's sense of duty did not affect both his decision of 1861 and his overall strategic view of the war. For a century, Lee biographers have written of the special agony and sacrifice in his decision of 1861 to resign his commission and lead the Virginia state forces.

How generations of writers came to decide that Lee loved the Union more than others is difficult to understand. Other officers of the old army were torn by similar doubts. Allan Nevins recalled the agony of Virginia-bred General Joseph Johnston, descendant of Patrick Henry and quartermaster general of the American army in 1861. Amidst tears and after much thought, Johnston murmured, "To leave the service is a hard necessity, but I must go." George Thomas was disowned by his Virginia family for remaining loyal to the Union, and Tennessee-born David Glasgow Farragut also opted for the North. The travail was not unusual for men from the border country who had homeland ties in the South.[137]

In fact, Lee's decision may have been easier. Douglas Freeman wrote two chapters to argue for what he called "the answer he was born to make." Freeman believed there was no doubt as to Lee's eventual decision because it was a product of an instinctive sense of duty to his Virginia environment.

There was a peculiar contradiction in Lee's behavior after he resigned from the United States army. His biographers have always lauded both Lee's deep grief at leaving the army and his immediate vigor in preparing the defense of Virginia.

It was not merely Lee's haste but, more important, the apparent sudden change in his attitude. Almost instantaneously, the secession movement which he supposedly abhorred was a holy cause, and the Union he loved had become a deadly enemy. Soon he would speak of "the evil designs of the North," of "a cruel enemy," and of a Federal army which sought to reduce the Confederate populace "to abject slavery." By 1862 Lee would declare that "no civilized nation within my knowledge has ever carried on war as the U.S. Government has against us."

To oppose such aggressors, Lee found hope in a Rebel cause "sacred and worthy." Three months after his resignation from the United States army, he swore to oppose it to the last. Lee wrote:

> As far as my voice and counsels go, they will be continued on our side, as long as there is one horse that can carry his rider and one arm that can wield a sword I prefer annihilation to submission . . .[138]

Even if his anguish of 1861 has not been overstated, this would not necessarily contradict Lee's sudden conversion to the Rebel effort. Both decisions were in part motivated by a sense of duty to his native state. They were products of his ability to isolate his thinking process and move by instinct. Contradictions in his behavior pattern were less important to Lee than his overwhelming concern for duty to Virginia.

Lee's personality also appears to have influenced his strategic outlook. His concept of the war effort was almost totally identified with Virginia, and he felt that other theaters were secondary to the eastern front. While Lee's love for Virginia helped engender this parochialism, his personality was also responsible. After his decision of 1861, Lee's commitment to duty centered narrowly upon the fatherland. As T. Harry Williams observed, Lee "was a product of his culture, and that culture, permeated in its every part by the spirit of localism, dictated that his outlook on war should be local."[139]

Lee's biographers have dismissed the charges of localism by evoking the image of the "bridled general" whose power to fashion broad strategic plans was held in check by Jefferson Davis. The concept is vulnerable. Throughout the war Lee exercised broad official and unofficial influence. His son described him in 1861 as the President's "constant and trusted adviser." Later, in March 1862, Davis assigned Lee to "the conduct of the military operations in the armies of the Confederacy."

Lee's biographers have often derided this appointment, describing it as a clerkship without authority. They have cited a letter from Lee to his wife in which he admitted he saw no pleasure or advantage in his duties. Yet Lee never denied that he had influence, and Freeman acknowledged that during his term of office, Lee passed upon military operations in every Confederate state and was consulted on large strategic issues.

When Lee took command of the Army of Northern Virginia, he remained Davis's military adviser. The President's orders emphasized that the new command "renders it necessary to interfere temporarily with the general service, but only so far as to make you available for command in the field of a particular army." Robert E. Lee, Jr., recalled later that "at all times [Lee] advised with the President and Secretary of War as to the movements and dispositions of the other armies of the Confederacy." In fact, young Lee recalled that "one is astonished" at the amount of such correspondence.[140]

The amount—and scope—of Lee's advice was considerable. In the summer of 1862, he suggested that Georgia and the Carolinas be stripped of troops for a second front in Virginia, and later that the western armies should invade Kentucky. From March through May 1863, he conferred with the government as to the proper strategy for both the relief of Vicksburg and the Tennessee front. In August—

October 1863, he advised Davis on plans for the Tennessee–Georgia theater. In early 1864, he helped shape the strategy to be used by General Joseph E. Johnston in the Atlanta campaign.

In early 1863, he made suggestions for the defense of the North Carolina coast and later recommended that the departmental army of the Carolinas be shipped to Virginia. In 1864 and 1865, he proposed that both the Carolina and Tennessee armies be sent to the Virginia front. Four times he gave advice on the question of a new commander for the Army of Tennessee; once in 1864 he was even consulted about the choice of a corps officer in that western army.

Lee's advice was consistent: Virginia was the main war zone. Any suggested reinforcement was almost inevitably a one-way matter—that the rest of the Confederacy was a manpower pool for the Virginia front. In the early autumn of 1862, when the Federal army in Tennessee was poised for an advance on the vital Chattanooga–Atlanta corridor, Lee suggested that the Confederate Army of Tennessee be sent eastward to guard Richmond while he invaded Maryland. In December 1862, when the Federals again threatened Chattanooga, Lee again recommended that the Army of Tennessee reinforce him in Virginia.

In May 1863, Union armies in the West were ready for a massive double offensive: Grant's Army of Tennessee to take Vicksburg and Rosecrans's Army of Cumberland to seize Chattanooga. Lee was telling Davis that "it would seem . . . that Virginia is to be the theater of action, and this army, if possible, ought to be strengthened." In the spring of 1864, the Federal Military Division of the Mississippi had gathered three armies under General William Sherman for the push from Chattanooga to Atlanta. But in April, Lee argued that "the great effort of the enemy in this campaign will be made in Virginia," and insisted that the western army must take the offensive against Sherman in order to halt it.[141]

LEE'S SELF-CONTROL has been so often discussed by his biographers that some vignettes about it have become legendary. One of them has been recounted by Colonel Walter Taylor. In 1862, when his daughter Annie died in North Carolina, Lee received the word by mail in his tent, along with some military correspondence. Taylor saw that Lee read the tragic news, and then calmly continued examining the army correspondence of the morning. Taylor left the tent, and when he returned minutes later, unannounced, he found Lee weeping. Given the deep sense of loss Lee must have felt, his demeanor was extraordinary.

Sometimes Lee's emotions broke through his self-imposed barrier. He could be brought to tears quickly, and the examples are not infrequent—such as in 1861 when he heard a sermon by Bishop Meade, in

1862 when the question of evacuating Richmond was discussed, and in 1864 when he learned of the deaths of J. E. B. Stuart and A. P. Hill.

Lee displayed his inner feelings in other ways. He would lapse into an angry depression, described by a staff officer as "one of his savage moods." When this occurred, his aides left him alone, for "when these moods were on him it was safer to keep out of his way."[142]

Lee also could show a savage temper. He exploded when he failed to trap McClellan on the Peninsula at Frayser's Farm, shortly before his suicidal attack at Malvern Hill. He lost his temper at Sharpsburg when he sighted a straggler carrying a pig, and ordered the soldier to be shot as a warning to the army. He became angry at the misplacement of a battery at Fredericksburg. The back of his neck reddened and his head jerked, mannerisms which Douglas Freeman admitted indicated "another familiar omen of an inward battle."[143]

Lee was aware of his temper. Once he told his aide, Walter Taylor, "When I lose my temper, don't let it make you angry." On another occasion he became angry at a visitor to his tent, and stormed at an aide: "Why did you permit that man to come to my tent and make me show my temper?"[144]

But such public scenes were exceptional. Usually Lee's strong inner disposition was hidden beneath the serene pose so often described by his biographers. This clamp on his inner nature, combined with years of unhappiness, may have affected his conception of the war.

Several generations of psychological researchers have seen some relationship—however often they disagree on its nature—between inner moods and aggressive or warlike tendencies. In 1920 Sigmund Freud put forth his concept of the "death instinct," which related aggressive behavior to inner guilt. In 1937 a group of Yale scholars published *Frustration and Aggression,* which attempted to establish a causal relationship between these two factors. In a work begun in 1926 as *A Study of War,* Professor Quincy Wright described these relationships. His section, "Analysis of Psychological Drives and Motives," saw an interaction between inner drives and a love of war. Professors E. F. M. Durbin and John Bowlby, in their 1939 *Personal Aggressiveness and War,* supported this theory. And in his recent *Power and Innocence: A Search for the Sources of Violence,* Rollo May perceived a myriad of psychological drives which produced either a tendency toward general violence or a love of war in particular.

The image of Lee has always been that of a war hater. Certain of his utterances regarding his dislike of war have become traditional. One was his famous Christmas letter to Mary Lee in 1862:

But what a cruel thing is war, to separate and destroy families and friends, and mar the purest joys and happiness God has granted us in this world; to fill our hearts with hatred instead of love for our neighbors, and to devastate the fair face of this beautiful world.[145]

Still one returns to Porter Alexander's haunting question about the mystery of Lee's "phenomenal audacity." What inner forces joined with Lee's military abilities in prompting the bold division of force that brought victory at the Seven Days, Second Manassas, and Chancellorsville? What drove Lee to launch repeated headlong assaults of the type that wrecked his army at Gettysburg? Why was his normally serene demeanor fired with excitement when under combat conditions?

While he hated war in the abstract, there is some evidence that, for Lee, aggression, audacity, and the offensive in combat may have been not only consciously developed military attributes but also the symptoms of a repressed personality. War thus provided an emotional release for a man who had contained strong emotions beneath a mantle of reserve.

Another personality element may have contributed to Lee's behavior in combat. In some respects he resembled his last opponent, Ulysses Grant. Both men either saw themselves as failures in the prewar days or were so. Lee's constant concern with his unhappy army life, slowness of promotion, his moral inadequacies, his melancholy family situation, the pleasant release of death—all bespoke a man who believed his life had failed.

Grant's prewar career had been an unbroken string of failures in various enterprises—the army, farming, tanning, real estate, storekeeping, and others. His biographer Lloyd Lewis described him in 1860:

> Seventeen years! The older he got the more rapidly failure seemed to strike. Eleven years in the Army; four years farming; two years collecting rents and hunting jobs. In April he would be thirty-eight, with no prospects at all.

Grant himself once wrote his father in exasperation, "I don't want to fly from one thing to another, but I am compelled to make a living . . ."[146]

There were also similarities in their generalship. Like Lee, Grant showed boldness in maneuver, a willingness to take chances, and a persistent desire to mount the offensive in battle. And when the fight came, Grant's demeanor also changed. More than one observer commented upon how his usual calm, almost torpid nature became restless and exhilarated in combat.

Perhaps the key rests in one last similarity. Like Lee, Grant possessed an unshakable self-confidence which did not fear committing a mistake. General John Schofield later recalled that Grant had "absolute confidence in his own judgement." In a wartime letter to Grant, Sherman spoke of how "when you have completed your last preparations you go into battle without hesitation," relying upon a "simple faith in success." And a Grant biographer, Adam Badeau, wrote that "he had no fear of not doing all that he was put in his place to do," because "there was no moment, however dark or distressing, when he was not more than hopeful."[147]

One might conjecture that part of this audacity, self-confidence, and warlike spirit in combat arose from Lee's and Grant's prewar experiences. In a sense, both men—at least in their own eyes—had never had success, so they did not fear failure. For Grant and Lee in 1861 there were no vast reputations to uphold, no fear of damaging the status quo by failure. In fact, there may have been an inherent willingness to act boldly in order to prove they had the capacity for success.

Other Civil War generals showed that there may be a correlation between prewar failure and wartime success. Sherman's career before 1861 was marked by repeated business misfortunes and changes of career. Albert Sidney Johnston's course before the war had been a mélange of disappointments in both military service and business life. At least a dozen times Johnston had embarked on some new enterprise only to encounter personal defeat. And though his war career was cut short by death, Johnston exhibited remarkable boldness in the surprise attack at Shiloh, while his second-in-command, Beauregard, was still protesting the attack fifteen minutes before it was launched. Another example was Stonewall Jackson's long struggle from prewar misfortunes to military glory. In 1860 Jackson had been written off by even his friends as a dull, eccentric failure. His war career also was characterized by aggressiveness in combat and a fiery change in personality when in battle.

Some who came to the war with a record of success proved to be mediocre leaders. General Henry Halleck was a total failure as a field commander. Halleck's celebrated twenty-mile "slow march" from Shiloh to Corinth in 1860 highlighted a wartime career of indecision, caution, and the inability to make a commitment. General George McClellan's star was in the ascendant by late 1861. His career before Fort Sumter was that of a brilliant young army officer and a successful railroad executive. His victory in the 1861 West Virginia campaign catapulted McClellan into the job of commander in chief of Union forces. McClellan's subsequent actions were marked by a caution and fear of failure that have become legendary.

It may appear heretical to suggest that Lee was exhilarated by combat. Even if one cannot concede a relationship between Lee's repressed personality and prewar lack of distinction on the one hand and his audacious spirit on the other, he seemed to be rejuvenated in battle.

Traces of this were apparent during the Mexican War. In 1847 he wrote a long, enthusiastic letter to his friend Jack Mackay, recounting the campaign from Veracruz to Mexico City. It was not a case of boyish enthusiasm. Lee was a mature soldier of forty. Yet his language displayed enthusiasm for combat:

> ... the troops moved to the assault. It was carried in beautiful style ... our men becoming impatient, turned to and after killing some 500 of the mob and deserters from the Army, who had not courage to fight us lawfully ... it is a miserable populace ... idle worthless and vicious. Should they give us another opportunity, they will be taught a lesson. Since this Army landed at Vera Cruz ... it has captured over 600 guns, many thousand *Stand of Arms* ... taken more prisoners than it numbers men, defeated every army that has been brought against it ... They will oblige us in spite of ourselves to overrun the country and drive them into the sea. I believe it would be our best plan to commence at once ...[148]

Lee could tell Mackay, "I think a little lead, properly taken, is good for a man," and in speaking of Cerro Gordo, he used such language as "when the musket balls and grape were whistling over my head in a perfect shower." He wrote his wife of Mexico and of how "we have ... drubbed her handsomely and in a manner no man might be ashamed of," and exulted that "we are the victors in a regular war ... and they are whipped in a manner of which women might be ashamed." In fact, if the peace terms did not suit him, Lee "would fight them ten years ..."[149]

In the Civil War, Lee's own statements and the comments of observers indicated his warlike spirit. Surveying the slaughter at Fredericksburg, he mused, "It is well that war is so terrible—we would grow too fond of it." Angry when Sedgwick's forces escaped after Salem Church, Lee raged, "Why, General Pender? That is the way you young men always do. You allow those people to get away.... Go after them, and damage them all you can." And when he lay ill in bed on the North Anna River, mindful of an opportunity to defeat Grant, Lee would murmur repeatedly, "We must strike them a blow—we must never let them pass us again—we must strike them a blow." When an observer visited Lee during the slaughter at Cold Harbor, remarking that the waves of Rebel musket fire sounded like the ripping of a bed sheet, Lee observed, "It is that that kills men."[150]

Lee appeared to change under combat conditions. A staff officer recalled that "General Lee in a drawing-room was a very different man from General Lee in the field." The English observer Francis Lawley remembered Lee in the Wilderness:

No man who, at the terrible moment, saw his flashing eyes and sternly-set lips, is ever likely to forget them . . . the light of battle still flaming in his eyes.[151]

Lee's aggressive nature bled the Confederacy of manpower. In his first two years as commander of the Virginia army, Lee threw his men into combat in furious assaults. His offensive tactics were dreadfully expensive, and the British historian Liddell Hart wrote that a wiser course might have been to combine offensive strategy and defensive tactics, "to lure the Union armies into attacking under disadvantageous conditions . . . ."[152]

But Lee, fired with a combative spirit, attacked. In his first four months of command in 1862, he suffered over 47,000 casualties, more men than there were at that time in the whole Army of Tennessee. At Gettysburg alone Lee lost more men than General Albert Sidney Johnston led on the western front in the autumn of 1861.

Finally, in his 1864 campaign against Grant, Lee was forced to adopt a defensive policy because of dwindling manpower. His successes at Spottsylvania and Cold Harbor, where the fortified Rebels inflicted heavy casualties upon Grant, should have given Lee pause for reflection. Instead, until the very end, he was obsessed with the hope that his army could be the aggressor and attack Grant. Even on the eve of Appomattox, when his paltry forces faced enormous odds, Lee would exclaim, "I will strike that man a blow in the morning . . . I will strike that man a blow in the morning."[153]

BUT THE BLOW did not come, and a weary Robert Lee went to the Shenandoah Valley to take up a new challenge. As president of Washington College, he did much to merit the appraisal of Marshall Fishwick, that to know the real Lee was to watch the old man moving among Lexington's children.

This image of the Lee after Appomattox has provided support for his mystique since the late nineteenth century. As mentioned, it also did much to assure Lee's status as a national figure after 1900. Then as now Americans reacted warmly to the sacrifice, dedication, and patience seen in Lee's last years.

The strength of this image has rested upon Lee as *the example,* a non-corporeal sculpture of dignity and humanity. Thus, Lee was the epitome of restraint in his public attitudes toward the trials of the Reconstruction. Lee was no doubt cognizant of his potential for setting an important example for a defeated Confederacy. His public statements at Lexington focused upon the need for himself and other prominent ex-Rebels to guide young Southerners.

And always the emphasis was upon two critical areas, education and attitude. Education to Lee was crucial because he considered younger Southerners to be the region's hope for recouping its fortunes. One senses that Lee had almost lost faith in the older generation which had brought the South to war. His irritation with the leadership of the lower cotton South had been clear in his correspondence of 1860–61. It seems ironic that these people would choose Lee as their major hero figure, for in many ways he was unlike them. Lee did not fit either the Southern stereotype of the hell-for-leather cavalier or that of the belligerent politician committed to preserve slavery. He was completely unlike those proud, haughty products of an inbred plantation culture who often lacked self-discipline or the willingness to subordinate their own sense of command to the common good.

Such men would not do to remold the South, and Lee looked elsewhere. His hope lay in Southern youth, for "we must look to the rising generation for the restoration of the country." And men such as Lee must set the example because "now more than at any other time, Virginia and every State in the South needs us."

They also needed him to serve as an example of moderation. Decades after Appomattox, historian Charles Francis Adams would hail Lee's demeanor after the war as a critical factor in the reunification of North and South. While Adams was no doubt exaggerating it is true that Lee was conscious of the need for ex-Confederate leaders to display a conciliatory attitude. Again the marble mantle drew tightly around his inner feelings, and Lee's utterances, while wise, were tinged with a cold formality. Typical was a formula for Southern conduct which he explained to Governor John Letcher. Ex-Confederates should "remain if possible in the country; promote harmony and good feeling; qualify themselves to vote; and elect to the State and General Legislature wise and patriotic men . . ."[154]

Yet Lee's image of greatness in the hard years after Appomattox tells us little of the inner man. One suspects that the mantle of reserve has cloaked his humanity. How did he feel, concluding a career of over thirty years' army service with military failure? How much was he like other ex-Confederates who discovered that the American dream of success had evaded them, and that hope of God's aid had brought nothing? In the Lexington years, troubled with failing health and immersed in the duties of the college presidency, did he feel resentment at the vain boastings of some other ex-Rebel generals and their admirers? Did he chafe when he saw his invalid wife's health continue to decline, far from the lost Arlington lands?

Occasionally Lee's inner spirit broke through to reveal hidden frustration. Certainly his status as a potential defender of the Lost Cause must have troubled him. No doubt he shared the feelings of other ex-Confederates who insisted that defeat had in no way proved the illegality of secession and that the South's version must be told to the nation. These beliefs were complicated by Lee's apparent realization that he was a public man who could do much to defend secession. His files of correspondence are filled with notes from admirers urging that he do so. Typical was a plea from one Virginian who implored Lee to write a defense so that "we may have truth where so much falsehood has already been published." And a Pennsylvania correspondent urged him, "not so much for your own sake, as for the sake of your Southern country," to write such a history.

Lee publicly avoided a defense of the South's position. His refusal to become involved in politics, fearing that his presence would prove harmful to Virginia, is well known. His voluminous correspondence is filled with advice to young men "not to be turned aside by thoughts of the past," but to rebuild the South. He shunned public ceremonies which he feared would rekindle sectional animosity. He refused to attend a meeting of the Gettysburg Battlefield Memorial Association, disliking "to keep open the sores of war."

But privately, and not infrequently, Lee commented forcefully on the secession issue. Lee appeared to believe that any statements he uttered in private would be kept confidential by his listeners. For example, in late 1865 a British writer, Herbert Saunders, spent an evening with Lee in Lexington, talking of the war and of the secession movement. Lee was evidently surprised when Saunders later sent a manuscript of the conversation, requesting permission to publish it. Lee explained that "I have an objection to the publication of my private conversations, which are never intended but for those to whom they are addressed." Whether conditioned by his deep humility, Lee's belief that comments to a traveling British writer and admirer would be kept confidential seems almost naïve. This same simple faith was evident when Lee responded to some queries about the Gettysburg campaign. A Virginia author, William McDonald, was preparing a school textbook and requested Lee to provide some observations. Lee's reply was concluded with the admonition: "I must ask that you will consider what I have said as intended solely for yourself."[155]

The underlying depth of Lee's feelings on the secession issue after the war has been neglected as an element of his personality. It is important to remember that Lee's views on secession in 1861 were not those he possessed after Appomattox. Too often Lee's anguish over the secession issue in 1861—which may itself have been exaggerated—has been regarded as a permanent state of mind. Others may have been misled by a terse statement on the secession issue which Lee made after the war to General Wade Hampton. Then Lee remarked, "I did only what my duty demanded . . . and if it was all to do over I should act precisely as I did."

However sorrowful Lee may have been in 1861, however much his decision then was a reaction to his credo of duty, Lee after Appomattox felt keenly about the secession issue. By 1866 he had traveled far from his prewar belief that the authors of the Constitution would not have expended so much labor "if it was intended to be broken by every member of the Confederacy at will," and that the Constitution was intended for " 'perpetual union.' " Even Douglas Freeman admitted that Lee's position had changed, noting that during the war "Lee absorbed the Southern constitutional argument and was convinced of it."[156]

It does not require Freeman's testimony to observe that, after Appomattox, Lee, however reserved his demeanor, was a strong adherent of the Lost Cause argument. As has been mentioned, Lee's opinion of the Union war effort underwent rapid change after his resignation in 1861. Within months he spoke of "the evil designs of the North" and of how he preferred "annihilation to submission."

After the surrender, Lee's feelings intensified. From his postwar correspondence one can reconstruct almost a stereotype of the Lost Causist who justified the war on constitutional grounds. Lee saw the war as the result of conflicting theories of the proper roles of central and state governments. The Confederates were the true preservers of the constitutional tradition, people "who considered their rights attacked & their Constitutional liberties invaded." Lee regarded the war as "our struggle for State Rights and Constitutional Government." As he suggested to Governor John Letcher, the South's loss told nothing of the merits of secession, and only indicated that the dispute was "decided against us" by force.[157]

Thus Lee reacted to some postwar Northern attitudes with a bitterness difficult to conceal. He resented the self-righteousness of writers who assumed that Northern victory was synonymous with right. Particularly Lee railed against the New England states, "whose citizens are the fiercest opponents of the Southern states." Because New Englanders had spoken of secession almost fifty years before the war, Lee saw them as inconsistent.

Lee was also disillusioned by what he believed to be harsh treatment of ex-Rebels by the North. He felt betrayed by Reconstruction policies. During an 1868 conversation with a Lexington colleague, Colonel William Preston Johnston, Lee spoke with feeling about the Reconstruction, and recounted a conversation he had had with General Winfield Scott in 1861. Scott attempted to convince Lee that President Abraham Lincoln intended a policy of pacification for the South. Instead, now Lee spoke of the "vindictiveness and malignity of the Yankees, of which he had no conception before the war."[158]

Lee also shared the fear of other ex-Rebels that unless the Southern version of the crisis were published, the secession effort would be interpreted by hostile historians. He was not the "silent Lee" so often depicted by historians, the man counseling reticence. In quite human fashion he tried to encourage others to defend the South. He praised Albert Bledsoe's planned *Southern Review* as an organ to present the South to the American people "in an agreeable and convincing manner"; encouraged historian Edward Pollard to give "a full and true account" of the Confederate saga; and agreed with a Georgia admirer that "a truthful history" needed to be written. And to his cousin Cassius, Robert Lee expressed hope for "a true history" of the South's "defense of the rights," that "justice be done them."[159] Lee's desire to justify secession was tied closely to his strong wish to write a history of the Army of Northern Virginia's exploits.

In Lee's own words, "soon after the cessation of hostilities" he was beginning to prepare that account. He was visited in Richmond sometime after the surrender by C. B. Richardson of the University Publishing Company of New York. Though no contract was signed, an informal agreement was reached during the summer of 1865 whereby Richardson's company would have publication privileges if Lee completed the manuscript. For the next five years Richardson and Lee conducted a heavy correspondence, with the publisher furnishing needed materials and gently prodding Lee to hasten his work. Lee's files contain dozens of entreaties from other publishing firms, many being turned aside by explanations that the General was already committed. Typical was a response in late 1865 to one publisher in which Lee explained that Richardson had made "such proposals" that if the book were finished "I feel that I ought first to offer it to him for publication."

Until his death Lee sought both materials and time to finish his cherished project. Numerous requests for documents and recollections were sent to his former officers, including a widely distributed circular letter in July 1865. Lee especially looked for information relating to the campaign against Grant, since most of his own papers on the subject had been lost in the confusion of the fall of Richmond in 1865.

That the book was not written is not surprising. Increasing ill health and the demands of the college presidency took up Lee's time and strength. Save for a secretary, Lee had virtually no administrative assistance at Washington College. It must have been a source of frustration that a general who once had a large staff must now busy himself with the details of selecting kitchen utensils and stovepipes for dormitory rooms.

Even had time been available, Lee never believed he possessed accurate documentation for the project. His frequent letters to old army colleagues requesting their aid are spiced with the frustration of a researcher without materials. Not only were "all my records, books, orders, etc. . . . destroyed in the conflagration and retreat from Richmond," but Lee was also without accurate official army returns that were among the captured Rebel documents in Washington, which few Southerners were allowed to view. With sadness, he wrote his cousin Cassius Lee, only a few months before his death, that while some materials had been collected, he lacked "so much that I wish to obtain that I have not commenced the narrative."[160]

Lee's unfulfilled dream of writing his army's history revealed again, beneath the rigid exterior, his inner sense of unfulfillment.

Why did Lee wish to write the book? No doubt he desired to pay tribute to the rank and file of the Army of Northern Virginia. He loved the army dearly, agonized at the travails suffered by old comrades after the surrender, and determined that the book would be "the only tribute that can now be paid to the worth of its noble officers and soldiers."[161] Though his inability to pay this homage must have troubled him, Lee experienced other personal frustrations over the unfinished project which cut more deeply.

A desire to serve the Lost Cause as a historian of the war was no less fervent than his hopes that secession would be justified. Yet for Lee and other Southerners the extolling of war exploits ran counter to the grain of American pragmatism. Long before the era of Social Darwinism, the national doctrine of progress preached that Americans gained success because their precepts were more noble. After the Confederate surrender, Northern authors, flushed with patriotic fervor, applied this formula of American innocence to the Civil War. The success of Union arms proved the Southern cause to be evil.

Defenders of the Confederacy claimed that its defeat was not due to poor generalship or lack of providential aid, but was attributable to superior Northern manpower and rations. Lee believed this strongly, and yearned to prove it in his manuscript. His comments on the book reflected his frustration, if not desperation. To Jubal Early, Lee wrote that "it will be difficult to get the world to understand the odds against which we fought." The loss of his army's official returns "embarrasses me very much." Perhaps, Lee complained, "the public mind is not prepared to receive the truth." To a correspondent he explained that "I want that the world shall know what my poor boys, with their small numbers and scant resources, succeeded in accomplishing." And to his beloved Markie Williams he confided that "my only object in writing is that truth should descend to posterity."[162]

Lee's comment to Markie Williams that he wanted the "truth" preserved revealed an even deeper source of frustration. His great humility has so long been emphasized that much of his humanity has been separated from the image. Yet he was also proud of his family heritage, his army, and himself. His pride has often been overlooked because he contained it beneath consideration and dignity, living always his clearly defined definition of a gentleman. His close friend William Preston Johnston commented after one long interview that no man talked with Lee "when he opens his mind" without feeling that he "is a proud, pure strong man . . . confident of his own ability on the battlefield."[163]

Lee's private conversations and letters after the war sometimes exhibited a very human trait, that of a man concerned for his own reputation. He did not say much about the matter, only enough to indicate that concern for his own good name also inspired him to write about the army's campaign.

It is not surprising that Lee sometimes sought to defend his reputation—though this may appear heretical to his image. What was remarkable was his restraint, that he said no more than he did. As seen in earlier chapters, the history of the war had often gone hard against Lee in the first years after Appomattox. The leading early war historians, Edward Pollard and William Swinton, had been published by 1867. Both had faulted Lee for Gettysburg and the Seven Days, and praised Stonewall Jackson excessively for Chancellorsville.

Beleaguered by ill health and his duties at Lexington, Lee also saw other ex-Confederates—or their admirers—augment or reconstruct wartime reputations. By 1865 Beauregard's circle of devotees was damning Jefferson Davis and transforming the Creole into the one indispensable Confederate. The Jackson family's handpicked biographer, Major R. L. Dabney, issued his prestigious life of Stonewall which censured Lee for the Seven Days campaign and made his subordinate the genius of Chancellorsville. James Longstreet furnished material to journalist William Swinton which doubtless was used in the segment on Gettysburg so critical of Lee. General Daniel Harvey Hill published an article defending the incident of the famous "Lost Dispatch" in the Sharpsburg campaign, asserting that McClellan's discovery of Lee's dispositions should have worked to the South's advantage in the campaign.

While he usually kept his own counsel, Lee occasionally revealed a frustration that would have proved unbearable to weaker men. He read in manuscript Major Dabney's biography of Jackson, and sent Jackson's widow some corrections. In 1867 he dispatched an unusually strong letter to A. T. Bledsoe, editor of the *Southern Review,* which disputed the notion that Jackson conceived the flanking march at Chancellorsville. There was a conversation in 1868 with William Preston Johnston on the Wilderness campaign in which Lee criticized Richard

Ewell's "vacillation" and Longstreet's "slowness." Lee, in fact, re-marked that "Longstreet was often slow." There was another conversa-tion recorded that year by Lee's secretary, E. C. Gordon, after publication of General Hill's article on the Maryland campaign. Gordon recounted that Lee "was excited & somewhat indignant with Gen. Hill" for his version of the "Lost Dispatch" controversy.

On that same day, February 15, another confidant, Colonel William Allan, recorded the first of several conversations with Lee on the war. Allan's fascinating memoranda remained in private hands until well over a decade after Douglas Freeman observed in *R. E. Lee* that "Lee's reticence in discussing the war was always noticeable."

There was no reticence in the interviews which Colonel Allan recorded meticulously. That Allan was a trusted friend who listened to remarks which Lee did not intend for the public ear is not the point. Important here is that the intensity of Lee's comments to Allan on several occasions disclosed a deep level of frustration, as shown in these excerpts from several interviews.

March 3, 1868. On the Wilderness campaign:

On May 12 Lee found Ewell perfectly prostrated by the misfortune of the morning, and too much overwhelmed to be efficient, and on May 17 or 18 . . . he lost all presence of mind, and Lee found him prostrate on the ground . . .

April 15, 1868. On Gettysburg:

He did not know the Federal army was at Gettysburg, *could not believe it,* as Stuart had been specially ordered to . . . keep him informed of the position of the enemy, and [Stuart] had sent no word.

Victory could have been won if he could have gotten one decided simultaneous attack on the whole line. This he tried his utmost to effect for three days and failed. Ewell he could not get to act with decision . . . Then Longstreet & Hill etc. could not be gotten to act in concert.

Stuart's failure to carry out his instructions *forced the battle of Gettysburg, and the imperfect, halting way in which his corps commanders [especially Ewell] fought the battle, gave victory . . . finally to the foe.*

General Lee talked feelingly of the criticism to which he had been subjected, said "critics" talked much of that which they knew little about . . .

December 17, 1868.
On war history in general:

He talked of the difficulties and referred to the many errors which had become rife, and which it would be necessary for him to correct ... He spoke of the mistakes in Dabney's Life of Jackson.

On Mechanicsville:

He was disappointed in not finding Jackson ... and so he attacked at Ellerson's and Mechanicsville with what troops he had ... So again the next day Jackson was still not up ...

On Fredericksburg:

He referred to the pieces lately in the papers about a proposed night attack at Fredericksburg on Jackson's part. He said this was not so, and that when he and Jackson were talking over the matter the day after the fight, he asked J. if it would be possible to pick a body of troops and attack in the night, and that Jackson advised against it ...

On Petersburg:

He also referred to the fall of Petersburg, and said the immediate occasion was Longstreet's delay in coming over ...

February 19, 1870. On Gettysburg:

He spoke feelingly of Gettysburg ... Said he had urged the Government before going to Pennsylvania in 1863, to bring Beauregard to Manassas ... and threaten Washington in that quarter. Mr. Davis promised to do so, but it was never done.[164]

LEE'S LAST YEARS in Lexington have usually been portrayed as a near-idyllic existence. Here Lee was at rest, living out his last five years amidst the satisfaction provided him by his family and the Washington College community.

There is much truth in this image, at least until his health broke badly in 1869. After years of absence in army service, he was at least reunited with his family in the comfortable president's home on the college slope. Here Lee must have found relief from the loneliness one observes in his earlier letters.

The family circle at Lexington was large and alive with activity. It included Lee's wife, three unmarried daughters, Agnes, Mildred, and Mary, and sons Custis, Rooney, and Robert, Jr. In 1867, when Rooney married and Agnes went to live in Baltimore, their departure scarcely diminished the household. For that same autumn three children of Lee's brother Carter enrolled in Lexington schools and became part of the family.

The Lee house was a focus of that social contact so essential to Robert Lee's gregarious nature. Lexington summers and autumns brought a constant flow of relatives and intimate friends to visit. During the spring commencement season the home was filled with young women friends of his daughters. Robert Lee found great pleasure in their company, and his son recalled that "the girls enjoyed his society more than they did that of their college adorers."

Almost nightly young men from local colleges paid court to Lee's daughters, and their visits provided him with an opportunity for mild jesting. There were many trips to spas such as the Rockbridge Baths and White Sulphur Springs. Though the excursions were for the purpose of improving Mary Custis Lee's health, they were also festive occasions with crowds of kin and close friends.

And until his health failed, Lee must have found inner peace on his frequent rides into the countryside around Lexington. His love for the Virginia land, a central element in his prewar homesickness, had never diminished. Now, astride Traveler, he often forayed through Rockbridge County, talking with farmers and inspecting livestock, and he soon knew every homestead and farmer's name in the county. There were also expeditions. Lee often rode the twenty-two-mile round trip to visit his ailing wife at the Rockbridge Baths. And in 1866, after the return of his favorite mare, Lucy Long, which had been lost during the war, Lee's daughters accompanied him on long forays, even into the Blue Ridge Mountains.

Lee's frequent comments on his code defined true happiness as the satisfaction of having performed one's duty. And his voluminous correspondence described his service at Lexington as inspired by a duty to train young men to rebuild the South.

So even in the tedium of his obligations in the president's office, Lee felt he was obeying a life's credo. He was simultaneously dean, director of college development, advisor to students and faculty, registrar, and college purchasing agent. He seldom mingled with the students, and rarely spoke to them in public except at commencement.

Instead he worked at reconstructing the curriculum, replacing the frills of classical education with more practical courses in mechanics, business, and engineering. He meticulously followed the progress of the students. Every week the faculty submitted to Lee progress reports on each pupil. The president not only tabulated these grades, but spent a great deal of time in consultation with erring students. None of these matters provided the excitement of a Second Manassas, but doubtless gave Lee much inward pleasure.

Yet some comments, often by Lee himself, suggest that even in his last years at Lexington he remained the unfulfilled man. Once he wrote a daughter that his long rides on Traveler "give me abundant opportunity for quiet thought." His son Robert, Jr., later wished "we could only obtain some records of his thoughts as he rode all along the mountain roads." Robert, Jr., was convinced that his father had yet to find peace, and remarked that no one "ever knew what that great heart suffered" on those long rides.

And once Robert Lee himself momentarily lifted his mantle of reserve in a note to his old comrade Richard Ewell. He spoke of his enjoyment of "the charms of civil life," but added thoughtfully, "I . . . find too late that I have wasted the best years of my life."[165]

WHAT HAD BEEN WASTED? What remained unfulfilled in Lee beneath the gentle reserve of the Lexington years?

Some new inner frustrations Lee encountered after Appomattox have already been discussed. He grieved deeply over the South's plight during the Reconstruction. And like any adherent of the Lost Cause, he longed impatiently for Southerners to publish justifications for secession. Lee also grieved over his inability to complete his own history of the war, a project that may have involved a very human desire for self-justification.

There were also unresolved matters in Lee's earlier personality which followed him to Washington College. For years he had spoken of settling with his family on a piece of his beloved Virginia. But obviously he felt that duty first to the Confederacy and then to Washington College demanded otherwise. Thus, Lee died without possessing his own land, a tenant in the house of his college.

This was no small frustration. For almost twenty years before his death, Lee's frequent letters to his sons were filled with detailed advice on farming, and one detects an underlying wish that Lee himself could work on the land. In 1865, shortly after accepting the college presidency, Lee confided to one son that if his new position proved unsatisfactory, he intended to procure a small farm—"the course to which my inclinations point." Lee once said to his children, "I wish I had a little farm of my own, where we could live in peace to the end of our days." And in 1867 he told his son Rooney that he planned to leave the college presidency the following year, "to retire to some quiet spot, east of the mountains," where he could farm the land and "earn my daily bread."[166]

Lee's allusion to a home east of the Blue Ridge underscored a strong note of personal sadness in his last years. He watched Mary Custis pass her final years in a condition which he described as "a state of helplessness." He could not have been unaware of his wife's and his daughters' dislike of their austere Lexington surroundings, nor of his wife's homesickness for her native eastern Virginia society. And his lack of success in attempting to regain either Arlington or its treasured Washington relics was no doubt a sore disappointment.

In fact, so many were his postwar family burdens that one senses again his personal unfulfillment. Markie Williams remained in the last years a vital source of pleasure. Lee could write her that "there is nothing . . . that I want, except to see you, and nothing you can do for me, except to think of and love me."

But even Markie could not remove his continued sense of other-worldliness, his long-held conviction that life was designed by the Creator as a transient, unhappy existence. His weariness increased after his health began to deteriorate in 1869. The malady that had disabled him during the war now bothered him severely. No longer could he take long rides in the country. He was often in intense pain, and the slightest exertion made it difficult for him to breathe. One expert has suggested that Lee suffered from angina pectoris, complicated by a hypertension associated with hardening of the arteries.

He was depressed during these seizures and spoke of his transient state in life, and of how he would soon die. Once in those last days he again drew aside his reserve and spoke to Markie of "the only thing I long for"—quiet.

HE DONNED the tattered military cape, listened as his daughter played the "Funeral March," and then walked out into the rainy Lexington night.

A NOTE ON SOURCES
NOTES
INDEX

A NOTE ON SOURCES

R ESEARCH FOR THIS VOLUME has required a survey of numerous collections of manuscripts, hundreds of books and articles concerned with Lee and the Civil War in general, and many monographs and pamphlets. The reader is advised to consult the Notes for specific citations.

Manuscripts concerned with the Lee image are widely scattered. Among the most important consulted were the several collections of Lee Papers and the Douglas Southall Freeman Papers in the Library of Congress; the several Lee collections at the Virginia Historical Society, Richmond; the extensive manuscript and pamphlet collection in the Lee Papers of the McCormick Library of Washington and Lee University; the George and Katharine Davis Collection at the Howard-Tilton Library, Tulane University; the Robert E. Lee Papers at the Missouri Historical Society, St. Louis; the Robert E. Lee Papers in the Colonial Dames Collection, Georgia Historical Society, Savannah; and smaller collections at the Department of Archives, Louisiana State University; Mississippi State Department of Archives; Duke University Library; University of North Carolina; Tennessee State Archives; National Archives, Western Reserve Historical Society, Cleveland, Ohio; Chicago Historical Society; New York Public Library; Pennsylvania Historical Society, Philadelphia; and others.

As cited in the text, a wide range of contemporary newspaper sources was utilized. For information on the progression of the Lee image since the Civil War, practically every popular American magazine and historical periodical was perused.

Hundreds of books concerned with Lee, the Civil War, and the literary impact of the war were examined. Writings about Lee are voluminous, as the notes will illustrate. For concise bibliographies, the reader is advised to consult: William Hollis and Marshall Fishwick, *A Preliminary Checklist of Writings about R. E. Lee* (Charlottesville, 1951); Douglas Southall Freeman, *R. E. Lee* (4 vols., 1934–35), Vol. IV; Margaret Sanborn, *Robert E. Lee* (2 vols., Philadelphia, 1966); Clifford Dowdey, *Lee* (Boston, 1965); Allan Nevins et al., *Civil War Books: A Critical Bibliography* (2 vols., Baton Rouge, 1967, 1969); Ollinger Crenshaw, *General Lee's College: The Rise and Growth of Washington and Lee University* (New York, 1969).

NOTES

CHAPTER I

1. Augusta *Chronicle and Sentinel*, May 21, 1862.
2. Columbus *Daily Enquirer*, April 24, 1862, September 13, 1863, May 24, 1864.
3. Atlanta *Daily Intelligencer*, April 15, 17, 1863, June 17, 1863; Atlanta *Southern Confederacy*, March 25, 1863; Memphis *Daily Appeal*, April 9, 1863.
4. Chattanooga *Daily Rebel*, March 23, April 1, 1864.
5. Charleston *Mercury*, May 13, 1863.
6. Edward Pollard, *The First Year of the War* (Richmond, 1862), p. 168.
7. Robert E. Lee, Jr., *Recollections and Letters of General Robert E. Lee* (Garden City, N.Y., 1924), p. 18.
8. Burke Davis, *Gray Fox: Robert E. Lee and the Civil War* (New York, 1956), pp. 57, 77.
9. Columbus *Daily Enquirer*, July 24, 1862; Macon *Daily Telegraph*, Aug. 11, 1862.
10. Macon *Daily Telegraph*, June 1, 16, 1862, May 27, 1863; Richmond *Whig*, May 27, 28, June 12, 1862; Memphis *Daily Appeal*, June 1, 11, 1862; Columbus *Daily Enquirer*, June 9, 1862; Atlanta *Daily Intelligencer*, June 13, 1862; Savannah *Morning News*, June 11, 1862.
11. Augusta *Chronicle and Sentinel*, June 28, 29, July 18, 1862, May 8, 1863; Memphis *Daily Appeal*, July 8, 1862; Richmond *Sentinel*, March 13, 1863.
12. Richmond *Whig*, July 1, 1862, July 7, 1863; Macon *Daily Telegraph*, September 23, 1862, July 16, 1862; Augusta *Chronicle and Sentinel*, August 15, 17, 28, 1862; Memphis *Daily Appeal*, September 1, 11, 1862; Atlanta *Southern Confederacy*, September 6, 1862.
13. Richmond *Examiner*, October 27, 1862; Chattanooga *Daily Rebel*, November 2, 12, 20, 1862; P. W. Alexander, "Confederate Chieftains," *Southern Literary Messenger*, XXXV (January 1863), 37.
14. Richmond *Sentinel*, May 5, 11, 12, 13, 1863; Atlanta *Southern Confederacy*, May 12, 1863; Atlanta *Daily Intelligencer*, May 12, 13, 17, 1863; Richmond *Whig*, May 12, 1863; *Southern Literary Messenger*, XXXV (June 1863), 374; Richmond *Examiner*, May 11, 14, 1863.
15. James Dabney McCabe, *The Life of Thomas J. Jackson, by an Ex-Cadet* (2nd ed., Richmond, 1864), p. 191.
16. John Beaty, *John Esten Cooke, Virginian* (New York, 1922), pp. 78–80, 45.
17. John Esten Cooke, *Stonewall Jackson and the Old Stonewall Brigade*, Richard Harwell (ed.) (Charlottesville, n.d.), pp. 49–72.
18. James Dabney McCabe, *Aide-de-Camp: A Romance of the War* (Richmond, 1863); T. Harry Williams, *P. G. T. Beauregard: Napoleon in Gray* (Baton Rouge, 1955), pp. 91–92; Memphis *Daily Appeal*, September 1, 1861.
19. Atlanta *Southern Confederacy*, September 4, 1862; Atlanta *Daily Intelligencer*, October 16, 1862; Chattanooga *Daily Rebel*, November 5, December 12, 1862.
20. Alexander, "Confederate Chieftains," p. 55; Chattanooga *Daily Rebel*, November 25, December 7, 1862; Columbus *Daily Enquirer*, May 18, 1864; Atlanta *Southern Confederacy*, January 22, 1865; Atlanta *Daily Intelligencer*, December 6, 1862; Richmond *Examiner*, December 1, 1863.

21. Memphis *Daily Appeal*, September 10, 12, 1861, February 23, 1862; Atlanta *Southern Confederacy*, March 20, 1862.

22. Macon *Daily Telegraph*, April 8, 15, 1862; Savannah *Morning News*, April 8, 1862; Columbus *Daily Enquirer*, April 8, 1862; Atlanta *Daily Intelligencer*, October 18, 1862; Augusta *Chronicle and Sentinel*, April 8, 1862.

23. *Southern Historical Society Papers*, VI (October 1878), 167, hereinafter cited as *SHSP*; Jefferson Davis, *The Rise and Fall of the Confederate Government* (2 vols., New York, 1881), II, 69; Charles P. Roland, *Albert Sidney Johnston: Soldier of Three Republics* (Austin, 1964), pp. 347, 353; C. A. Culberson, *The Greatest Confederate Commander* (n.p., n.d.), pp. 8, 21.

24. New York *Times*, April 23, 1865.

25. Roland, *Johnston*, pp. 347, 353.

CHAPTER II

1. D. H. Hill to editor, *Century*, in *Century* Collection, New York Public Library; Dabney Maury to Jefferson Davis, November 2, 1877, in Dunbar Rowland (ed.), *Jefferson Davis, Constitutionalist: His Letters, Papers, and Speeches* (10 vols., Jackson, Miss., 1923), VIII, 39–40; Davis to J. William Jones, November 22, 1883, *ibid*, IX, 269; Arthur Shaw (ed.), "Some Post-War Letters from Jefferson Davis to His Former Aide-de-Camp, William Preston Johnston," in *Virginia Magazine of History and Biography*, LI (April 1943), 158–59.

2. Charles Venable to Jubal Early, February 15, 1871, in Jubal Early Papers, Library of Congress; all collections in this library cited hereinafter as DLC. See also Hunter McGuire to Early, April 16, 1871, in Early Papers, DLC, and John Imboden, "Lee at Gettysburg," *Galaxy*, XI (April 1871), 507–13.

3. John Letcher to Lee, August 5, 1865, in Lee Papers, McCormick Library of Washington and Lee University, hereinafter cited as W&L.

4. John Brockenbrough to Lee, August 10, 1865, Lee to Brockenbrough, March 1, 1866, in Lee Papers, W&L; Ollinger Crenshaw, *General Lee's College: The Rise and Growth of Washington and Lee University* (New York, 1969), pp. 148, 169–70.

5. Pendleton to John Brockenbrough, November 16, 1865, in Lee Papers, W&L.

6. *Circular of Board of Trustees of Washington College in Regard to the Enlargement of the Scientific Schools* (n.p., n.d.); Lee to Board of Trustees, January 8, 1869, Faculty Committee to Lee, January 8, 1869, in Lee Papers, W&L.

7. Mildred Lee Journal, January 22, 1887, in Lee-DeButts Papers, DLC.

8. J. Lewis Howe, "George Washington Custis Lee," *Virginia Magazine of History and Biography*, XLVIII (October 1940), 324–25; Crenshaw, *General Lee's College*, pp. 179–80.

9. *Ibid.*, p. 177.

10. Circular copy in Lee Papers, W&L.

11. Joseph Taylor, *Address Before the Literary Societies of Washington and Lee University* (Baltimore, 1871), copy in Lee Papers, W&L.

12. *Ibid.*

13. Crenshaw, *General Lee's College*, pp. 185–86, 192.

14. William Allan to Jubal Early, December 16, 1870, in Early Papers, DLC.

15. Mary Custis Lee, "My Reminiscences of the War Waged Against the South . . . ," ms. in Lee-DeButts Papers, DLC.

16. Mary Custis Lee to "Cousin Ellen," February 22, 1867, in Robert E. Lee Papers, Missouri Historical Society, St. Louis, hereinafter cited as Lee Papers, Missouri.

17. Rose M. MacDonald, *Mrs. Robert E. Lee* (Boston, 1939), p. 245.
18. Mildred Lee's appendix to Mary Custis Lee's "My Reminiscences...," December 11, 1874, also Mildred Lee Journal, January 22, 1887, both in Lee-DeButts Papers, DLC; Mary Custis Lee to "Cousin Ellen," February 22, 1867, in Lee Papers, Missouri; Mary Custis Lee to Edward Turner, n.d., in MacDonald, *Mrs. Robert E. Lee*, pp. 244–45.
19. MacDonald, *Mrs. Robert E. Lee*, pp. 295, 299; Mildred Lee's appendix to Mary Custis Lee's "My Reminiscences...," and Mildred Lee Journal, February 5, 1885, both in Lee-DeButts Papers, DLC.
20. MacDonald, *Mrs. Robert E. Lee*, pp. 244–45.
21. Mary Custis Lee to Mrs. William H. Stiles, February 9, 1861, typescript in Robert E. Lee Papers, Colonial Dames Collection, Georgia Historical Society, Savannah, hereinafter cited as Lee Papers, Colonial Dames, Georgia.
22. Margaret Sanborn, *Robert E. Lee: The Complete Man, 1861–1870* (Philadelphia, 1967), p. 62.
23. Mary Custis Lee, "My Reminiscences...," in Lee-DeButts Papers, DLC.
24. Mary Custis Lee to Mrs. A. L. Long, November 29, 1870, in Lee Papers, W&L; Mary Custis Lee to Miss Mary Meade, November 12, 1870, in *Virginia Magazine of History and Biography*, XXXV (January 1927), 23–24.
25. *Ibid.*
26. Mary Custis Lee to Mrs. William H. Stiles, March 8, 1862, in Lee Papers, Colonial Dames, Georgia.
27. MacDonald, *Mrs. Robert E. Lee*, p. 288.
28. Mary Custis Lee to Mrs. Susanna Blain, January 9, 1871, in Lee Papers, W&L.
29. Mary Custis Lee to Mrs. A. L. Long, November 20, 1870, in Lee Papers, W&L.
30. MacDonald, *Mrs. Robert E. Lee*, p. 299. Mildred Lee Journal, January 22, 1887, in Lee-DeButts Papers, DLC; J. William Jones, *Personal Reminiscences, Anecdotes and Letters of General Robert E. Lee* (New York, 1874), p. vi, cited hereinafter as Jones, *Personal Reminiscences; Southern Magazine*, III (January 1872), 122.
31. Susan Pendleton Lee, *Memoirs of William Nelson Pendleton* (Philadelphia, 1893), pp. 39–40, 48, 58, 66, 71, 108, 172, 279–80.
32. *Ibid.*, p. 414.
33. *Ibid.*, p. 337; William N. Pendleton, "Personal Recollections of General Lee," *Southern Magazine*, XV (December 1874), 634.
34. Lee, *Pendleton*, pp. 343–55, 456, 461; Glen Tucker, *Lee and Longstreet at Gettysburg* (Indianapolis, 1968), pp. 13, 43; Donald Sanger and Thomas R. Hay, *James Longstreet* (Baton Rouge, 1952), pp. 412, 415; Pendleton, "Personal Recollections," p. 613; *Historical Magazine*, 3rd ser., II (July 1873), 40.
35. "Sketch of the Lee Memorial Association," *SHSP*, XI (August–September 1883), 406–07.
36. *To the Alumni, Students and Friends of Washington College, November 15, 1870,* and *Announcement, October, 1870,* copies in Lee Papers, W&L; Charles Venable to Jubal Early, May 15, 1871, J. William Jones to Early, July 9, 25, 1873, in Early Papers, DLC.
37. J. William Jones to Jubal Early, July 9, 1873, in Early Papers, DLC; Jones, *Personal Reminiscences*, p. vi; *Virginia Magazine of History and Biography*, XVIII (April 1910), xviii.
38. J. William Jones, *The Davis Memorial Volume* (Richmond, 1890), p. v; Jones, *Personal Reminiscences*, p. v; *Confederate Veteran*, I (December 1893), 357.
39. J. William Jones to W. T. Walthall, February 4, March 11, 1879, in W. T. Walthall Papers, Mississippi Department of Archives and History; Rowland, *Davis*, IX, 197; J. William Jones to Jubal Early, March 20, 26, 1878, in Early Papers, DLC.

40. Dabney Maury to Jubal Early, October 26, 1870, in Early Papers, DLC.
41. See *Organization of the Lee Monument Association and the Association of the Army of Northern Virginia* (n.p., n.d.), copy in Lee Papers, W&L.
42. William Allan to Jubal Early, October 25, 1870, in Early Papers, DLC.
43. W. P. Johnston to Jubal Early, December 16, 1870, March 2, 14, 1871, William Allan to Early, December 16, 1870, March 15, 1871, John C. Breckinridge to Early, December 20, 1870, Charles Venable to Early, February 16, May 15, June 12, 1871, all in Early Papers, DLC; Crenshaw, *General Lee's College*, pp. 191–92.
44. Crenshaw, *General Lee's College*, pp. 191–92.
45. Basset French to Mayor of Mobile, Alabama, December 18, 1875, and circular (n.p., n.d.), both in Walthall Papers, Mississippi.
46. *Lee Monument Association*, pp. 31, 49.
47. "The Monument to General Robert E. Lee," *SHSP*, XII (January–December 1889), 285–86.
48. Charles Marshall, *Address Delivered before the Lee Monument Association* ... (Baltimore, 1888), p. 51, copy in Lee Papers, W&L; Charles Marshall, *An Aide-de-Camp of Lee, Being the Papers of Colonel Charles Marshall*, Sir Frederick Maurice (ed.) (Boston, 1927), pp. 178–81.
49. Walter Taylor, *Four Years with General Lee* (New York, 1877), pp. 155, 162–86, 188.
50. *Lee Monument Association*, pp. 18–19.
51. "Sketch of the Lee Memorial Association," p. 408.
52. *Ibid.*, pp. 408–09; G. Moxley Sorrel, *Recollections of a Confederate Staff Officer* (New York, 1905), pp. 238–39; Henry Wise, *End of an Era* (Boston, 1889), pp. 227–29.
53. Lee to Jubal Early, November 22, 1865, March 15, 1866, in George and Katharine Davis Collection, Howard-Tilton Library, Tulane University, hereinafter cited as Davis Collection, Tulane; Lee to "Whom It May Concern," copy in Lee Papers, W&L; Early to Lee, January 25, 1866, in Early Papers, DLC; Early to Thomas Rosser, May 10, 1866, typescript in Douglas Southall Freeman Papers, DLC, hereinafter cited as Freeman Papers, DLC.
54. J. William Jones to Jubal Early, March 20, 1872, Francis Lawley to Early, March 14, 1872, William Allan to Early, July 28, 1873, Jefferson Davis to Early, October 21, 1873, W. P. Johnston to Early, March 2, 1871, Charles Venable to Early, February 16, 1871, all in Early Papers, DLC.
55. Robert Stiles, *Four Years under Marse Robert* (New York, 1903), p. 190.
56. For example, see *Historical Magazine*, 3rd ser., I (January 1872), 1–2.
57. Edward Pollard, *Lee and His Lieutenants* (New York, 1867), pp. 476–77.
58. Jubal Early, *The Campaigns of Gen. Robert E. Lee* (Baltimore, 1872), p. 47.
59. William Swinton, *Campaigns of the Army of the Potomac* (2nd ed., New York, 1882), p. 17.
60. Francis Lawley, "General Lee," *Blackwood's Edinburgh Magazine*, CXI (March 1872), 361–63.
61. Charles Venable to Jubal Early, May 15, 1871, W. P. Johnston to Early, March 2, 1871, Francis Lawley to Early, May 14, 1872, Fitzhugh Lee to Early, January 29, May 6, 1871, all in Early Papers, DLC; Emily Mason, *Popular Life of Gen. Robert Edward Lee* (Baltimore, 1877), p. 359.
62. John Esten Cooke, *A Life of Gen. Robert E. Lee* (New York, 1871), pp. 155, 306–07, 317–18.
63. Rowland, *Davis*, VIII, 259; Ray M. Atchison, "Southern Literary Magazines, 1865–1877," Ph.D. dissertation, Duke University, 1956, p. 283.
64. Edward Pollard, *The Southern History of the War: The Third Year of the War* (New York, 1865), pp. 15–16; Pollard, *Lee and His Lieutenants*, pp. 110–11, 116.

65. James McCabe, *Life and Campaigns of General Robert E. Lee* (New York, 1867), pp. 49–50.
66. *Ibid.*, pp. 98, 236, 241, 319, 349, 394–95.
67. Swinton, *Campaigns of the Army of the Potomac*, pp. 163, 124–25, 142–65.
68. John Esten Cooke, *Stonewall Jackson: A Military Biography* (New York, 1866), pp. 410, 464.
69. Swinton, *Campaigns of the Army of the Potomac*, pp. 340–41, 356; William Swinton, *The Twelve Decisive Battles of the War* (New York, 1867), pp. 352–53; McCabe, *Life of Thomas J. Jackson*, pp. 179, 196.
70. Pollard, *Lee and His Lieutenants*, p. 229.

CHAPTER III

1. For information on postwar magazines, the author is heavily indebted to Rayburn Moore's excellent "Southern Writers and Northern Literary Magazines, 1865–1890," Ph.D. dissertation, Duke University, 1956. Moore's bibliography of articles on Southern culture is invaluable. Other important studies heavily used include Mary Covington, *"The Atlantic* and *Harper's* in Relation to Southern Literature, 1865–1900," and Atchison's "Southern Literary Magazines," already cited.
2. See *Historical Magazine*, 3rd ser., I (January 1872), 1–2.
3. For examples of Cooke's work, see "Virginia Partisans," Philadelphia *Times,* October 29, 1881, and "Stuart and the Lady Prisoners," Philadelphia *Times,* October 5, 1878, copies in Henry McClellan Papers, Virginia Historical Society.
4. *Southern Review,* V (April 1869), 443–45; *Southern Review,* n.s., XIX (April 1876), 325.
5. Quoted in Dorothy Smith, "Attitudes Toward the Civil War and the Reconstruction Period by Southern Novelists," M.A. thesis, University of Southern California, 1939, p. 21.
6. Beaty, *John Esten Cooke,* p. 98.
7. *Ibid.*, p. 100.
8. John Esten Cooke, "The Personal Character of General Lee," *Appleton's,* XII (January 9, 1875), 47–50.
9. *SHSP*, n.s., I (April 1914), 215.
10. *SHSP*, V (April 1878), iv; *Southern Magazine,* n.s., VII (January 1874), appendix p. "A."
11. *Southern Magazine,* n.s., VII (January 1874), appendix page "A,"; John Caldwell to Jubal Early, May 27, 1873, in Early Papers, DLC; New Orleans *Picayune,* June 15, 1869, clipping in Lee Papers, W&L.
12. J. William Jones to Jubal Early, March 26, 1878, July 26, September 21, December 7, 1877, in Early Papers, DLC; *SHSP*, XI (April–May 1883), 239; *SHSP*, IX (July–August 1881), 382–83.
13. J. William Jones to Jubal Early, November 15, 1876, in Early Papers, DLC.
14. J. William Jones to Jubal Early, March 9, 1875, in Early Papers, DLC.
15. *Ibid.*
16. J. William Jones to Jubal Early, May 21, December 7, 1877, in Early Papers, DLC.
17. William Allan to Jubal Early, March 26, 1872, Charles Marshall to Early, August 7, 1873, March 13, 1878, Walter Taylor to Early, February 26, 1878, all in Early Papers, DLC.
18. Charles Marshall to Jubal Early, August 7, 1873, March 13, 1878, Walter Taylor to Early, February 26, 1878, all in Early Papers, DLC.
19. Rowland, *Davis,* IX, 167.
20. *Ibid.*, IX, 269; Arthur Shaw (ed.), "Some Post-War Letters from Jefferson Davis to

His Former Aide-de-Camp, William Preston Johnston," *Virginia Magazine of History and Biography,* LI (April 1943), 158–59.

21. Rowland, *Davis,* IX, 524–25, 522, 551, VII, 379 ff.; Jefferson Davis, "Robert E. Lee," *North American Review,* L (January 1890), 64–65.

22. Rowland, *Davis,* VIII, 56, 141, IX, 470–71.

23. J. William Jones to W. T. Walthall, February 4, March 24, 1879, in Walthall Papers, Mississippi.

24. See *SHSP,* VIII (August–September 1880), 409; see also Alfred Roman to P. G. T. Beauregard, January 14, 1866, typescript in Alfred Roman Papers, Louisiana State Department of Archives; Rowland, *Davis,* VIII, 340, 344.

25. Williams, *Beauregard,* p. 309; Roman to Beauregard, March 1, 1883, copy in Alfred Roman Papers, LSU.

26. J. William Jones to Jubal Early, May 21, December 7, 1877, William Allan to Early, March 26, 1872, Charles Marshall to Early, August 7, 1873, all in Early Papers, DLC.

27. See *The Nation,* XXXVIII–XXXIX (March 6, 1884), 215; *Harper's New Monthly Magazine,* LXVIII (April 1884), 808; Williams, *Beauregard,* p. 315.

28. Memphis *Daily Appeal,* December 30, 1881, clipping in Association of the Army of Northern Virginia Papers, Louisiana Historical Association Collection, LSU.

29. *SHSP,* I (June 1876), 412–13, 423.

30. Mrs. T. J. Jackson to Lee, October 20, 1865, January 9, 1866, in Lee Papers, W&L.

31. Lee to Mrs. Jackson, January 25, 1866, in Lee Papers, W&L; Robert L. Dabney, *Life and Campaigns of Lieut.-Gen. Thomas J. Jackson (Stonewall Jackson)* (New York, 1866), p. 484.

32. Lee to Albert Bledsoe, October 28, 1867, in J. William Jones, *Life and Letters of Robert Edward Lee, Soldier and Man* (New York, 1906), 236.

33. *Ibid.*

34. Fitzhugh Lee, "Chancellorsville," *SHSP,* VII (December 1879), 545–85.

35. J. William Jones, "Reminiscences," *SHSP,* IX (Oct.–Dec. 1881), 558, 565.

36. *SHSP,* II (July 1873), 33, VIII (April 1880), 92; Charles Marshall to Jubal Early, May 24, 1877, March 23, 1876, in Early Papers, DLC.

37. *Southern Magazine,* 3rd ser., I (January 1872), 1–2.

38. Glenn Tucker, *Lee and Longstreet at Gettysburg* (Indianapolis, 1968), pp. 13, 43; Donald Sanger and Thomas R. Hay, *James Longstreet* (Baton Rouge, 1952), pp. 412, 415; *Historical Magazine,* 3rd ser., II (July 1873), 40; Pendleton, "Personal Recollections," p. 603.

39. Sanger and Hay, *Longstreet,* pp. 410–36.

40. Robert Park to J. William Jones, May 1, 1877, in Southern Historical Society Papers, VHS; Jones to Jubal Early, March 21, 22, 1877, Charles Marshall to Early, May 24, 1877, in Early Papers, DLC.

41. *SHSP,* III (March 1877), 154.

42. J. William Jones to Jubal Early, March 22, 1887, Charles Marshall to Early, May 24, 1877, in Early Papers, DLC.

43. Walter Taylor, "The Campaign in Pennsylvania," Philadelphia *Times,* August 27, 1877.

44. *SHSP,* IV (August 1877), 89–90.

45. *SHSP,* V (January–February 1878), 90–93; Charles Venable to Jubal Early, April 28, 1875, in Early Papers, DLC.

46. *SHSP,* IV (August 1877), 50–87, IV (December 1877), 241, 281.

47. Henry McClellan to Jubal Early, February 6, 1878, in Early Papers, DLC.

48. Jubal Early to Henry McClellan, February 11, 1878, in McClellan Papers, VHS.

49. Jubal Early to Henry McClellan, February 13, 1878, in McClellan Papers, VHS.

50. Fitzhugh Lee to Henry McClellan, July 31, 1878, in McClellan Papers, VHS;

Fitzhugh Lee to Jubal Early, January 29, 1878, in Early Papers, DLC.

51. *SHSP*, V (June 1878), 257–69, 270–87.
52. *SHSP*, XVI (January–December 1886), 102–18.
53. Jones, *Life and Letters*, p. 275.
54. Atlanta *Southern Confederacy*, May 22, September 10, 12, 1862; Columbus *Daily Enquirer*, April 8, 1864; Atlanta *Daily Intelligencer*, July 4, 1862.
55. Richmond *Sentinel*, July 17, May 16, 1864.
56. *SHSP*, VI (December 1878), 243, XI (January 1883), 247, IX (October–December 1881), 573.
57. Quoted in Jones, *Personal Reminiscences*, pp. 51, 49.
58. *SHSP*, VII (February 1879), 59, 63.
59. John Hampden Chamberlayne, "Address on the Character of General R. E. Lee," *SHSP*, III (January 1877), 30.
60. *Ceremonies Connected with the Unveiling of the Statue of General Robert E. Lee* (New Orleans, 1884), p. 38, copy in Custis-Lee Mansion, Arlington.
61. *SHSP*, IX (January 1881), 36.
62. Hugh Pleasants, "Character of the Southern People," *The Land We Love*, IV (June 1868), 243; *SHSP*, XIV (January–December 1886), 464–95; Pollard, *Lee and His Lieutenants*, p. 94.
63. "Editor's Comment," *Southern Magazine*, III (January 1872), 122; see also Chamberlayne, "Address," p. 31.
64. Jones, *Life and Letters*, pp. 148, 247, 147; Lee to wife, November 13, 1862, General Orders 5, May 7, 1863, both in Lee Papers, DLC.
65. John Daniel, *Robert Edward Lee: An Oration* (Savannah, 1883), pp. 13–14.
66. *SHSP*, I (January 1876), 51–52.
67. Mason, *Popular Life*, p. 351; Jones, *Personal Reminiscences*, pp. 488–89, 491.
68. The relationship of the Lee image to Daniel's political fortunes is discussed in Richard Doss, "John Warwick Daniel: A Study in the Virginia Democracy," Ph.D. dissertation, University of Virginia, 1955.
69. Daniel, *Lee Oration*, pp. 13–14, 66–67, 25, 23, 29.

CHAPTER IV

1. For newspaper comments, see *Public Opinion*, IX (June 7, 1890), 189–90.
2. *Ibid.*; see also *Harper's Weekly*, XXXIV (June 14, 1890), 470.
3. A. J. McKelway, "Appomattox: An Anniversary," *Harper's Weekly*, LXII (April 15, 1916), 411–12; Wallace Rice, "Hero of a Lost Cause," *Dial* (October 16, 1904), 233; E. F. Andrews, "The Surrender of Lee," *Chautauquan*, XXXI (August 1900), 523.
4. Theodore Roosevelt, "Robert E. Lee and the Nation," *Sewanee Review*, XVI (April 1907), 173 ff.; Woodrow Wilson, "Robert E. Lee: An Interpretation," *Journal of Social Forces*, II (March 1924), 321, a reprint of a 1909 address at the University of North Carolina. See also Laura Spencer Porter and Charles Graves, "His Love for His Old Gray Horse," *The Ladies' Home Journal*, XXV (January 1908), 20; "Robert E. Lee," *Outlook*, LXXXIV (December 22, 1906), 956; "North and South Fifty Years after Appomattox," *Literary Digest*, L (May 1, 1915), 1000–1003; A. J. McKelway, "Appomattox: An Anniversary," *Harper's Weekly*, LXII (April 15, 1916), 411–12; Julia Ward Howe, "Robert E. Lee," *Current Literature*, XLII (March 1907), 342; Charles F. Smith, "Robert E. Lee Once More," *South Atlantic Quarterly*, VII (October 1908), 359–69; John J. Halsey, "Grant and Lee as National Heroes," *Dial*, LII (March 1, 1912), 159–62; "The Soul of Honor," *Outlook*,

LXXXV (January 5, 1907), 48–59; Charles Graves, "Recollections of General Robert E. Lee," *Harper's Weekly*, LI (February 2, 1907), 172.

5. For examples, see A. R. H. Ranson, "General Lee as I Knew Him," *Harper's New Monthly Magazine*, CXXII (February 1911), 327–36; John B. Gordon, "Gettysburg," *Scribner's Magazine*, XXXIV (July 1903), 2–24; Captain Robert E. Lee, "With My Father on the Battlefield," *The Ladies' Home Journal*, XXI (October 1904); Mrs. George Pickett, "The Wartime Stories of General Pickett," *Cosmopolitan Magazine*, LV (November 1913), 752–60; Thomas Nelson Page, "General Lee and the Confederate Government," *Scribner's Monthly*, L (November 1911), 581–92; and Edward Porter Alexander, "Lee at Appomattox," *Century*, LXIII (April 1902), 921–31.

6. John Irion, "Sketch of the Fifth Tennessee Infantry," in Tennessee State Library and Archives; *SHSP*, XIV (January–December 1886), 31.

7. Quoted in Majorie Craig, "Survivals of the Chivalric Tournament in Southern Life and Literature," M.A. thesis, University of North Carolina, 1935, pp. 158–61.

8. *Ibid.*, pp. 60–61.

9. *Ibid.*, pp. 91–92.

10. *SHSP*, XXI (July–September 1898), 467.

11. *SHSP*, IX (May 1881), 194, n.s., IV (October 1905), 305, 315, IX (April 1881), 190.

12. Bradley T. Johnson, *The Constitution of the Confederate States* (Baltimore, 1891), copy in Louisiana Historical Association Collection, Tulane.

13. *SHSP*, VII (August 1879), 381–82, XVI (January–December 1888), 424; *Chautauquan*, XV (May 1892), 150.

14. John Esten Cooke, "Virginia in the Revolution," *Harper's New Monthly Magazine*, LIII (June 1876), 2–3.

15. Covington, "*The Atlantic* and *Harper's* in Relation to Southern Literature," pp. 138–44.

16. Thomas Nelson Page, *The Old Dominion* (New York, 1908), pp. 58, viii, 311–12, 327.

17. Moore, "Southern Writers and Northern Literary Magazines," pp. 246–57; Sara Pryor, *My Day: Reminiscences of a Long Life* (New York, 1908), pp. 9–12.

18. *Ibid.*, p. 82.

19. Sara Pryor, *Reminiscences of Peace and War* (New York, 1904), pp. 101, 58, 119, 136–42.

20. See cover advertisement for both books by Sara Pryor.

21. George Cary Eggleston, *Recollections of a Varied Life* (New York, 1910), pp. 46, 47, 49; Eggleston to John Esten Cooke, April 26, 1874, quoted in Moore, "Southern Writers and Northern Literary Magazines."

22. George Cary Eggleston, "A Rebel's Recollections," *The Atlantic Monthly*, XXXIII (June 1874), 734.

23. George Cary Eggleston, *A Rebel's Recollections* (New York, 1875), p. 6.

24. Smith, "Attitudes Toward the Civil War and the Reconstruction Period by Southern Novelists," pp. 5–6, 47–48; George Cary Eggleston, *History of the Confederate War* (2 vols., New York, 1910), I, 167–68.

25. *SHSP*, XVI (January–December 1888).

26. Henry Shepherd, *Life of Robert Edward Lee* (New York, 1906), pp. 247–62.

27. William P. Trent, *Robert E. Lee* (New York, 1899), pp. 34, x–xi.

28. John Deering, *Lee and His Cause* (New York, 1907), pp. 180–81, 27, 29.

29. Stiles, *Four Years under Marse Robert*, p. 35.

30. *Ibid.*, p. 20.

31. Darrell Rutman, "Philip Alexander Bruce: A Divided Mind of the South," *Virginia Magazine of History and Biography*, LXVIII (October 1960), 390.

32. Thomas Nelson Page, "Lee in Defeat," *South Atlantic Quarterly*, VI (January 1907), 1.

33. S. F. R. Henderson, "Review of General Long's Book," *SHSP*, n.s., I (April 1914), 104 ff.; for other articles on Gettysburg, see *SHSP*, XXXVIII (January–December 1910), 312 ff., n.s., II (September 1915), 253 ff., XXXI (January–December 1903), 288 ff., XXXVII (June 1897), 323.

34. *Confederate Veteran*, V (June 1897), 323, also pp. 317, 326.

35. *Official Program of the Twentieth Annual Reunion of the Army of the Cumberland* (n.p., 1889), *Southern Battlefields* (Nashville, n.d.), *Cockade City of the Union* (Petersburg, 1907), copies in Louisiana Historical Association Collection, Tulane; *Confederate Veteran*, V (June 1897), 31.

36. *Ibid.*, VIII (August 1900), 341.

37. *Ibid.*, I (December 1893), 361.

38. *SHSP*, XXXVI (January–December 1908), 156.

39. *Confederate Veteran*, XXIX (June 1921), 208.

40. Susan P. Lee, *New School History of the United States* (2nd ed., Richmond, 1900).

41. Mary Williamson, *The Life of General Robert E. Lee* (2nd ed., Richmond, 1918), pp. 43, 75, 102, 122, 171.

42. *Memorial Day Annual*, pp. 31, 92–93.

43. *SHSP*, XVII (January–December 1890), 136.

44. *Confederate Veteran*, IX (February 1901), 59, also p. 58.

45. W. B. Merritt, *Selections for the Observance . . . of the Birthday of Robert E. Lee in the Schools of Georgia* (Atlanta, 1905), copy in Lee Papers, W&L.

46. Alabama Department of Education, *Program and Selections for the Celebration . . . of the One Hundredth Anniversary of the Birthday of Robert Edward Lee* (Montgomery, 1907), copy in Lee Papers, W&L.

47. *Suggestions for the Celebration of the One Hundredth Anniversary* (New Orleans, 1907), copy in Custis-Lee Mansion, Arlington.

48. Cozette Keller, *Sword of Robert E. Lee: Poses and Directions for Pantomiming and Reciting* (n.p., 1911), copy in Lee Papers, W&L.

49. New York *Times*, January 19, 1908.

50. *The Atlantic Monthly*, XCV (January 1905), 133–34.

51. *Dial*, XXXVIII (October 16, 1904), 233–35; *Current Literature*, July 1905, p. 33; *Independent*, November 16, 1905, p. 1157.

52. *The Nation*, LXXX (January 19, 1905), 55.

53. *Outlook*, LXXVIII (November 26, 1904), 782.

54. For examples of Adams's approach, see "A Great Historic Character and *Vae Victis,*" in *Trans-Atlantic Historical Solidarity* (Oxford, 1913), pp. 154–57; *Shall Cromwell Have a Statue?* (Boston, 1902); *Lee's Centennial: An Address . . . Delivered at Lexington, Virginia, Saturday, January 19, 1907* (Boston, 1907); *Lee at Appomattox and Other Papers* (Boston, 1902); and *The Confederacy and the Transvaal: A People's Obligation to Robert E. Lee* (Boston, 1901).

55. *Dial*, XXXIII (July 16, 1902), 52.

56. Crenshaw, *General Lee's College*, pp. 282–83.

57. Lee to Mary Lee, January 18, 1862, in Lee Papers, VHS; for altered version, see Robert Lee, Jr., *Recollections and Letters*, pp. 60–61. Lee to Mary Lee, July 12, 1861, in Lee Papers, VHS; for altered version, see *Recollections and Letters*, p. 36. Lee to Mary Lee, April 30, 1861, in Lee Papers, DLC; for altered version, see *Recollections and Letters*, p. 29. For further alterations, see Jones, *Life and Letters*, pp. 143, 139.

58. Lee to Mary Lee, December 27, 1856, in Freeman, *Lee*, I, 371–73; for altered version, see Jones, *Life and Letters*, p. 82; see also Lee to W. H. F. Lee, February 16, 1862, in Lee Papers, VHS.

59. Lee to W. H. F. Lee, July 9, 1860, in Bolling Lee Papers, VHS.
60. Lee to W. H. F. Lee, May 30, 1858, in Bolling Lee Papers, VHS; for Jones's alteration, see *Life and Letters*, p. 94. Lee to Mary Lee, October 26, 1862, in Lee Papers, VHS; for altered version see Lee, *Recollections and Letters*, pp. 79–80.
61. Lee to Mary Lee, September 9, 1861, in Lee Papers, VHS.
62. See Thomas Nelson Page, *Robert E. Lee: The Southerner* (New York, 1909), and *Robert E. Lee: Man and Soldier* (New York, 1911).
63. *Library of Southern Literature* (Atlanta, 1907), XIII, 5955.
64. For discussion of national attitudes, see Russel B. Nye, *The Unembarrassed Muse: The Popular Arts in America* (New York, 1970); Roderick Nash, *The Call of the Wild, 1900–1916* (New York, 1970); Neil Harris, *The Land of Contrasts, 1880–1901* (New York, 1970); David Noble, *The Progressive Mind, 1890–1917* (Chicago, 1970).
65. See Gamaliel Bradford, *Lee the American* (Boston, 1912).
66. New York *Sun*, January 21, 1906, clipping in Freeman Papers, DLC; Wayne Whipple, *The Heart of Lee* (Philadelphia, 1918); E. F. Andrews, "The Surrender of Lee," *Chautauquan*, XXXI (August 1900), 523.
67. Garland Greever, "Southern Leadership Since the Civil War," *North American Review*, CXCII (August 1910), 272; Frederick T. Hill, *On the Trail of Grant and Lee* (New York, 1911), p. 288.
68. *Harper's Weekly*, LI (February 2, 1907), 172; Lee, "With My Father on the Battlefield," pp. 11 ff.; Edwin Mims, "General Lee's Place in History," *Outlook*, LXXXIV (December 22, 1906), 978–82; Roosevelt, "Robert E. Lee and the Nation," pp. 173–76; McKelway, "Appomattox: An Anniversary," pp. 411–12.

CHAPTER V

1. See Roderick Nash, *The Nervous Generation: American Thought and Culture, 1917–1930* (Chicago, 1969).
2. *The Nation*, CXXIV (February 9, 1927), 135.
3. *The Atlantic Monthly*, CXXXVIII (August 1926), 182.
4. *American Mercury*, XVIII (March 1929), 358.
5. Sara Haardt, "Southern Credo,"*American Mercury*, XX (May 1930), 110.
6. Charles Hosmer, Jr., *The Presence of the Past: A History of the Preservation Movement in the United States before Williamsburg* (New York, 1965), pp. 131–32.
7. See Anne M. Washington, *History of the George Washington Bi-Centennial* (3 vols., Washington, 1932).
8. Mary Flournoy, *Essays: Historical and Critical, Twin Patriots, Washington and Lee* (Freeport, N.Y., 1967), pp. 41–47.
9. *Restoration of the Lee Mansion* (Washington, 1924), copy in Custis-Lee Mansion, Arlington.
10. New York *Times*, March 25, 1929, April 14, 1930; *Congressional Record*, January 20, 1930.
11. Lucy Shelton Stewart, *The Reward of Patriotism* (New York, 1930), pp. 406–08.
12. *Ibid.*, p. 406.
13. *Ibid.*, pp. 410–11.
14. *Ibid.*, p. 412.
15. *Ibid.*, pp. 445–47; New York *Times*, April 8, 1928.
16. *Washington and Lee University Bulletin*, XX (November 25, 1921), copy in Lee Papers, W&L; Crenshaw, *General Lee's College*, p. 301.
17. *Washington and Lee University Bulletin*, XXII (September 1, 1923), copy in Lee Papers, W&L.

18. New York *Times*, January 21, 1924; Crenshaw, *General Lee's College*, p. 303.
19. Nash, *The Nervous Generation*, contains a full discussion.
20. Nye, *The Unembarrassed Muse*, pp. 76–87.
21. Boy Scouts of America, *Handbook for Patrol Leaders* (New York, 1933), p. i.
22. *Washington and Lee University Bulletin*, XX (November 6, 1921), copy in Lee Papers, W&L.
23. J. G. de Roulhac and Mary Hamilton, *The Life of Robert E. Lee for Boys and Girls* (New York, 1917); William Johnstone, *Robert E. Lee: The Christian* (New York, 1933); James Young, *Marse Robert: Knight of the Confederacy* (New York, 1929), p. 345; William Brooks, *Lee of Virginia* (New York, 1932), pp. xii–xiii; Robert Winston, *Robert E. Lee: A Biography* (New York, 1934).
24. "Marse Robert," *Collier's*, LXXIX (March 5, 1927), 32, 34.
25. For a full discussion, see Charles Alexander, *Nationalism in American Thought, 1930–1945* (Chicago, 1969), pp. 25–59; David Shannon, *Twentieth Century America* (Chicago, 1963), pp. 397–413.
26. *Saturday Review*, XV (March 6, 1937), 8.
27. Nye, *The Unembarrassed Muse*, pp. 379–84, 393–96.
28. Margaret Mitchell, *Gone With the Wind* (New York, 1936), p. 63.
29. New York *Times*, June 30, 1936.
30. Stark Young, *So Red the Rose* (New York, 1934), pp. 5, 30, 90; Francis Griswold, *Tides of Malvern* (New York, 1930), p. 215; Craig, "Survivals of the Chivalric Tournament," pp. 99–105.
31. Shannon, *Twentieth Century America*, pp. 428–30; Alexander, *Nationalism in American Thought*, pp. 164–75.
32. James Randall, "The Blundering Generation," *Mississippi Valley Historical Review*, XXVII (June 1940), 3–28; Charles Ramsdell, "The Natural Limits of Slavery Expansion," *Mississippi Valley Historical Review*, XVI (September 1929), 151–71; Charles Ramsdell, "Lincoln and Fort Sumter," *Journal of Southern History*, III (August 1937), 259–88.
33. *Saturday Review*, XV (March 6, 1937), 8.
34. Clifford Dowdey, *Bugles Blow No More* (Boston, 1937), pp. 201, 213, 300, 380; Young, *So Red the Rose*, p. 248; Joseph Hergesheimer, *Swords and Roses* (New York, 1929), p. 169.
35. *Scholastic*, March 9, 1942, p. 11.
36. *Confederate Veteran*, XXXVII (December 1930), 458; *Washington and Lee University Bulletin*, XXXII (May 1, 1933), copy in Lee Papers, W&L.
37. Johnstone, *Robert E. Lee: The Christian;* Charles Rhodes, *R. E. Lee: The West Pointer* (Richmond, 1932), p. 16.
38. Copy of radio broadcast in Lee Papers, W&L.
39. Copy of radio broadcast in Lee Papers, W&L.
40. Winston, *Lee*, p. 89.
41. Copy of speech in Lee Papers, W&L.
42. *Address of Hon. Henry T. Wickham* (Richmond, 1940), copy in Custis-Lee Mansion, Arlington.
43. See Francis Griswold, *A Sea Island Lady* (New York, 1939).
44. Hergesheimer, *Swords and Roses*, pp. i, 169.
45. Donald Davidson, "A Note on American Heroes," *Southern Review*, I (1935–36), 436–38.
46. S. A. Steel, *Lee: The Passing of the Old South* (Atlanta, 1932), pp. 55, 9, 31.
47. L. W. Allen, *An Epic Trilogy* (New York, 1929), p. 34.
48. Flournoy, *Washington and Lee*, p. 42; William Folsom, "Robert E. Lee: An Appreciation," in *Vermonters in Battle and Other Papers* (Montpelier, 1953), p. 172; Brooks, *Lee of Virginia*, p. 31.

49. *Robert E. Lee Week* (n.p., n.d.), copy in Lee Papers, W&L.
50. *Scribner's Magazine*, LXXXVIII (December 1930), 587–88.
51. Brooks, *Lee of Virginia*, p. 236.
52. Freeman, *Lee*, III, 106, 153.
53. Copy of address in Lee Papers, W&L.
54. Bernard De Voto, "Gettysburg," *Harper's*, CLXXV (August 1937), 333–36.
55. Donald Davidson, *Lee in the Mountains and Other Poems* (New York, 1949), pp. 5–6.

CHAPTER VI

1. See Ambler Johnston, *Reminiscences* (Richmond, n.d.), p. 50: New York *Times*, February 10, 1935; *Time*, LII (October 18, 1949), 108.
2. Lee Memorial Fund, *Robert E. Lee: Soldier, Patriot, Educator* (n.p., 1921), copy in Lee Papers, W&L; *The Lee Memorial School of Journalism: Washington and Lee University Bulletin*, XXI (December 20, 1922), copy in Lee Papers, W&L.
3. Henry L. Smith, *Lee the Educator* (Lexington, 1929), copy in Lee Papers, W&L.
4. Francis Pendleton Gaines, *Lee: The Final Achievement, 1865–1870* (Lexington, Va., 1933), copy in Lee Papers, W&L.
5. *Gifts That Can Mold a Future* (n.p., n.d.) and *Two Great Investments in Faith* (n.p., n.d.), copies in Lee Papers, W&L.
6. *Joint Resolution, 80th Congress, June 14, 1948*, copy in Lee Papers, W&L.
7. *Robert E. Lee: Innovative Educator* (Lexington, Va., 1970), copy in Lee Papers, W&L.
8. Douglas Southall Freeman, "The Lengthening Shadow of Lee," copy in Freeman Papers, DLC.
9. Douglas Southall Freeman, "Your Age: An Address Before the Columbia School of Journalism, May 14, 1936," copy in Freeman Papers, DLC.
10. Freeman, "Lengthening Shadow of Lee."
11. Douglas Southall Freeman, "Address Before the Institute of Arts and Sciences of Columbia University, October 23, 1935," copy in Freeman Papers, DLC.
12. Freeman, "Lengthening Shadow of Lee."
13. Douglas Southall Freeman, "Barbed-Wire Horizons—Commencement Address at Marshall College, June 4, 1940," copy in Freeman Papers, DLC; Douglas Southall Freeman, "Old Ramparts and New," copy in Freeman Papers, DLC.
14. *Time*, LII (October 18, 1948), 109; Freeman, "Lengthening Shadow of Lee."
15. Freeman, "The Battlefields Around Richmond," *Stars and Bars*, April 1925, copy in Freeman Papers, DLC.
16. Freeman, "Lengthening Shadow of Lee"; Freeman, *Lee*, I, 489; Douglas Southall Freeman, "The Cornerstones of Stratford," copy in Freeman Papers, DLC.
17. Copy of speech, July 30, 1919, in Freeman Papers, DLC.
18. Freeman, "The Cornerstones of Stratford."
19. Freeman, *Lee*, II, 462.
20. Douglas Southall Freeman, "Virginia: A Gentle Dominion," *The Nation*, CXIX (July 16).
21. Freeman, "The Battlefields Around Richmond"; Douglas Southall Freeman, "The Confederate Tradition of Richmond," *Civil War History*, III (December 1957), 369.
22. Freeman, *Lee*, I, 459.
23. *Ibid.*, II, 19–20, 231, 259.
24. *Ibid.*, II, 277.
25. *Ibid.*, I, 68, 449–50; see also pp. 84–85.
26. *Ibid.*, I, 85, 451–56.

27. *Ibid.*, I, 351–52; II, 106, 260, 267, 276, 345.
28. *Ibid.*, I, 359, 428.
29. *Ibid.*, I, 432, 484.
30. *Ibid.*, I, 459–60, 477–78.
31. *Ibid.*, I, 21, 44–46, 92–94, 109–10, 131, 169, 440, 453.
32. *Ibid.*, I, 415–16.
33. *Ibid.*, I, 434–45.
34. *Ibid.*, I, 440.
35. *Ibid.*, II, 6–7.
36. *Ibid.*, III, 165, 259–60.
37. Douglas Southall Freeman and Elbridge Colby, "Robert E. Lee: Is His Military Genius Fact or Fiction?", *Current History*, XXIX (October 1928), 45–46.
38. *Ibid.*, p. 45.
39. *Ibid.*, p. 46.
40. Freeman, *Lee*, II, 347.
41. *Ibid.*, III, 149–60.
42. *Ibid.*, II, 40.
43. Douglas Southall Freeman, *Lee's Lieutenants* (3 vols., New York, 1942–44), I, 83.
44. Freeman, *Lee*, II, 247.
45. *Ibid.*, II, 418, 218.
46. *Ibid.*, I, 480, 485; II, 321, 343, 498.
47. Freeman, *Lee's Lieutenants*, I, 485–86.
48. Freeman, *Lee*, II, 109, 520–21, 523; III, 2–4.
49. T. Harry Williams, "Freeman: Historian of the Civil War: An Appraisal," *Journal of Southern History*, XXI (February, 1955), 93.
50. See reviews by Henry Steele Commager in *Yale Review*, n.s., XXIV (Spring 1935), 594–97, and by Dumas Malone in *American Historical Review*, XLI (October 1935), 164–68. For other examples, see *The Nation*, CXXXIX (December 26, 1934), 747; *Time*, XL (October 26, 1942), 106; *Catholic World*, CXL (March 1935), 752–53; *Review of Reviews*, XCI (January 1935), 5–6; Allen Tate, "The Definitive Lee," *New Republic*, LXXXI (December 19, 1934), 171–73; Charles Willis Thompson, New York *Times*, February 10, 1935; *North American Review*, CCXL (June 1935), 184–90.
51. New York *Times*, February 10, 1935.
52. Freeman, *Lee*, I, 452.
53. See *Civil War History*, I (March 1955), 10.
54. Freeman, *Lee*, I, 446, 459; II, 67.
55. Williams, "Freeman: Historian of the Civil War," p. 99.
56. Freeman, "Your Age."
57. Freeman, "Lengthening Shadow of Lee."
58. Freeman, *Lee*, IV, 501–02.
59. *Ibid.*, IV, 503, 505.
60. J. F. C. Fuller, *Grant and Lee: A Study in Personality and Generalship* (2nd ed., Bloomington, Ind., 1957).
61. See B. H. Liddell Hart, *Sherman: Soldier, Realist, American* (New York, 1929).
62. See B. H. Liddell Hart, "Lee: A Psychological Problem," *Saturday Review*, XI (December 15, 1934), 365 ff.; and "Why Lee Lost Gettysburg," *Saturday Review*, XI (March 23, 1935), 561 ff.
63. Williams, "Freeman: Historian of the Civil War," pp. 96, 100.
64. Allan Nevins, *The War for the Union* (4 vols., New York, 1959, 1971), I, 110–11; II, 84.
65. Avery Craven, "Lee's Dilemma," *Virginia Magazine of History and Biography*, LXIX (April 1961), 131–32.

66. Joseph Harrison, Jr., "Harry Williams, Critic of Freeman: A Demurrer," *Virginia Magazine of History and Biography*, LXIV (January 1956), 72–75.
67. For other attacks upon Lee critics, see Donald Davidson, "A Note on American Heroes," *Southern Review*, I (1935–36), 436–38; Kirkwood Mitchell, "Lee and the Bullet of the Civil War," *William and Mary Quarterly*, 2nd ser., XVI (January 1936), 26–37; Charles Roland, "The Generalship of Robert E. Lee," in Grady McWhiney (ed.), *Grant, Lee, Lincoln and the Radicals* (New York, 1964), pp. 33–71.
68. Marshall Fishwick, "The Virginia Tradition," *American Heritage*, V (Spring 1954), 55.
69. Marshall Fishwick, *Lee after the War* (New York, 1963), pp. 225–26.
70. *Ibid.*, p. 227.
71. See Dowdey's review in *Virginia Magazine of History and Biography*, LXXI (July 1963), 376–78.
72. Dixon Wecter, *The Hero in America* (Ann Arbor, 1966), p. 8.
73. *Ibid.*, pp. 143–44.
74. *Ibid.*, pp. 14–15.
75. *Ibid.*, p. 15.
76. *Harper's*, CCXXII (April 1961), 4; *Newsweek*, LVII (March 27, 1961), 76–78.
77. See *Civil War History*, II (March 1956), 110; *Civil War History*, IV (December 1958), 448; *American Heritage*, XIV (October 1963), 32; *Saturday Review*, XLIV (June 10, 1961), 47; *The Saturday Evening Post*, CCXXXV (August 11, 1962), 10.
78. *Time*, LXVII (June 4, 1956), 26.
79. *The Saturday Evening Post*, CCXXII (April 7, 1951), 31.
80. British Travel Association, *Explore the Lee Country in Britain* (n.p., n.d.), copy in Lee Papers, W&L.
81. Bruce Catton, *This Hallowed Ground: The Story of the Union Side of the Civil War* (Garden City, N.Y., 1956), p. 316.
82. Bruce Catton, *Glory Road* (Garden City, N.Y., 1962), p. 337.
83. Catton, *This Hallowed Ground*, pp. 128, 135, 252, 316.
84. Clifford Dowdey, "General Lee's Unsolved Problem," *American Heritage*, VI (April 1955), 34–35.
85. *Ibid.*, p. 35; Clifford Dowdey, *The Land They Fought For* (Garden City, N.Y., 1955), pp. 93, 157, 160–61, 182, 194, 196; Clifford Dowdey, *Lee's Last Campaign* (Boston, 1960), pp. 10–11, 15; Clifford Dowdey, *Lee* (Boston, 1965), p. xi.
86. Virginius Dabney, "An Approach to Virginia," *Saturday Review*, XVI (January 23, 1943), 18; see also Virginius Dabney, "Recess from Battle," *Saturday Review*, XLIV (September 30, 1961), 32; and Virginius Dabney, "Appomattox: Epic Surrender," *Saturday Review*, XXXVIII (March 19, 1955), 34–35.
87. Oscar Handlin, "Why Lee Attacked," *The Atlantic Monthly*, CXCV (March 1955), 65–66.
88. Bruce Catton, "Where the Great Change Took Place," *The New York Times Magazine*, February 5, 1961, pp. 11–13, 68–69; Catton, *This Hallowed Ground*, pp. 235, 256–57.
89. Catton, *Glory Road*, pp. 360–31.
90. *Saturday Review*, XXXVIII (October 29, 1955), 12, and XLIII (July 16, 1960), 20; *American Heritage*, VII (October 1956), 59.
91. Dixon Wecter, *The Hero in America*, pp. 478–87.
92. Marshall Fishwick, "Lee's Mistake," *Saturday Review*, XLV (December 1, 1962), 23.
93. Interlaken Mills, *The Noble Lee* (n.p., 1961), copy in Lee Papers, W&L.
94. Stanley Horn, "Robert E. Lee," *American Heritage*, III (Winter 1952), 16.
95. Allan Nevins, "The Glorious and the Terrible," *Saturday Review*, XLIV (September 2, 1961), 48.

EPILOGUE

1. Margaret Sanborn, *Robert E. Lee* (2 vols., Philadelphia, 1966), I, 77.
2. Mildred Lee Journal, January 22, 1867, in Lee-DeButts Papers, DLC.
3. Sanborn, *Lee*, I, 97.
4. MacDonald, *Mrs. Robert E. Lee*, pp. 37–38.
5. Sanborn, *Lee*, I, 91.
6. MacDonald, *Mrs. Robert E. Lee*, p. 41.
7. *Ibid.;* see also Lee to Mary Lee, June 2, 1832, in Bolling Lee Papers, VHS.
8. MacDonald, *Mrs. Robert E. Lee*, p. 42.
9. Lee to Andrew Talcott, October 21, November 9, 1835, in Lee-Ludwell Papers, VHS.
10. Lee to Andrew Talcott, February [illegible], February 13, May 5, 1836, Lee-Ludwell Papers, VHS; Lee to Talcott, February 1, 1838, in Lee Papers, Missouri.
11. Sanborn, *Lee*, I, 127; Lee to Mary Lee, March 20, 1839, in Bolling Lee Papers, VHS.
12. Lee to wife, August 4, 1840, in Bolling Lee Papers, VHS.
13. Lee to wife, September 5, 1853, in Lee Papers, VHS.
14. *Ibid.;* see also Lee to wife, January 9, March 7, July 27, 1857, in Lee Papers, VHS.
15. Lee to wife, March 3, 1860, in Lee Papers, VHS.
16. Lee to wife, November 18, 1861, Lee to daughters, November 22, 1861, Lee to Agnes Lee, March 2, 1862, all in Lee Papers, DLC.
17. Lee to wife, June 25, 1862, in Lee Papers, VHS.
18. Sanborn, *Lee*, I, 66, 39.
19. Jones, *Life and Letters*, pp. 25–26.
20. Lee to Jack Mackay, February 17, October 18, June 26, 1834, in Lee Papers, Colonial Dames, Georgia.
21. Lee to Margaret Elliott, October 18, 1853, in Lee Papers, Colonial Dames, Georgia.
22. Lee to Eliza Mackay, April 13, 1831, January 4, 1832, in Lee Papers, Colonial Dames, Georgia.
23. Lee to Jack Mackay, October 18, 1834, Lee to Eliza Stiles, May 24, 1856, in Lee Papers, Colonial Dames, Georgia.
24. Lee to Mary Custis, November 7, 1839, in Bolling Lee Papers, VHS.
25. Lee to wife, May 2, 10, 1853, in Bolling Lee Papers, VHS.
26. Sanborn, *Lee*, I, 74; Freeman, *Lee*, I, 164.
27. Freeman, *Lee*, I, 169, 453.
28. Edward Childe, *Life and Campaigns of General Lee* (London, 1875), p. 24.
29. Freeman, *Lee*, III, 236.
30. *Ibid.*, I, 20–21, 45–46, 32, 22; Mary Powell, *History of Old Alexandria in Virginia* (Richmond, 1928), pp. 87–99, 124–35.
31. Sanborn, *Lee*, I, 37–38.
32. Freeman, *Lee*, I, 109–10.
33. Lee to wife, April 24, 1832, in Bolling Lee Papers, VHS.
34. Lee to Jack Mackay, June 26, 1834, in Lee Papers, Colonial Dames, Georgia.
35. Lee to Andrew Talcott, February 10, 1835, in Lee-Ludwell Papers, VHS.
36. Lee to Jack Mackay, February 14, 1835, in Lee Papers, Colonial Dames, Georgia.
37. Lee to Andrew Talcott, May 5, 1836, in Lee-Ludwell Papers, VHS.
38. Lee to wife, August 5, 1837, August 4, 1850, in Lee-Ludwell Papers, VHS; Lee to Jack Mackay, March 18, 1841, in Lee Papers, Colonial Dames, Georgia; Douglas Freeman, "Lee and the Ladies," *Scribner's Magazine*, LXXVIII (October 1925), 347–48.
39. Lee to Andrew Talcott, November 1, 1834, October 14, 21, November 9, 17, 25, 1835, June 22, 1836, in Lee-Ludwell Papers, VHS.

40. Lee to Harriet Talcott, May 5, 1836, in Lee-Ludwell Papers, VHS.
41. Lee to Martha Williams, September 2, 1844, in Avery Craven (ed.), *"To Markie":
    The Letters of Robert E. Lee to Martha Custis Williams* (Cambridge, Mass., 1933),
    p. 4; see also letters of December 14, 1844, *ibid.*, pp. 6–7; May 26, 1845, *ibid.*, pp.
    10–11; September 17, 1845, *ibid.*, p. 13; April 1, 1849, *ibid.*, pp. 22–23.
42. May 10, 1851, *ibid.*, p. 24.
43. *Ibid.*, p. 26.
44. May 26, 1854, *ibid.*, pp. 45–46.
45. August 27, 1870, *ibid.*, p. 89.
46. Freeman, "Lee and the Ladies," p. 465.
47. Lee to Margaret Stuart, December 25, 1863, in Lee Papers, W&L; see also Lee to
    Misses Stuart, September 8, 1863, Lee to "Carrie," November 21, 1863, March
    19, 1864, Lee to Margaret Stuart, March 20, April 28, 1864, all in Lee Papers, W&L.
48. Lee to Charlotte Lee, April 26, 1862, in Jones, *Life and Letters*, p. 183.
49. Lee to Andrew Talcott, February 2, 1837, in Lee-Ludwell Papers, VHS.
50. Lee to W. H. F. Lee, April 2, 1860, in Jones, *Life and Letters*, p. 112.
51. Lee to Cassius Lee, August 20, 1838, in Fitzhugh Lee, *Lee*, p. 29; Lee to Andrew
    Talcott, October 3, 1838, May 18, 1839, in Lee-Ludwell Papers, VHS.
52. Sanborn, *Lee*, I, 69–70; Freeman, *Lee*, I, 97–98.
53. Lee to [?], April 2, 1860, in Jones, *Life and Letters*, p. 112.
54. Lee to wife, October 16, 1837, in Bolling Lee Papers, VHS.
55. Jones, *Life and Letters*, p. 39.
56. *Ibid.*, p. 40.
57. *Ibid.*
58. *Ibid.*
59. *Ibid.*, p. 67.
60. *Ibid.*, p. 94.
61. Robert E. Lee Diary, 1855–1861, in Lee Papers, VHS.
62. Robert E. Lee, Jr., *Recollections and Letters*, pp. 13–14, 9.
63. Agnes Lee Diary, July 20, 1853, in Lee-DeButts Papers, DLC.
64. *Ibid.*, March 21, 23, 1856.
65. Annie Lee to Helen Bratt, August 30, 1857, typescript in Lee Papers, W&L.
66. Lee to wife, March 7, 1857, in Lee Papers, VHS.
67. Lee to wife, July 27, 1857, in Lee Papers, VHS.
68. Lee to A. S. Johnston, October 25, 1857, in M. S. Sibley (ed.), "Robert E. Lee to
    Albert Sidney Johnston, 1857," *Journal of Southern History*, XXIX (February
    1963), 103–04.
69. Jones, *Life and Letters*, pp. 81–82.
70. Lee to Mary Lee, March 3, 1860, in Lee Papers, VHS.
71. Lee to Annie Lee, August 27, 1860, in Lee Papers, VHS.
72. Lee to Martha Williams, May 26, 1854, in Craven, *"To Markie,"* p. 46.
73. Jones, *Life and Letters*, p. 113.
74. Lee to wife, May 25, August 4, 1861, Lee to Annie Lee, December 8, 1861, Lee
    to wife, December 22, 1861, in Lee Papers, DLC; Lee to daughter, December
    25, 1861, in Jones, *Life and Letters*, p. 154.
75. Lee to wife, June 14, 1863, in Lee Papers, VHS; Fitzhugh Lee, *Lee*, p. 354.
76. Mildred Lee Journal, July 20, 1890, in Lee Papers, VHS.
77. Mary Lee to Mrs. William H. Stiles, February 9, 1861, in Lee Papers, Colonial
    Dames, Georgia.
78. Lee to wife, May 8, 11, 25, 1861, in Lee Papers, DLC.
79. Jones, *Life and Letters*, p. 156.
80. *Ibid.*

81. Fitzhugh Lee, *Lee*, p. 129.
82. For examples, see Lee to Reverdy Johnson, January 27, 1866, Lee to J. L. Black, January 13, March 12, 1869, in Lee Papers, VHS; Freeman, *Lee*, IV, 393–94.
83. Lee to Jack Mackay, June 27, 1838, November 8, 1839, in Lee Papers, Colonial Dames, Georgia.
84. Jones, *Life and Letters*, p. 146.
85. *Ibid.*, p. 154.
86. Lee to wife, September 5, 1855, in Lee Papers, VHS.
87. Lee to wife, March 3, 1860, in Lee Papers VHS.
88. Lee to wife, September 29, 1862, in Lee Papers, VHS.
89. Jones, *Life and Letters*, p. 154.
90. Robert E. Lee, Jr., *Recollections and Letters*, p. 20.
91. Fitzhugh Lee, *Lee*, p. 43.
92. Robert E. Lee, Jr., *Recollections and Letters*, pp. 20–21.
93. Jones, *Life and Letters*, p. 94.
94. Fitzhugh Lee, *Lee*, p. 43.
95. Freeman, *Lee*, IV, 499.
96. Robert E. Lee, Jr., *Recollections and Letters*, pp. 8, 17.
97. *Ibid.*, p. 46.
98. Fitzhugh Lee, *Lee*, pp. 234–35.
99. Richard Ketchum, "Faces from the Past," *American Heritage*, XII (June 1961), 29.
100. Robert E. Lee Diary, 1855–1861, in Lee Papers, VHS.
101. Notes in Lee Diary, in Lee Papers, VHS.
102. George T. Lee, "Reminiscences of General Robert E. Lee," *South Atlantic Quarterly*, XXV (July 1927), 244.
103. Lee to wife, April 27, May 2, 1853, in Lee Papers, VHS; Fitzhugh Lee, *Lee*, p. 51.
104. Jones, *Life and Letters*, p. 80.
105. Lee To Mildred Lee, January 9, 1857, in Lee Papers, VHS.
106. Lee to Mary Lee, January 9, 1857, in Lee Papers, VHS.
107. Lee to wife, July 27, 1857, in Lee Papers, VHS; Lee to Johnston, October 25, 1857, in Sibley, "Robert E. Lee to Albert Sidney Johnston," pp. 103–04.
108. Jones, *Life and Letters*, pp. 81, 116; Lee to wife, July 27, 1857, in Lee Papers, VHS; Lee to wife, May 25, 1861, in Lee Papers, DLC; Lee to wife, March 12, 1860, in Bolling Lee Papers, VHS.
109. Lee to wife, May 2, July 27, 1861, in Bolling Lee Papers, VHS; Jones, *Life and Letters*, pp. 147–48, 185, 244; Lee to wife, April 29, 1862, in Lee Papers, VHS; Lee to wife, November 13, December 16, 1862, April 3, July 7, 12, 1863, in Lee Papers, DLC.
110. Lee to wife, May 2, 25, 1861, February 8, 1862, in Lee Papers, DLC; Fitzhugh Lee, *Lee*, pp. 131, 305; Jones, *Life and Letters*, pp. 160, 185, 148.
111. Lee to wife, April 27, 1853, in Lee Papers, VHS; Lee to wife, September 20, 1857, in Bolling Lee Papers, VHS; Lee to Eliza Stiles, August 14, 1856, in Lee Papers, Colonial Dames, Georgia.
112. Lee to Mildred Lee, November 10, 1862, Lee to wife, October 26, 1862, in Lee Papers, DLC.
113. Lee to wife, July 27, 1861, in Lee Papers, DLC.
114. Jones, *Life and Letters*, pp. 84, 380, 299; Freeman, *Lee*, IV, 121.
115. Lee to wife, May 8, November 22, 1861, Lee to Agnes Lee, March 2, 1862, in Lee Papers, DLC; Lee to wife, June 25, November 6, 1862, in Lee Papers, VHS; Lee to wife, December 16, 1862, March 9, September 29, 1863, in Lee Papers, DLC; Jones, *Life and Letters*, p. 211.

116. Charles Anderson, *Texas Before and on the Eve of the Rebellion* (Cincinnati, 1884), p. 24.

117. John Bell Hood, *Advance and Retreat: Personal Experiences in the United States and Confederate States Armies* (2nd ed., Bloomington, Ind., 1959), p. 98.

118. Eben Swift, "The Military Education of Robert E. Lee," *Virginia Magazine of History and Biography*, XXXV (April 1929), 106–07; *SHSP*, XI (October 1883), 448, 446; see also Erasmus Keyes, *Fifty Years' Observations of Men and Events* (New York, 1884), pp. 206–07.

119. Freeman, *Lee*, IV, 432; *SHSP*, XI (October 1883), 447.

120. Freeman, *Lee*, IV, 436–37.

121. Robert Lee to W. H. F. Lee, January 29, 1861, in Bolling Lee Papers, VHS; Jones *Life and Letters*, p. 119.

122. T. Harry Williams, "The Military Leadership of the North and South," in David Donald (ed.), *Why the North Won the Civil War* (New York, 1962), p. 47.

123. *Ibid.*, p. 35.

124. Bruce Catton, *Never Call Retreat* (Garden City, N.Y., 1965), p. 315; Freeman, *Lee*, IV, 499.

125. Frank Vandiver, *Mighty Stonewall* (New York, 1957), p. 329.

126. Williams, "Military Leadership of the North and South," p. 35.

127. E. Porter Alexander, *Military Memoirs of a Confederate* (New York, 1918), pp. 110–11.

128. Fitzhugh Lee, *Lee*, p. 68.

129. *SHSP*, VI (July 1878), 94.

130. *Ibid.*, pp. 144, 147; Bradford, *Lee the American*, p. 154.

131. Jones, *Life and Letters*, pp. 84, 278, 247; Lee to Cora Ives, January 25, 1868, in Lee Papers, VHS; Lee to wife, December 16, 1862, Lee to Mildred Lee, November 10, 1862, in Lee Papers, DLC.

132. Lee to wife, January 7, 1856, April 19, 1867, in Lee Papers, VHS; Lee to wife, September 20, 1857, in Bolling Lee Papers, VHS.

133. Jones, *Personal Reminiscences*, p. 144.

134. *Ibid.*, pp. 142, 145; Jones, *Life and Letters*, p. 211.

135. Lee to wife, January 3, 1857, in Lee Papers, VHS.

136. Bradford, *Lee the American*, p. 89.

137. Nevins, *The War for the Union*, I, 108–10.

138. Lee to "Cousin Jane," July 1861, copy in Wigfall Family Papers, DLC; Lee to wife, July 27, 1861, in Lee Papers, DLC; Jones, *Life and Letters*, p. 158.

139. Williams, "Military Leadership of the North and South," p. 48.

140. Robert E. Lee, Jr., *Recollections and Letters*, p. 103; Thomas L. Connelly, "Robert E. Lee and the Western Confederacy: A Criticism of Lee's Strategic Ability," *Civil War History*, XV (June 1969), 121–22.

141. *Ibid.*, pp. 122–27.

142. Freeman, *Lee*, IV, 145.

143. *Ibid.*, 202, 443.

144. *Ibid.*, II, 488; III, 243.

145. Jones, *Life and Letters*, p. 213.

146. Lloyd Lewis, *Captain Sam Grant* (Boston, 1950), pp. 371, 369.

147. Bruce Catton, *Grant Takes Command* (Boston, 1969), pp. 134–35.

148. Lee to Jack Mackay, October 2, 1847, in Lee Papers, Carlisle Barracks, Penn.

149. Jones, *Life and Letters*, pp. 53, 57; Fitzhugh Lee, *Lee*, p. 43.

150. Davis, *Gray Fox*, pp. 168, 203, 315, 322.

151. A. R. H. Ranson, "General Lee as I Knew Him," *Harper's New Monthly Magazine*,

CXXII (February 1911), 336; Francis Lawley, "General Lee," *Blackwood's Edinburgh Magazine*, CXI (March 1872), 356–57.

152. B. H. Liddell Hart, "Why Lee Lost Gettysburg," *Saturday Review*, XI (March 23, 1935), 569.

153. Davis, *Gray Fox*, p. 315; Ranson, "General Lee," p. 336.

154. Lee to John Letcher, August 28, 1865, in Lee Papers, VHS; see also Lee to Richard Ewell, March 3, 1868, in Lee Papers, W&L.

155. Lee to Herbert Saunders, August 22, 1868, Lee to William McDonald, April 15, 1868, in Lee Papers, VHS.

156. Freeman, *Lee*, IV, 303.

157. Rowland, *Davis*, VII, 258; Lee to John Letcher, August 28, 1865, in Lee Papers, VHS.

158. William Preston Johnston, "General R. E. Lee, Memoranda of Conversation, May 7, 1868," copy in Lee Papers, W&L; *Confederate Veteran*, XXXV (January 1927), 6.

159. Lee to A. T. Bledsoe, October 8, 1866, Lee to Cassius Lee, June 6, 1870, in Lee Papers, W&L; Lee to Edward Pollard, October 12, 1865, Lee to L. W. Whittle, November 29, 1866, in Lee Papers, VHS.

160. Lee to Cassius Lee, Jr., June 6, 1870, copy in Lee Papers, W&L. The same collection should be consulted for extensive correspondence on both Lee's search for materials and his dealings with publishers.

161. Lee to Walter Taylor, July 31, 1865, in Lee Papers, VHS.

162. Lee to Jubal Early, March 15, 1866, in Lee Papers, VHS; Allen W. Moger, "General Lee's Unwritten 'History of the Army of Northern Virginia,'" *Virginia Magazine of History and Biography*, LXXI (July 1963), 342–43.

163. Johnston, "General R. E. Lee, Memoranda of Conversation, May 7, 1868."

164. *Ibid.;* see also "Conversations with General R. E. Lee," manuscript in Lee Papers, W&L.

165. Lee to Richard Ewell, March 3, 1868, in Lee Papers, W&L.

166. Robert E. Lee, Jr., *Recollections and Letters,* pp. 260, 266; Freeman, *Lee*, IV, 258.

167. Craven, *"To Markie,"* pp. 63, 85; Freeman, *Lee*, IV, 524–25.

INDEX

Adams, Charles Francis, 116–20
Alexander, General E. Porter, 19, 62–3, 197–8
Allan, Colonel William, 75, 87–90 *passim*, 215
Allen, Frederick Lewis, 123
Allen, L. W., 137
Anderson, Charles, 193
"Annals of the Civil War," 69, 71, 85
Arlington (estate), 34–7, 126, 165, 171–2, 182–4
Association of the Army of Northern Virginia, 46–8, 82

Badeau, Adam, 206
Barton, Bruce, 129
Battle Abbey, 112
Beauregard, General P. G. T., 8, 33, 76–80 *passim*
Benét, Stephen Vincent, 138, 163
Blair, Francis, 194
Bledsoe, Albert, 70–1, 81–2, 96, 214
Bradford, Gamaliel, 120–1
Breckinridge, General John C., 33
Brock, Robert, 110
Brockenbrough, John, 28–9
Brooks, William, 135–9
Bruce, Philip A., 109–10

Cameron, T. J., 135
Campaigns of the Army of the Potomac (Swinton), 83–4
Catton, Bruce, 158–9, 161, 163
Cavalcade of America (radio series), 135, 158
Centennial, of 1876, 66–8
Chancellorsville, battle of, 81–2
Chesnut, Mary Boykin, 163
Churchill, Winston, 138–9
Civil War Centennial, 157–8
Comte de Paris (Louis Philippe d'Orléans), 75, 85–90 *passim*
Confederated Memorial Association of the South, 111–12

Confederate newspapers
  on T. J. Jackson's popularity, 18–19
  on R. E. Lee's popularity, 16–18
  opinions on relative importance of western and eastern zones, 15–16
Confederate public opinion
  on "Stonewall" Jackson, 18–19
  on R. E. Lee's popularity, 16–18
  on western front, 13–15
Cooke, John Esten
  biographer of "Stonewall" Jackson, 19–20, 60
  critic of Lee, 25, 57–60
  defends Virginia image, 69–72, 103–4
Craven, Avery, 155
Custis, George Washington Parke, 7, 165
Custis, Mary (Mrs. George Washington Parke Custis), 190

Dabney, Major Robert L., 20, 80–1
Dabney, Virginius, 160
Dabney, William Pope, 104
Daniel, Major John, 65, 95, 97–8
Davidson, Donald, 137, 139–40
Davis, Jefferson
  dislike of Beauregard and Johnston, 76–80 *passim*
  on Lee cult, 25
  and Lost Cause mentality, 92, 96
  opinion of Lee, 76–7
  postwar bitterness, 42
  his *Rise and Fall*, 96
Davis, Winnie, 65
Dawson, Henry, 68–9
Deering, John, 108
De Voto, Bernard, 131, 133, 139
Dowdey, Clifford, 133–4, 156, 159–60

Early, General Jubal A.
  appearance, 52
  flees South after war, 52–3
  in Gettysburg debate, 54–6, 84–90 *passim*

leader of Richmond cult, 47–61
  passim
leads Southern Historical Society, 55,
  73–8 *passim*
Lee birthday address (1872), 55–6, 84
organizes Lee Monument Association,
  43–6
personality, 51–5
war career, 52–5
Washington raid, 52, 55
Eggleston, George Cary, 68, 71, 106–7
Evans, General Clement, 112
Ewell, General Richard, 54, 218

Farragut, David G., 201
Faulkner, William, 131, 133
Fenner, Charles, 93
Fishwick, Marshall, 95, 208
Freeman, Douglas S., 138–9, 211
  background, 143
  critic of Jackson, 149–51
  critic of Longstreet, 149
  impact of writings, 141, 151–2
  on Lee's character, 144–7
  on Lee's personality, 152–3, 164
  on Lee's resignation from U.S. army,
    148–9
  opinion of Lee's generalship, 144–50
  publishes *R. E. Lee*, 143–5
  stresses Lee's genealogy, 146
  on superiority of Virginians, 143–6
  views on western theater, 146–7
French, Colonel Basset, 46
Fuller, General J. F. C., 153–5

Gaines, Francis P., 134, 142–3
Gettysburg, battle of, 54–9, 62, 70–1,
  83–90 *passim*
"Gettysburg Series," 87–90 *passim*
Golden, Harry, 157
Gone With the Wind (Mitchell), 131–2
Gordon, E. C., 215
Gordon, General John, 43, 61, 92, 100,
  112
Grant, General Ulysses S., 4, 9, 14, 62,
  161, 205–8
Graves, Charles, 121
"Great South" series, 67
Griswold, Francis, 136

Halleck, General Henry W., 206
Hamilton, J. G. de Roulhac, 130
Handlin, Oscar, 160–1
Harrison, Joseph, Jr., 155–6
Harwell, Richard, 19–20
Hergesheimer, Joseph, 134, 136
Heth, General Henry, 68, 73, 88
Hill, Senator Ben H., 94
Hill, General Daniel Harvey, 25, 94, 96,
  102
Hill, Frederick, 121
Historical Magazine, 68–9, 84
Hollywood Memorial Association, 45
Hood, General John Bell, 193
Hooker, General Joseph, 195
Horn, Stanley, 134, 162
Howard, General Oliver Otis, 62–3
Howe, Julia Ward, 121–2
Hughes, Rupert, 156

Imboden, General John B., 25, 69

Jackson, General Thomas Jonathan
  criticized by Freeman, 149–52
  early biographers of, 19–20, 76
  postwar image, 80–2
  wartime comparisons with Lee, 18–19
  wartime popularity, 18–20
Jackson, Mrs. Thomas Jonathan, 80–1
Johnson, General Bradley, 46, 48, 102
Johnston, General Albert Sidney, 23–5,
  181, 206
Johnston, General Joseph E.
  attacked by Lee cult, 75–80 *passim*
  postwar image, 79–80
  service in U.S. army, 10
  wartime popularity, 22–3
  writes memoirs, 79
Johnston, William Preston, 33, 44, 78,
  211
Johnstone, William, 130, 134
Jones, Jesse, 136
Jones, John William, 39–40, 82, 85, 102
  alters Lee's letters, 118–19
  criticizes "Stonewall" Jackson, 83
  curries Jefferson Davis' favor, 78
  in Gettysburg debate, 85–90 *passim*
  leader of Southern Historical Society,
    39, 41–2, 73–8 *passim*

Lee biographer, 39–42, 93, 110
and Lee Memorial Volume, 41–2
personality, 41–2

King, Edward, 67

Lee, Agnes (daughter of R. E. Lee), 31, 35, 180, 182–3
Lee, Anne Carter (mother of R. E. Lee), 5–6, 177
Lee, Annie Carter (daughter of R. E. Lee), 180, 193, 203
Lee, Charles, 5
Lee, Charlotte Wickham (daughter-in-law of R. E. Lee), 176
Lee, General Fitz (nephew of R. E. Lee), 46–8, 73, 82–3, 87–90 passim, 107
Lee, General George Washington Custis (son of R. E. Lee), 30–2, 179
Lee, General Henry (Light-Horse Harry, father of R. E. Lee), 5–6, 176–7, 182
Lee, Major Henry (Black-Horse Harry, half brother of R. E. Lee), 5–6, 177
Lee, Mary (daughter of R. E. Lee), 65
Lee, Mary Anne Randolph Custis (wife of R. E. Lee)
and Lee Memorial Association, 33–7 passim, 44
health, 7, 32, 35, 165–9 passim, 172
life and personality, 7, 33–7 passim, 172
loses Arlington, 34–5
Lee, Matilda (Mrs. Henry Lee), 5
Lee, Mildred Childe (daughter of R. E. Lee), 11, 31, 35
Lee, Richard, 4
Lee, Richard Henry, II, 68
Lee, General Robert Edward
accepts Washington College presidency, 28–9
aggressive spirit in combat, 203–8
appointed commander of 2nd Cavalry, 9
attitude toward his children, 176–80
attitude toward secession, 194–5, 198–202
becomes national hero, 99–122 passim
belief in Divine Providence, 94, 190–1
career in U.S. army, 6–9, 193
centennial birthday celebration, 100, 113–15
as chivalry symbol, 101–2
as Christ symbol, 94–5, 98
and Civil War Centennial, 158–62
colonial ancestry, 5–6
compared with George Washington, 7, 90, 96–8, 125–6, 148, 171–2
criticizes subordinates, 214–16
death, 11–12, 28
duty in Savannah, Ga., 169–70
as educator, 208–9, 212, 217
flexibility of image, 161
funeral, 12
habits of command, 195–8
in Hall of Fame, 4
health, 216–19
image during Depression years, 134–40 passim
as Lost Cause symbol, 91–8 passim, 100–10 passim
marriage, 7, 90
memorial half dollar, 4
in Mexican War, 7–8, 193
as middle-class hero, 156–62 passim
modern critics of, 153–6
obsession with death, 191–3
obsession with duty, 188–9, 199–202
opinion of battle of Chancellorsville, 214
opinion of battle of Gettysburg, 215–16
opinion of "Stonewall" Jackson, 80–2, 214
opinion of J. E. Johnston, 9
personality, 164–219 passim
popularity after Seven Days campaign, 17–18
postwar image, 90–8
as Reconstruction symbol, 91–8
relationship to mother, 169–72
relationship to mother-in-law, 171, 190
relationship to Winfield Scott, 7, 193–4
relationship to staff, 48–51
relationship to wife, 165–76 passim
religious views, 189–93
resigns from U.S. army, 194–5, 198–202
sense of failure as officer, 180–2
Stone Mountain Memorial to, 126–7
as strategist, 202–3
as tactician, 203–8
tries to write war history, 211–16

Lee, General Robert E. (*continued*)
  unhappiness after Civil War, 209–16,
    218–19
  unhappiness with early army life, 8–9,
    166–86 *passim*
  unpopularity during wartime, 16–17
  views on the war, 213–16
  views on the years after 1865, 209–13,
    218
  wartime comparison with Jackson,
    18–19
  at West Point, 6
Lee, Captain Robert Edward, Jr. (son of
  R. E. Lee), 31, 108, 115–19, 179, 218
Lee, Captain Sidney Smith (brother of
  R. E. Lee), 172
Lee, Susan Pendleton, 112–13
Lee, William Henry Fitzhugh (Rooney,
  son of R. E. Lee), 46, 176, 178–9
Lee Memorial Association, 12, 28, 39–40,
  65, 78, 97–8
Lee Memorial Chapel controversy, 127–8
Lee Memorial Foundation, 126
Lee Memorial University concept, 32
Lee Memorial Volume, 33, 37, 40, 78,
  128
Lee Monument Association, 43–61
  passim
Lewis, Lloyd, 205
Lilley, General R. D., 31–2, 40
Lindbergh, Charles, 128–9
Lloyd George, David, 141
London, Jack, 120
Long, Colonel Armistead L., 48, 50–1,
  77, 107
Longstreet, General James
  assists William Swinton, 84
  blamed for loss at Gettysburg, 83–90
    passim, 139
  criticisms of Lee, 84
  criticized by Freeman, 149
  disliked by postwar Southerners, 64,
    74–5
  at Gettysburg reunion, 62–3
  postwar popularity in North, 63–4, 85
Lost Cause rationale, 91–8, 100–3, 107

Mackay, Eliza, 170
Mackay, Jack, 6, 172–3, 207
Mackay family, 170

Mahone, General William, 54, 62, 97
Marshall, Colonel Charles, 40, 46, 48–9,
  61, 75, 84
Mason, Emily, 75, 90, 97
Maurice, Sir Frederick, 130
Maury, General Dabney, 25
May, Rollo, 214
McCabe, James, 19, 59–61, 77
McCabe, W. Gordon, 47
McCausland, General John, 124
McClellan, General George, 8, 9, 206
McClellan, Major Henry, 88, 90
McClelland, Mary, 104
McClure, Colonel Alexander, 69, 71, 85
Mencken, Henry L., 124
Mitchell, Margaret, 131–2
Mosby, Colonel John S., 88

Nevins, Allan, 155, 162, 201

Page, Thomas Nelson, 103–4, 110, 119
Palmer, Dr. Benjamin, 72
Pember, Phoebe Yates, 104
Pendleton, General William Nelson, 12,
  29, 37–40, 44–5, 84–5
Pickett, Mrs. George, 99–100
Pollard, Edward, 16, 58, 60–1, 77
Porter, Gene Stratton, 123
Pryor, Sara, 104–5

Ramsdell, Charles, 133
Randall, James, 133
Richardson, C. B., 212
Riley, Franklin, 129–30
Rives, Amélie, 104
Rives, W. C., 188
Rhodes, Charles, 134
"Robert E. Lee Week," 138
Roosevelt, Franklin D., 136
Roosevelt, Theodore, 4, 99, 120–1
Ryan, Father Abram, 114–15

Saunders, Herbert, 210
Scheibert, Captain Justus, 86–7
Schofield, General John, 205–6
Scott, General Winfield, 7–8, 193–5

Seawell, Molly, 104
Shepherd, Henry, 108
Sherman, General William T., 14
Sickles, General Daniel, 62–3
Smith, Henry L., 127–8, 142
Smith, Roswell, 65
So Red the Rose (Young), 131–2
Southern Historical Society, 41–2, 45, 72–3, 82
Southern Historical Society Papers, 41–2, 47, 72–8 *passim,* 85–90 *passim*
Southern literary magazines, 69–70
Southern Magazine, 84–5, 94
Southern Review, 70–1, 81–2
Stabler, Jennie, 68
Steel, S. A., 134, 137
Stephens, Alexander, 96
Stiles, Robert, 109
St. John, General I. M., 77
Stone Mountain memorial, 126–7
Stratford restoration, 126
Stuart, Caroline, 175
Stuart, General James Ewell Brown, 88–90
Stuart, Margaret, 175–6, 191
Stuart, Reverend Samuel, 29
Sullivan, Mark, 123
Swinton, William, 54, 56–7, 59, 83–4
    see also *Campaigns of the Army of the Potomac* and Longstreet, General James

Talcott, Andrew, 172–3, 176
Talcott, Harriet Hackley, 173–4
Talcott, Major T. M. R., 83
Taylor, Colonel Joseph, 32
Taylor, General Richard, 90
Taylor, Colonel Walter, 44, 46, 48, 50, 82, 86–7, 203–4
Thomas, General George, 201
Thompson, Lucy, 104
Trent, William P., 108
Trimble, General Isaac, 55

United Confederate Veterans, 110–13

Valentine, Edward V., dedication of his sculpture of Lee, 97–8
Vandiver, Frank E., 197
Venable, Colonel Charles, 25, 32–3, 40, 43–5, 48, 51, 73, 87
Virginia argument, 106–7
Virginia Division, of Association of Army of Northern Virginia, 46–7
Virginia writers in 19th century, 69–72

Walthall, Major W. T., 76
Walton, Reverend E. P., 29
Washington, George, 4, 7, 125
    see also Lee, General Robert Edward
Washington and Lee University
    and Lee Memorial University project, 32
    offers presidency to Lee, 28–9
    use of Lee name in fund-raising campaigns, 29–33, 40, 45, 64–5, 127–8, 142–3, 157
Wecter, Dixon, 156–62 *passim*
Whitman, Walt, 157
Williams, Martha Custis, 174–5, 219
Williams, T. Harry, 154–5, 163, 195, 202
Williamson, Mary, 113
Wilson, Woodrow, 4, 121, 128
Winston, Robert, 136, 139
Wise, General Henry, 16
Wister, Owen, 120
Wolseley, Lord Garnet, 114
Woodville, Jennie, 104
Woodward, William E., 156
Wright, Harold Bell, 129
Wright, General Marcus, 76
Wright, Quincy, 204

Young, James, 130
Young, Stark, 131–2, 136